CERTIFICATION CIRCLE™

MOUS

Microsoft Word 2002

Katherine T. Pinard

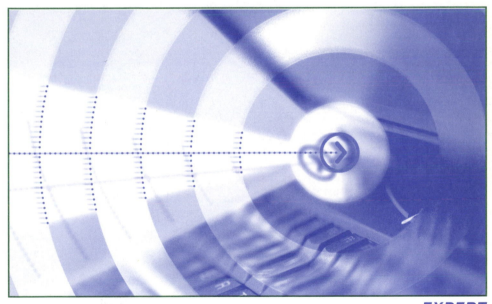

EXPERT

MICROSOFT OFFICE
USER SPECIALIST
Microsoft OFFICE
APPROVED COURSEWARE

THOMSON™
COURSE TECHNOLOGY

Australia • Canada • Mexico • Singapore • Spain • United Kingdom • United States

MOUS Microsoft Word 2002

CERTIFICATION CIRCLE™ *EXPERT*

Katherine T. Pinard

Managing Editor:
Nicole Jones Pinard

Product Managers:
Debbie Masi
Julia Healy

Editorial Assistant:
Christina Kling Garrett

Production Editor:
Debbie Masi

Contributing Author:
Carol Cram

Developmental Editors:
Laurie Brown, Kim Crowley

Composition House:
GEX Publishing Services

QA Manuscript Reviewers:
Nicole Ashton, John Freitas,
Jeff Schwartz, Alex White

Book Designers:
Joseph Lee, black fish design

COPYRIGHT © 2002 Course Technology, a division of Thomson Learning. Thomson Learning is a trademark used herein under license.

ISBN 0-619-05716-5

Printed in Canada

1 2 3 4 5 6 7 8 9 WC 06 05 04 03 02

For more information, contact Course Technology, 25 Thomson Place, Boston, Massachusetts, 02210.

Or you can visit us on the World Wide Web at www.course.com

Thank You, Advisory Board!

This book is a result of the hard work and dedication by authors, editors, and more than 30 instructors focused on Microsoft Office and MOUS certification. These instructors formed our Certification Circle Advisory Board. We looked to them to flesh out our original vision and turn it into a sound pedagogical method of instruction. In short, we asked them to partner with us to create *the* book for preparing for a MOUS Exam. And, now we wish to thank them for their contributions and expertise.

ADVISORY BOARD MEMBERS:

Linda Amergo	Old Westbury
Shellie Besharse	Mississippi County Community College
Margaret Britt	Copiah Lincoln Community College
Becky Burt	Copiah Lincoln Community College
Judy Cameron	Spokane Community College
Elizabeth T. De Arazoza	Miami-Dade Community College
Susan Dozier	Tidewater Community College
Dawna Dewire	Babson College
Pat Evans	J. Sargent Reynolds
Susan Fry	Boise State University
Joyce Gordon	Babson College
Steve Gordon	Babson College
Pat Harley	Howard Community College
Rosanna Hartley	Western Piedmont Community College
Eva Hefner	St. Petersburg Junior College
Becky Jones	Richland College
Mali Jones	Johnson and Wales University
Angie McCutcheon	Washington State Community College
Barbara Miller	Indiana University
Carol Milliken	Kellogg Community College
Maureen Paparella	Monmouth University
Mike Puopolo	Bunker Hill Community College
Kathy Proietti	Northern Essex Community College
Pamela M. Randall	Unicity Network
Theresa Savarese	San Diego City College
Barbara Sherman	Buffalo State
Kathryn Surles	Salem Community College
Beth Thomas	Hagerstown Community College
Barbara Webber	Northern Essex Community College
Jean Welsh	Lansing Community College
Lynn Wermers	North Shore Community College
Sherry Young	Kingwood College

Preface

Welcome to the *CERTIFICATION CIRCLE SERIES*. Each book in this series is designed with one thing in mind: preparing you to pass a Microsoft Office User Specialist (MOUS) exam. This strict focus allows you to target the skills you need to be successful. You will not need to study anything extra—it's like getting a peek at the exam before you take it! Read on to learn more about how the book is organized and how you will get the most out of it.

Table of Contents
This book is organized around the MOUS exam objectives. Each Skill on the exam is taught on two facing pages with text on the left and figures on the right. This also makes for a terrific reference; if you want to brush up on a few skills, it's easy to find the ones you're looking for.

Getting Started Chapter
Each book begins with a Getting Started Chapter. This Chapter contains skills that are *not* covered on the exam but the authors felt were vital to understanding the software. The content in this chapter varies from application to application.

Skill Overview
Each skill starts with a paragraph explaining the concept and how you would use it. These are clearly written and concise.

File Open Icon
We provide a realistic project file for every skill. And, it's in the form you need it in order to work through the steps; there's no wasted time building the file before you can work with it.

Skill Steps
The Steps required to perform the skill appear on the left page with what you type in green text.

Tips
We provide tips specific to the skill or how the skill is tested on the exam.

Skill Set 8
Integrating with Other Applications

Import Data to Access
Import Data from an Excel Workbook

You can import data into an Access database from several file formats, including an Excel workbook or another Access, FoxPro, dBase, or Paradox database. It is not uncommon for a user to enter a list of data into Excel and later decide to convert that data into an Access database, because the user wants to use Access's extensive form or report capabilities or wants multiple people to be able to use the data at the same time. (An Access database is inherently **multi-user**; many people can enter and update data at the same time.) Since the data in an Excel workbook is structured similarly to data in an Access table datasheet, you can easily import data from an Excel workbook into an Access database by using the **Import Spreadsheet Wizard**.

Activity Steps
Classes01.mdb

1. Click **File** on the menu bar, point to **Get External Data**, then click **Import**

2. Navigate to the drive and folder where your Project Files are stored, click the **Files of type list arrow**, click **Microsoft Excel**, click **Instructors**, then click **Import** to start the Import Spreadsheet Wizard
   See Figure 8-1.

3. Select the **First Row Contains Column Headings check box**, then click **Next**

4. Click **Next** to indicate that you want to create a new table, then click **Next** to not specify field changes

5. Click the **Choose my own primary key option button** to set InstructorID as the primary key field, then click **Next**

6. Type **Instructors** in the Import to Table box, click **Finish**, then click **OK**

7. Double-click **Instructors** to open it in Datasheet View
   See Figure 8-2. Imported data works the same way as any other table of data in a database.

8. Close the Instructors table

Step 4
You can also import Excel workbook data into an existing table if the field names used in the Excel workbook match the field names in the Access table.

Additional Projects

For those who want more practice applying the skills they've learned, there is a project for each skill set located at the back of each book. The projects ask you to combine the skills you've learned to create a meaningful document – just what you do in real life.

Project for Skill Set 1
Working with Cells and Cell Data

Sales Projection for Alaska Adventures

You work for Alaska Adventures, a small company based in Juneau, Alaska, that offers sea kayaking, mountain biking, and hiking tours. You've received a workbook containing a sales projection for the sea kayaking tours that the company hopes to sell in the busy summer months of June, July, and August. In this project, you will complete and format this worksheet. The workbook also contains a second worksheet that includes a list of the guests who purchased sea kayaking tours on a single day during the previous summer. You'll use the AutoFilter features on this list to determine the number of customers who came from countries other then the United States and Canada.

Activity Steps

open EC_Project1.xls

1. Clear the contents and formats of cell A3, drag cell A4 up to cell A3, then delete cell D14 and shift the cells left
2. Merge cell A3 across cells A3 to E3, then check the spelling in the worksheet and correct any errors
3. Enter **Total** in cell E5, use the **Go To** command to navigate to cell C13, then change the value in cell C13 to 1200
4. Use the **SUM** function in cell E12 to add the values in cells B12 through D12, then copy the formula to cells E13 through E15
5. Select cells B12 through B16, then use the **AutoSum button** to calculate the totals required for cells B16 through E16
6. In cell B18, enter the formula required to subtract the value in cell B16 from the value in cell B9, then copy the formula to cells C18 through E18
7. Use **Find and Replace** to locate all instances of 1500 and replace them with 500
8. Format cells B7 through E7, B9 through E9, B12 through E12, B16 through E16, and B18 through E18 with the **Currency style**, format cells B8 through E8 and cells B13 through E15 with the **Comma** style, then compare the completed worksheet to Figure EP 1-1
9. Switch to the **Customers worksheet**, then use AutoFilter to show only the **International** customers in the Category column. The filtered list appears as shown in Figure EP 1-2

close EC_Project1.xls

Step 8
To save time, press and hold the [CTRL] key, select each group of cells, and then click the Currency Style button.

Skill 1
Import Data to Access

Figure 8-1: **Import Spreadsheet Wizard dialog box**

Figure 8-2: **Imported Instructors table in Datasheet View**

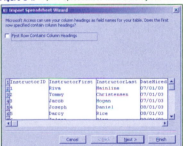

Seven records were imported

extra!

Using delimited text files

You can import data from a **delimited text file**, a file of unformatted data where each field value is delimited (separated) by a common character, such as a comma or a tab. Each record is further delimited by a common character, such as a paragraph mark. A delimited text file usually has a **txt** (for text) file extension. You can use delimited text files to convert data from a proprietary software system (such as an accounting, inventory, or scheduling software system) into a format that other programs can import. For example, most accounting software programs won't export data directly into an Access database, but they can export data to a delimited text file, which can then be imported by Access.

Figures

There are at least two figures per skill which serve as a reference as you are working through the steps. Callouts focus your attention to what's important.

Extra Boxes

This will *not* be on the exam—it's extra—hence the name. But, there are some very cool things you can do with Office xp so we had to put this stuff somewhere!

Target Your Skills

At the end of each unit, there are two Target Your Skills exercises. These require you to create a document from scratch, based on the figure, using the skills you've learned in the chapter. And, the solution is provided—there's no wasted time trying to figure out if you've done it right.

Additional Resources

There are many resources available with this book—both free and for a nominal fee. Please see your sales representative for more information. The resources available with this book are:

INSTRUCTOR'S MANUAL

Available as an electronic file, the Instructor's Manual is quality-assurance tested and includes unit overviews, lecture topics, solutions to all lessons and projects, and extra Target Your Skills. The Instructor's Manual is available on the Instructor's Resource Kit CD-ROM, or you can download if from www.course.com.

FACULTY ONLINE COMPANION

You can browse this textbook's password protected site to obtain the Instructor's Manual, Solution Files, Project Files, and any updates to the text. Contact your Customer Service Representative for the site address and password.

PROJECT FILES

Project Files contain all of the data that students will use to complete the lessons and projects. A Readme file includes instructions for using the files. Adopters of this text are granted the right to install the Project Files on any stand-alone computer or network. The Project Files are available on the Instructor's Resource Kit CD-ROM, the Review Pack, and can also be downloaded from www.course.com.

SOLUTION FILES

Solution Files contain every file students are asked to create or modify in the lessons and projects. A Help file on the Instructor's Resource Kit includes information for using the Solution Files.

FIGURE FILES

Figure Files contain all the figures from the book in bitmap format. Use the figure files to create transparency masters or in a PowerPoint presentation.

SAM, SKILLS ASSESSMENT MANAGER FOR MICROSOFT OFFICE XP SAM^xp

SAM is the most powerful Office XP assessment and reporting tool that will help you gain a true understanding of your students' proficiency in Microsoft Word, Excel, Access, and PowerPoint 2002.

TOM, TRAINING ONLINE MANAGER FOR MICROSOFT OFFICE XP TOM

TOM is Course Technology's MOUS-approved training tool for Microsoft Office XP. Available via the World Wide Web and CD-ROM, TOM allows students to actively learn Office XP concepts and skills by delivering realistic practice through both guided and self-directed simulated instruction.

Certification Circle Series, SAM, and TOM: the true training and assessment solution for Office XP.

Preparing for the MOUS Exam

Studying for and passing the Microsoft Office User Specialist (MOUS) exams requires very specific test preparation materials. As a student and reviewer of MOUS exam materials, I am proud to be a part of a team of creators that produced a new series specifically designed with the MOUS exam test taker in mind. The Certification Circle Series™ provides a fully integrated test preparation solution for MOUS Office[XP] with the powerful combination of its Core and Expert textbooks, testing software with Skills Assessment Manager (SAM[XP]) and Training Online Manager (TOM[XP]). This combination coupled with the Exam Reference Pocket Guide for quick test taking tips and Office[XP] materials will provide the skills and confidence a student will need to pass the MOUS exams.

How does the Certification Circle Series provide the best test preparation materials? Here's how:

▶ Core and Expert texts are based entirely on MOUS exam objectives.

▶ Table of Contents in each book maps directly to MOUS exam objectives in a one to one correlation.

▶ "Target Your Skills" exercises in the end of unit material presents problem solving questions in similar fashion to the MOUS 2002 exams.

▶ Skills Assessment Manager (SAM[XP]) provides a simulated testing environment in which students can target their strengths and weakness before taking the MOUS exams.

If you are an experienced Word user, you'll probably want to go directly to the Target Your Skills exercise at the end of the Skill Set and Test your mastery of the objectives in that Skill Set. If you are unsure about how to accomplish any part of the exercise, you can always go back to the individual lessons that you need to review, and practice the steps required for each MOUS objective.

If you are relatively new to Word, you'll probably want to complete the lessons in the book in a sequential manner, using Target Your Skills exercise at the end of each Skill Set to confirm that you've learned the skills necessary to pass each objective on the MOUS test.

The Target Your Skills exercises simulate the same types of activities that you will be requested to perform on the test. Therefore, your ability to complete them in a timely fashion will be a direct indicator of your preparedness for the MOUS exam.

Judy Cameron, Spokane Community College
and the Certification Circle Series Team

SAM, Skills Assessment Manager for Microsoft Office XP

SAM XP–the pioneer of IT assessment.

How can you gauge your students' knowledge of Office XP? SAM XP makes teaching and testing Office XP skills easier. SAM XP is a unique Microsoft Office XP assessment and reporting tool that helps you gain a true understanding of your students' ability to use Microsoft Word, Excel, Access, and PowerPoint 2002, and coming soon Outlook 2002, Windows 2000 and Windows XP.

TOM, Training Online Manager for Microsoft Office XP

TOM—efficient, individualized learning when, where, and how you need it.

TOM is Course Technology's MOUS-approved training tool for Microsoft Office XP that works in conjunction with SAM XP assessment and your Illustrated Office XP book. Available via the World Wide Web or a stand-along CD-ROM, TOM allows students to actively learn Office XP concepts and skills by delivering realistic practice through both guided and self-directed simulated instruction.

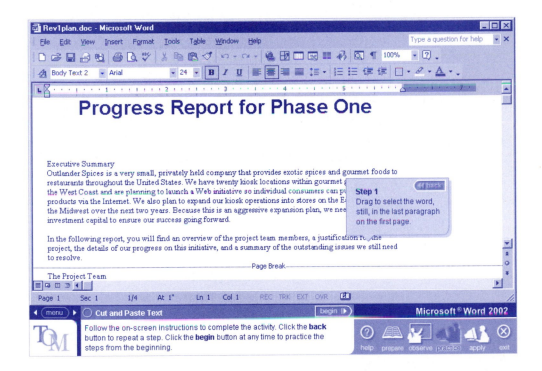

Certification Circle: Exam Reference Pocket Guide

The Microsoft Office ^{XP} Exam Reference Pocket Guide is a reference tool designed to prepare you for the Microsoft Office User Specialist (MOUS) exams. The book assumes that you are already familiar with the concepts that are the basis for the skills covered in this book. The book can therefore be used as a study companion to brush up on skills before taking the exam or as a desk reference when using Microsoft Office programs.

There are six chapters in this book. The first chapter in the book, *Exam Tips*, provides some background information on the MOUS Certification program, the general process for taking an exam, and some helpful hints in preparing and successfully passing the exams.

The remaining five chapters each cover a different Office program: Word, Excel, Access, PowerPoint, and Outlook. Each program-specific chapter begins by covering program basics in a brief *Getting Started* section. This section covers the basic skills that are not specifically covered in the MOUS exams, but that are essential to being able to work in the program. The *Getting Started* section is followed by the complete set of skills tested by the Microsoft MOUS Certification exams, starting with the Core or Comprehensive exam, and then followed by the Expert exam where applicable. These sections are labeled and ordered to exactly match the Skill Sets and Skill Activities tested in the MOUS Certification Exam. Clear, bulleted steps are provided for each skill.

Because there are often different ways to complete a task, the book provides multiple methods where appropriate for each skill or activity, including Menu, Button, Keyboard, Mouse, and Task Pane methods. The MOUS exams allow you to perform the skills using any one of these methods, so you can choose the method with which you are most comfortable to complete the task. It is the perfect companion to any of the Certification Circle Series textbooks or as a stand-alone reference book.

Contents

MOUS Microsoft Word 2002

CERTIFICATION CIRCLE™ EXPERT

MOUS Microsoft Word 2002

CERTIFICATION CIRCLE™ EXPERT

MOUS Microsoft Word 2002

CERTIFICATION CIRCLE™ EXPERT

MOUS Microsoft Word 2002

CERTIFICATION CIRCLE™ EXPERT

MOUS Microsoft Word 2002

CERTIFICATION CIRCLE™ EXPERT

Skill List

1. Start and exit Word
2. Understand toolbars
3. Understand task panes
4. Open and close documents
5. Work with more than one open document
6. Navigate in the document window
7. Understand views
8. Save the files you create
9. Use smart tags
10. Get help

Microsoft Word is a **word-processing program**, a program that makes it easy to enter and manipulate text in documents. A **document** is any file that you create using Word.

Before you can start creating your own documents, you need to learn a few fundamentals about working with Word, including how to start and exit the program, open and close documents, navigate in a document, open and close task panes, change views, save files, use smart tags, and use Help.

Getting Started

Getting Started with Word 2002

Start and Exit Word

Before you can create documents, you need to start Word. In this lesson, you will learn how to start and exit the Word program. When you start Word, you open the Word program window and a blank document window.

Activity Steps

Step 5
You can also click Exit on the File menu to exit Word.

1. Click the **Start button** [Start] on the Windows taskbar
2. Point to **Programs**
   See Figure GS-1.
3. Click **Microsoft Word**
4. If necessary, click the **Maximize button** [□] in the Word program window title bar
   See Figure GS-2.
5. Click the **Close button** [×] in the program window title bar

Figure GS-1: Starting Word

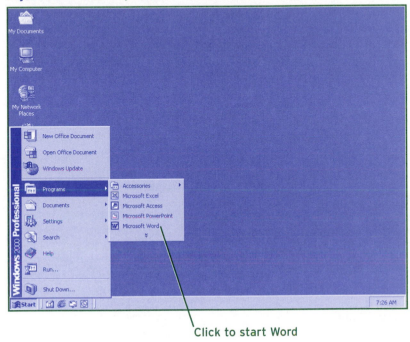

Click to start Word

Figure GS-2: Word program window

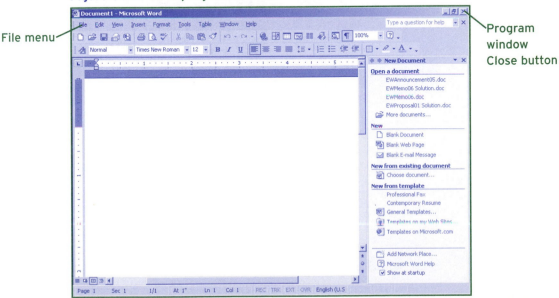

File menu

Program
window
Close button

Getting Started

Getting Started with Word 2002

Understand Toolbars

Toolbars contain buttons that provide one-click access to frequently used commands. When you start Word, usually only the Standard and Formatting toolbars are visible. Word provides 30 toolbars that contain buttons grouped by specific tasks. For example, the Tables and Borders toolbar contains buttons that you click when you are working with a table in a document. Toolbars are either **docked** along a screen edge, or they are **floating** in the middle of the screen.

If you keep the Standard and Formatting toolbars on one line, the button you want may not be visible, so click the Toolbar Options button on either toolbar, then click the button you need.

Activity Steps

1. Start Word

2. If the Standard and Formatting toolbars are on one line, as shown in Figure GS-3, click either **Toolbar Options button** , then click **Show Buttons on Two Rows**
   The figures in this book show the Standard and Formatting toolbars on two lines.

3. Click **Tools** on the menu bar, click **Customize** to open the Customize dialog box, then click the **Options tab**, if necessary

4. Make sure that the **Show Standard and Formatting toolbars on two rows** check box is selected, then click the **Always show full menus check box** to select it, if necessary

5. Click **Close** in the Customize dialog box

6. Right-click any toolbar, then click **Tables and Borders** to open the Tables and Borders toolbar
   See Figure GS-4.

7. If the Tables and Borders toolbar is not floating as shown in Figure GS-4, position the pointer over a blank area on the toolbar (not over a button), press and hold the mouse button so that the pointer changes to ┼, then drag the toolbar down into a blank area of the window and release the mouse button

8. Click the **Close button** ☒ in the Tables and Borders toolbar title bar, then exit Word

Figure GS-3: Word program window with Standard and Formatting toolbars on one line

Toolbars on one line

Toolbar Options buttons

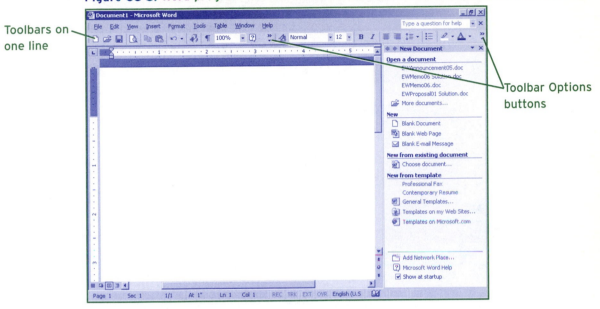

Figure GS-4: Standard and Formatting toolbars on two lines and a floating toolbar

Toolbars on two lines

Tables and Borders toolbar

Toolbar Close button

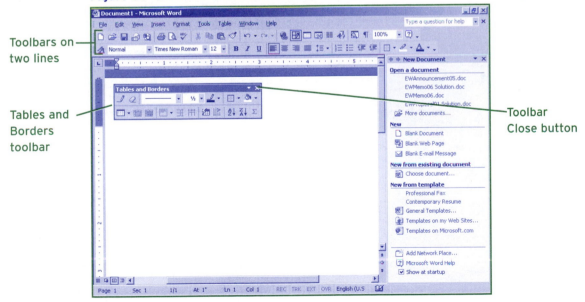

Getting Started

Getting Started with Word 2002

Understand Task Panes

Task panes provide lists of hyperlinks (links) to commonly used commands. They usually appear on the right side of the document window. When you move the pointer over a hyperlink in a taskpane, the pointer changes to 🖑 and the link becomes underlined (similar to links in your browser window). Clicking a link has the same effect as executing a command using the menus or toolbars. Word provides eight task panes (see Table GS-1).

Activity Steps

1. Start Word

2. If a task pane is not open, click **View** on the menu bar, then click **Task Pane**

3. Click the **Other Task Panes list arrow** ▼ in the task pane title bar, then click **Reveal Formatting** to open the Reveal Formatting task pane

4. Move the pointer over the **Font link** to see the pointer change to 🖑
   See Figure GS-5.

5. Move the pointer over the **Sample Text box** at the top of the task pane to see the list arrow appear

6. Click the **Back button** ◀ in the task pane title bar to return to the previously displayed task pane

7. Click the **Close button** ✕ in the task pane title bar to close the task pane
   See Figure GS-6.

8. Exit Word

tip

Right-click any toolbar, then click Task Pane to open or close task panes.

TABLE GS-1: Task panes in Word	
task pane	**description**
New Document	Contains commands for opening new and existing documents
Clipboard	Opens the Office Clipboard, a special area for holding text and objects that you want to paste into the document
Search	Contains commands and options for searching for files that meet specific criteria
Insert Clip Art	Contains commands for searching for clip art (saved images) that meet specific criteria
Styles and Formatting	Contains lists of Word styles (pre-defined formats for text)
Reveal Formatting	Displays a description of the formatting in the selected text
Mail Merge	A set of six panes that helps you merge names and addresses with a form letter
Translate	Contains commands for translating selected text or the entire document to and from French or Spanish

Figure GS-5: Reveal Formatting task pane open

Back button

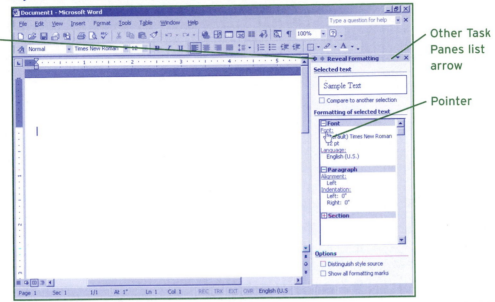

Other Task Panes list arrow

Pointer

Figure GS-6: Document window with no task pane open

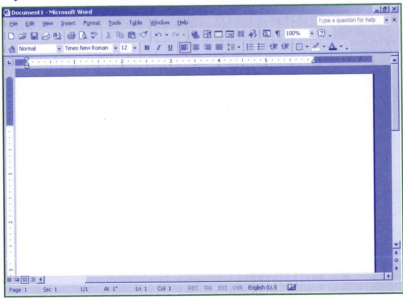

extra!

Using task panes versus using menus and toolbars

Some task pane commands are available on menus or toolbars; for example, you can click the New button ☐ to open a new, blank document, or you can click the Blank Document link on the New Document task pane. Other commands are available only on task panes; for example, when you click Search on the File menu, a Search task pane opens, because that is the only place you can enter your search criteria.

Getting Started

Getting Started with Word 2002

Open and Close Documents

In Word, you can create new, blank documents and you can open existing documents to edit them. When you open documents, you can click the list arrow next to the Open command in the Open dialog box to choose one of a variety of ways to open the document (see Table GS-2). When you have finished working on a document, you should close it. It's a good idea to close all open documents before exiting Word.

Activity Steps

1. Start Word, make sure the New Document task pane is open, then click the **Blank Document link** under **New** in the task pane as shown in Figure GS-7 to open another new, blank document

2. Click the **Close Window button** ☒ in the menu bar to close the document

3. Click the **Open button** ☞ to open the Open dialog box

4. Click the **Look in list arrow**, then select the drive or folder where your project files are stored

5. If your project files are stored within another folder, double-click that folder in the list to display its contents

6. Click the **CCAnnouncement01** file to select it
   See Figure GS-8.

7. Click **Open** to open the selected file

8. Click **File** on the menu bar, then click **Close** to close the document

   Note: In the rest of the book, we assume that you will have Word running or that you will start Word before completing the steps, and that you will exit Word when you have finished.

   When you need to open a file to complete a set of steps, the complete filename will appear next to 🗒 before Step 1. 🗒 will appear again at the end of the steps to remind you to close the file or files you worked on in the skill.

Click the New Blank Document button to open a new, blank document; click the More documents link in the New Document task pane to open the Open dialog box.

Figure GS-7: Closing a document

New Blank Document button

Open button

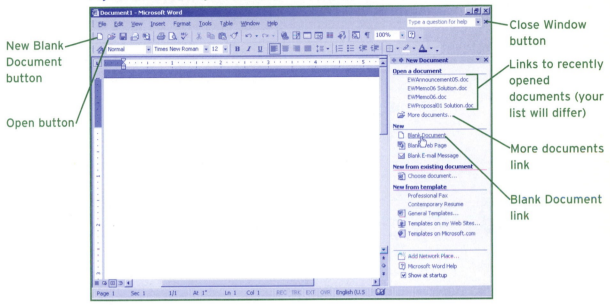

Close Window button

Links to recently opened documents (your list will differ)

More documents link

Blank Document link

Figure GS-8: Open dialog box

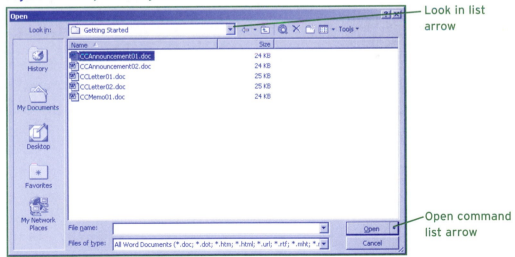

Look in list arrow

Open command list arrow

Getting Started

Getting Started with Word 2002

Work with More Than One Open Document

You can open more than one document at a time in Word. The **active document** is the document that you are currently working on. The other documents are **inactive**. You can switch between open documents by clicking the document button on the Windows task bar; by clicking Window on the menu bar, then clicking the document name; or by displaying all of the open document windows on the screen at once and clicking in the one you want to make active.

Activity Steps

 open CCAnnouncement01.doc

1. Make sure that Word is running, then make sure you opened the **CCAnnouncement01** file as indicated above

2. Click the **Open button** 📂, navigate to the drive and folder where your project files are stored, click the **CCMemo01** file, then click **Open** to open a second document

Step 3
You can also click the document button on the taskbar to switch to another document.

3. Click **Window** on the menu bar, then click **CCAnnouncement01**, as shown in Figure GS-9, to make it the active document

4. Click **Window** on the menu bar, then click **Arrange All** to display both documents at the same time
See Figure GS-10.

5. Click in the **CCMemo01 document window** to make it the active document

6. Press and hold **[Shift]**, click **File** on the menu bar in the CCMemo01 document window, then click **Close All**

7. Click the **Maximize button** ⬜ in the Word program window

Figure GS-9: Switching between documents using the Windows menu

Checkmark appears next to active document

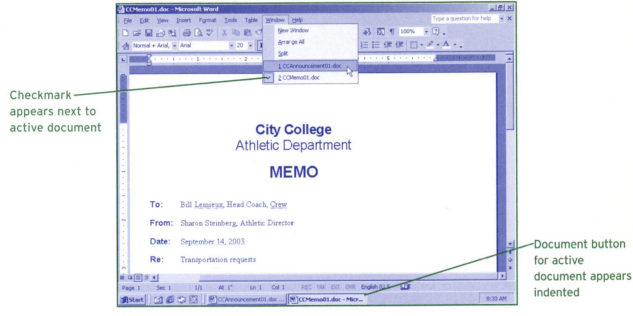

Document button for active document appears indented

Figure GS-10: Two open documents displayed on screen at the same time

Title bar of active document is blue

Title bar of inactive document is gray

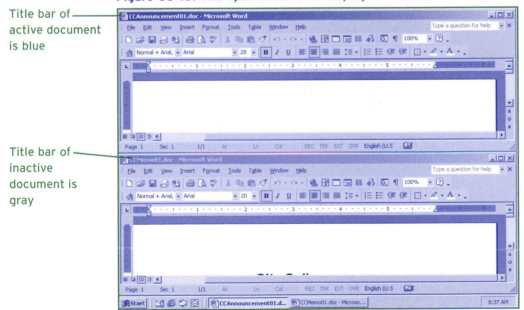

Getting Started

Navigate in the Document Window

One of the benefits of working with Word is how easy it is to move around and edit different parts of the document. You can click anywhere in the document to position the **insertion point**, the blinking vertical line that indicates where the text you type will appear. You can also use the keyboard to move the insertion point around in the document (see Table GS-3). Some keys need to be used together to move the insertion point. When you see two keys listed next to each other, such as [Ctrl][Home], you must press and hold the first key, in this case, the [Ctrl] key, then press the second key, in this case, the [Home] key, and then release both keys.

Activity Steps

 open CCLetter01.doc

1. Make sure that you opened the **CCLetter01** file as indicated above, then click immediately before **crew** in the first line of the body of the letter to position the blinking insertion point there *See Figure GS-11.*

The horizontal scroll bar works the same way as the vertical scroll bar except the document moves sideways in the window.

2. Press [➡] five times to move the insertion point to the word **program** in the next line

3. Press [Page Down] to move the insertion point down a screen

4. Drag the scroll box in the vertical scroll bar down to the bottom of the scroll bar to see the end of the document without moving the insertion point

5. Click above the scroll box in the vertical scroll bar to jump up a screen

6. Click the down scroll arrow in the vertical scroll bar to scroll down one line

7. Press [Ctrl][Home] to move the insertion point to the beginning of the document

8. Make sure you close the **CCLetter01** document as indicated below

 close CCLetter01.doc

Figure GS-11: Insertion point in document

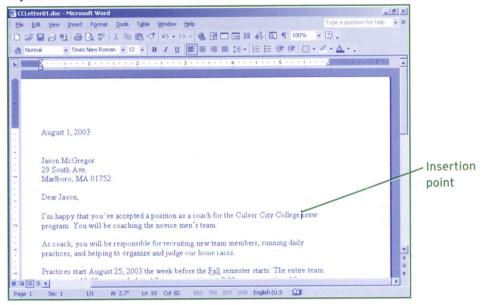

Insertion point

TABLE GS-2: Shortcut keys for moving the insertion point

key	effect
[→], [←]	Moves the insertion point to the right or left one character at a time
[Ctrl][→], [Ctrl][←]	Moves the insertion point to the right or left one word at a time
[↓], [↑]	Moves the insertion point down or up one line
[Page Down], [Page Up]	Moves the insertion point down or up one screen at a time
[Ctrl][Home]	Moves the insertion point to the beginning of the document
[Ctrl][End]	Moves the insertion point to the end of the document
[Home]	Moves the insertion point to the beginning of the current line
[End]	Moves the insertion point to the end of the current line

Getting Started

Understand Views

Word allows you to look at your document in different ways called **views** (see Table GS-3). The default view is Print Layout view. To change the view, you click one of the view buttons located to the left of the horizontal scroll bar. You can also change the **zoom**, the magnification of the document on screen, by clicking the Zoom button list arrow , then selecting another zoom setting from the list, or by clicking in the Zoom box, then typing a new magnification. Changing the view or zoom does not affect how the document will look when printed.

Activity Steps

📁 **open CCAnnouncement02.doc**

1. Make sure that you open the **CCAnnouncement02** file as indicated above, then click the **Normal View button** 📄 See Figure GS-12.

2. Click the **Web Layout View button** 🗔

3. Click the **Outline View button** 📄

4. Click the **Print Layout View button** 📄

5. Click the **Zoom button list arrow** , then click **Whole Page** See Figure GS-13.

6. Click in the **Zoom box**, type **60**, then press **[Enter]**

7. Click the **Zoom button list arrow** `60%`, then click **100%**

8. Make sure that you close the **CCAnnouncement02** document as indicated below

📁 **close CCAnnouncement02.doc**

tip

You can also change views by selecting a view on the View menu.

TABLE GS-3: Document views	
view	**what you see**
Print Layout view	All of the text, any graphical elements, and headers and footers as they appear on the printed page
Normal view	Formatted text, but not some graphical elements or headers and footers; does not show the document as it will look when printed
Web Layout view	Document as it would look if you published it to a Web page
Outline view	Headings indented to show the structure of the document

Figure GS-12: Document in Normal view

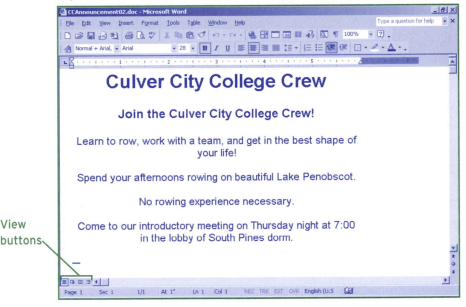

View buttons

Figure GS-13: Document at Whole Page zoom in Print Layout view

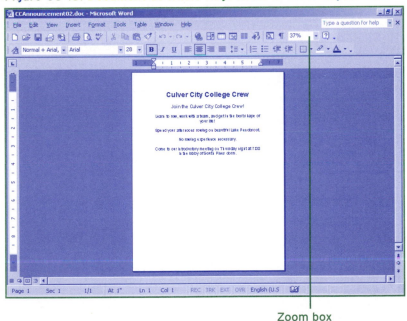

Zoom box

extra!

Splitting a document window into two parts

When you work with a long document, it can sometimes be helpful to split the document window into two panes, allowing you to jump back and forth quickly between two parts of the document. The easiest way to do this is to position the pointer on top of the thin split box, just above the up scroll arrow in the vertical scroll bar, so that the pointer changes to ⬍. Drag the split box down to create two panes in the document window. To close the second window, double-click the split box.

Getting Started

Getting Started with Word 2002

Save the Files You Create

As you work through the activities in this book, you might want to save your completed files. You will learn more about saving files in Skill Set 4, but in the meantime, you can save your files in one of two ways. If you want to leave the original files that you open unchanged, you can save your completed files with a new name by using the Save As command on the File menu. If you don't care if the original file changes, you can save the changes that you make when you complete the steps to the same file that you opened by clicking the Save button 🖫.

Activity Steps

 open CCMemo01.doc

1. Make sure that you opened the **CCMemo01** file as indicated above, click **File** on the menu bar, then click **Save As** to open the Save As dialog box

2. Click the **Save in list arrow**, then select the drive or folder where you want to store your files

3. If you are storing your files within another folder, double-click that folder in the list to display its contents

4. Select the text in the **File name box** if it's not already selected, then type **Intro Letter** in the Filename box
   See Figure GS-14.

5. Click **Save** to save the document with the new name and leave the original document unchanged

6. Type **Culver**, then press the **[Spacebar]**

7. Click the **Save button** 🖫 to save the changes to the document with the same filename
   See Figure GS-15.

8. Make sure that you close the **Intro letter** document as indicated below

 close Intro Letter.doc

tip

Copy all of the project files before you use them to complete the skills in this book. This will allow you to repeat the steps for any skills that you want to review.

---

extra!

Closing without saving
If you do not want to save the changes you made to the documents as you work through the activities, you can simply close the files without saving them first. When you do this, a warning box will appear asking if you want to save the changes to the file. If you click No, the file closes without saving your changes. If you click Yes, the changes you made are saved, then the file closes.

Figure GS-14: Save As dialog box

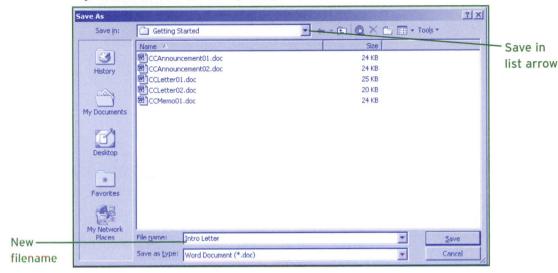

Save in list arrow

New filename

Figure GS-15: Using the Save button

New filename

Save button

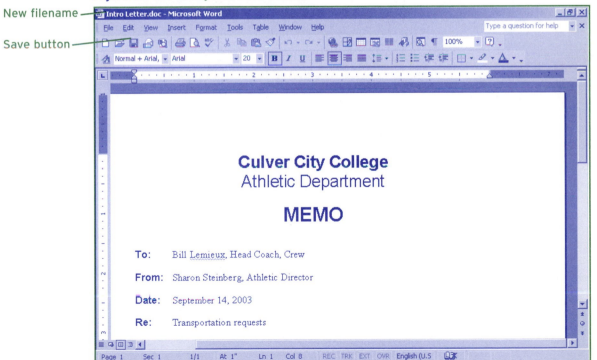

Use Smart Tags

A **smart tag** is a button that appears on screen when Word recognizes a word or phrase as belonging to a certain category, for example, names, addresses, and dates. When you click the button, you can choose to add the name or address to your electronic address book, or you can choose to add the date to your electronic scheduler. Some smart tags do not appear until you position the pointer over their locations, which are identified by a dotted red line under a word or phrase.

Activity Steps

 open CCLetter02.doc

1. Make sure that you opened the **CCLetter02** file as indicated above, then move the pointer over the **date** in the first line to see the smart tag ⓘ appear
   See Figure GS-16.

2. Point to the **smart tag** to make the Smart Tag Actions button ⓘ ▾ appear

3. Click the **Smart Tag Actions button** ⓘ ▾ to open the drop-down list
   See Figure GS-17.

4. Click **Schedule a Meeting** on the drop-down list to open your electronic calendar

5. Click the **Close button** ✕ in the calendar program window, then click **No** when asked if you want to save changes

6. Move the pointer over the **street address** in the inside address to display the smart tag, move the pointer over the **smart tag** ⓘ, then click the **Smart Tag Actions button** ⓘ ▾

7. Click **Remove this Smart Tag**

8. Make sure that you close the **CCLetter02** document as indicated below, clicking **No** when asked if you want to save changes

 close CCLetter02.doc

tip

Step 4
If the Outlook 2002 startup wizard screen appears, you will need to use it to set up Outlook before you can complete Steps 4 and 5. Follow the wizard steps, or click Cancel in the wizard, then continue with Step 6.

extra!

Changing smart tag options
You can change what type of text is labeled by Word with smart tags. Click Smart Tag Options on the Smart Tag Actions button drop down list, or click AutoCorrect Options on the Tools menu, then click the Smart Tags tab. Click the check boxes in the Recognizers list to select or deselect the types of text you want to be recognized. If you are connected to the World Wide Web, you can also click More Smart Tags on the Smart Tags tab in the AutoCorrect Options dialog box. This will connect you to a Microsoft Web site, where you can find more Smart Tags you can download.

Figure GS-16: Displaying a smart tag

Smart tag

Pointer

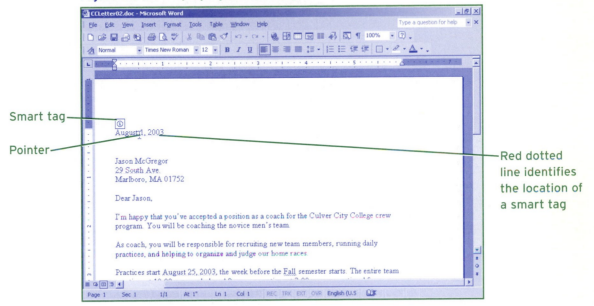

Red dotted line identifies the location of a smart tag

Figure GS-17: Using the Smart Tag Actions button

Smart Tag Actions button

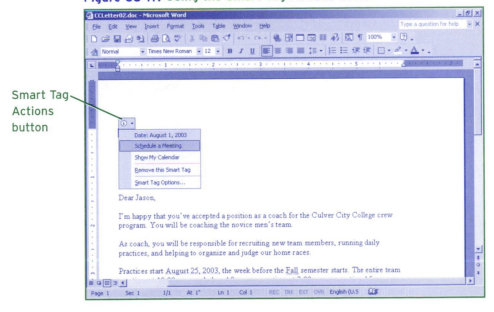

Get Help

Word provides an online Help system to help you find information about Word and instructions on how to use Word commands and features. The easiest way to access the Help system is to type a question in the Ask a Question box in the menu bar in the program window. You can also open the Help window by pressing [F1] or by clicking the Microsoft Word Help button ⍰.

Activity Steps

tip

Step 6
If the topics shown in Figure GS-19 do not appear on your screen, click the plus sign next to Microsoft Word Help in the Contents tab, then click the plus sign next to Viewing and Navigating Documents.

1. Click in the **Ask a Question box** `Type a question for help` in the menu bar

2. Type **Look at two parts of a document**, then press **[Enter]**
   See Figure GS-18.

3. Click the **See more link** at the bottom of the drop-down list

4. Click the **View two parts of a document simultaneously link** to open a Help window displaying this information

5. If the Help window is not expanded as shown in Figure GS-19, click the **Show button** ⊡ in the Help window toolbar to expand the Help window

6. Click the **Contents tab** in the pane on the left of the Help window, if necessary, then click **Move around in a document** as shown in Figure GS-19

7. Click the **plus sign** next to **Getting Started with Microsoft Word** in the Contents tab to expand that topic list

8. Click the **Back button** ⇐ at the top of the Help window to return to the previous Help screen, then click the **Close button** ⊠ in the Help window title bar to close the Help window

extra!

Using the Answer Wizard and Index tabs in the Help window
To use the Answer Wizard tab, you type a question in the box labeled What would you like to do? at the top of the tab, then click Search, and Word retrieves the same list of topics it would have retrieved if you had typed the question in the Ask a Question box. To find all the Help pages associated with a particular topic, click the Index tab, then type a key word into the Type keywords box at the top of the tab; this allows you to scroll quickly to the topic in the list in the middle box. When you see the correct topic in the list in the middle box, click Search, and a list of Help pages appears in the bottom box.

Figure GS-18: Selecting a Help topic from the Ask a Question box drop-down list

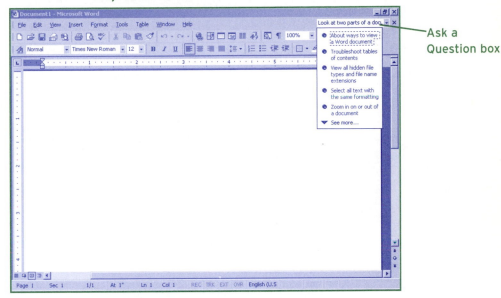

Ask a
Question box

Figure GS-19: Contents tab in the Help window

Click plus sign to
expand topic list

Click minus sign
to collapse topic
list

Click this topic
to display new
information in
pane on the right

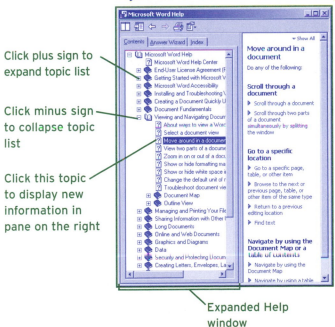

Expanded Help
window

Target Your Skills

Getting Started with Word 2002

Target Your Skills

If you know the answers to the following questions, then you are ready to move ahead to the rest of the chapters in this book. If you have trouble with any of the questions, refer to the page listed next to the question to review the skill.

1. How do you start Word? How do you exit Word? (p. 2)

2. What is the three-letter filename extension for Word documents? Name two other filename extensions that Word recognizes. (p. 3)

3. Describe a toolbar. How are toolbars positioned in the window? Describe two ways to close a toolbar. (p. 4)

4. Define **toggle**. (p. 5)

5. Describe task panes. How do you open a task pane? Describe three ways to close a task pane. (p. 6)

6. How do you open a new, blank document? How do you open an existing document? Describe two ways to close a document. (p. 8)

7. Define **active document**. Describe two ways to switch between open documents. Explain how to display two open documents on the screen at the same time. (p. 10)

8. to the beginning of a document? (p. 12)

9. Describe the four views in Word. Explain what the Zoom command does. (p. 14)

10. How do you split a document window in two? (p. 15)

11. How do you save changes to a document? How do you save a document with a new name? How do you save a new document for the first time? (p. 16)

12. Can you close a document without saving changes that you made? (p. 17)

13. Define **smart tag**. How are smart tags identified in a document? (p. 18)

14. How do you access Word's online Help system? (p. 20)

Skill List

1. Insert, modify, and move text and symbols
2. Apply and modify text formats
3. Correct spelling and grammar usage
4. Apply font and text effects
5. Enter and format date and time
6. Apply character styles

In Skill Set 1, you will learn how to create a document in Microsoft Word 2002. A **document** is any file that you create using Word. You can create many kinds of documents, including memos, letters, newsletters, resumes, brochures, and multi-page reports.

Once you insert text into a document, you can modify that text in several ways. You can change the words or the word order. If you want, you can change the way the text looks by modifying the format of the text. You can also use Word to check your spelling and grammar and to automatically insert the current date and time.

Skill Set 1
Inserting and Modifying Text

Insert, Modify, and Move Text and Symbols
Insert Text

The first thing you do when you create a document is insert text. To do this, you simply start typing using the keyboard. The blinking **insertion point** on the screen indicates where the text will appear. When you reach the end of a line, the insertion point automatically moves to the next line—you do not need to press [Enter]. This is called **word-wrap**. You press [Enter] when you want to start a new paragraph. To add a blank line between paragraphs, you can press [Enter] twice.

Activity Steps

You do not need to type two spaces after any punctuation, because Word adjusts the space automatically.

1. Create a new, blank document

2. Type **November 3, 2003**, then press **[Enter]** twice
   See Figure 1-1.

3. Type **Ms. Patsy Madison**, then press **[Enter]**

4. Type **503 Shore Drive**, then press **[Enter]**

5. Type **Charleston, SC 29407**, then press **[Enter]** twice

6. Type **Dear Ms. Madison:**, then press **[Enter]** twice

7. Type the body of the letter shown in Figure 1-2, then press **[Enter]** twice at the end of the paragraph

8. Type **Sincerely,** press **[Enter]** four times, then type your name

 close file

Figure 1-1: Text entered in a new document

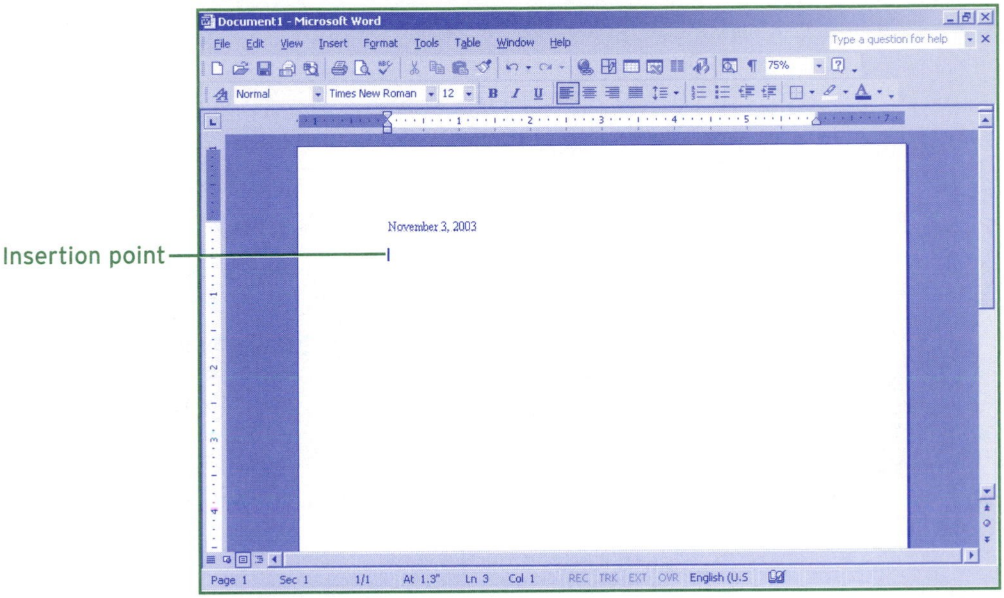

Insertion point ──────────

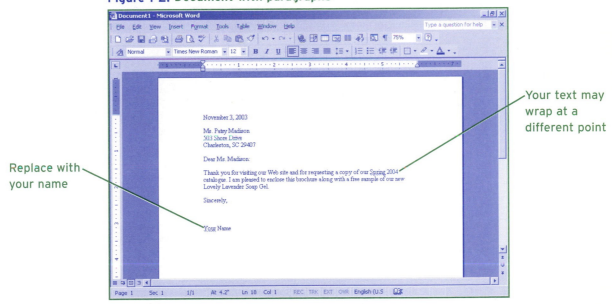

Figure 1-2: Document with paragraphs

Replace with your name

Your text may wrap at a different point

Skill Set 1
Inserting and Modifying Text

Insert, Modify, and Move Text and Symbols
Insert Symbols

In addition to letters and numbers, you can enter symbols in a document. A **symbol** is a character not included in the standard English alphabet or set of Arabic numbers. You enter symbols using the Symbol dialog box.

Click the Special Characters tab in the Symbol dialog box to see a short list of common symbols.

Activity Steps

 open EWLetter01.doc

1. Click immediately after the word **Soap** in the third line, so that the insertion point blinks to the left of the period

2. Click **Insert** on the menu bar, then click **Symbol** to open the Symbol dialog box

3. Click the **Font list arrow**, then click to select **Times New Roman**, if necessary

4. Drag the **scroll box** to the top of the scroll bar, then click the **down scroll arrow** three times

5. Click ©, the copyright symbol
   See Figure 1-3.

6. Click **Insert**, then click **Close**
   See Figure 1-4.

 close EWLetter01.doc

Figure 1-3: Symbol dialog box

Copyright symbol

Description of selected symbol

Shortcut key combination
to insert selected symbol

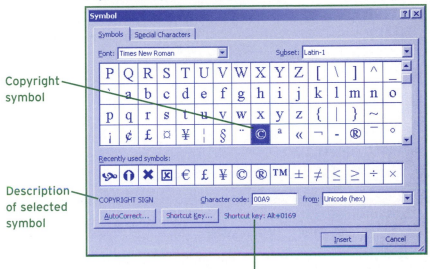

Figure 1-4: Symbol inserted in document

Copyright symbol inserted

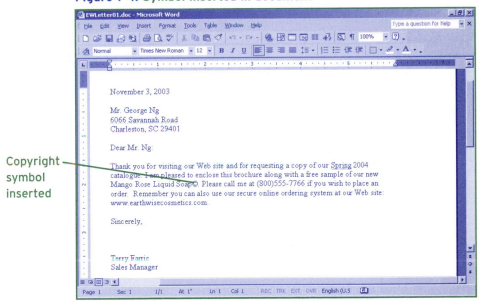

Skill Set 1

Inserting and Modifying Text

Insert, Modify, and Move Text and Symbols
Edit Text

With a word processor, you do not need to retype an entire document when you want to change a word or delete a sentence. The easiest way to edit text is to use the [Backspace] and [Delete] keys. When you press [Backspace], you delete the character immediately to the left of the insertion point. When you press [Delete], you delete the character immediately to the right of the insertion point. You can also **select**, or highlight, the text you want to change and then start typing, and the characters you type will replace all of the selected text.

If you make a mistake, you can "undo" it by clicking the Undo button. Undo any number of previous actions by clicking the list arrow next to the Undo button, then selecting as many actions as you want.

Activity Steps

 open EWMemo01.doc

1. Click immediately to the right of **Seaview** in the first paragraph in the body of the memo

2. Press **[Backspace]** seven times, then type **Riverside**

3. Click immediately to the left of **20** (after **June**) in the first paragraph

4. Press **[Delete]** twice, then type **19**

5. Double-click the word **three** in the first line in the first paragraph to select it

6. Type **four**
   See Figure 1-5.

 close EWMemo01.doc

Figure 1-5: Document with edited text

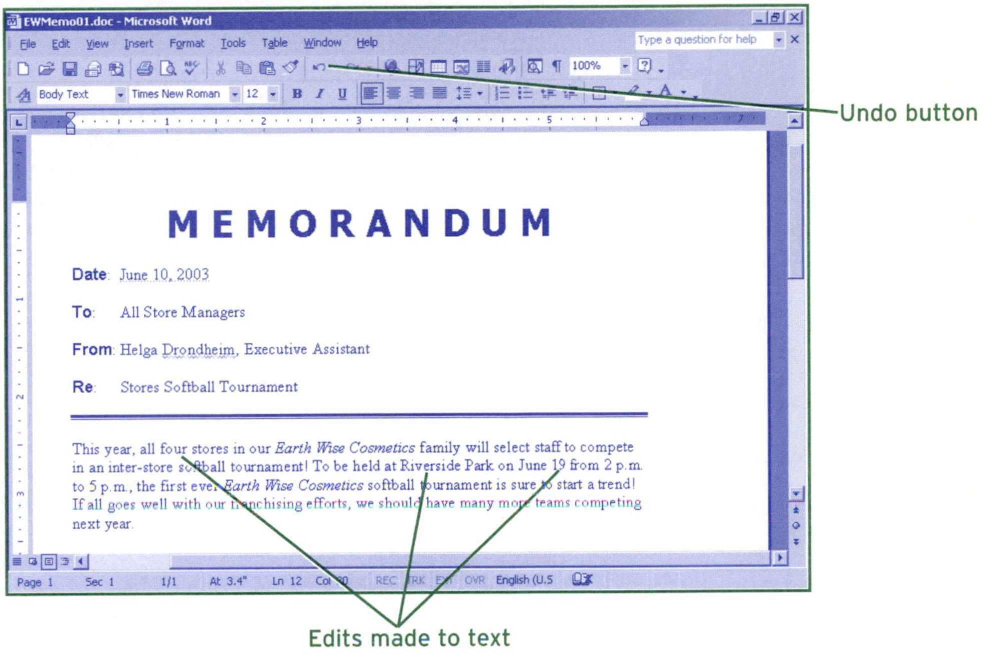

Undo button

Edits made to text

extra!

Selecting text

There are several ways to select text. You can position the pointer to one side of the text you want to select, press and hold the mouse button, drag the pointer across the text to select it, then release the mouse button. To select a word quickly, double-click it. To select a line of text, position the pointer in the blank area on the left side of the document to the left of the line, so that the pointer changes to ⌐, then click. To select a large body of text, click at the beginning of the text you want to select, press and hold [Shift], then click at the end of the text. You can also use the keyboard to select text. Position the pointer to the left or right of the text you want to select, press and hold [Shift], then press [➡] or [⬅] as many times as necessary to select the word or phrase. To select a word at a time, press and hold [Shift] and [Ctrl] while you press [➡] or [⬅].

Skill Set 1

Inserting and Modifying Text

Insert, Modify, and Move Text and Symbols
Cut and Paste Text

You use the Cut and Paste commands to move text from one place in a document to another, or even from one document to another. When you **cut** text, it is removed from the document and stored in the system **clipboard**. When you **paste** text, you are pasting whatever is stored on the clipboard. You can paste the text you stored on the clipboard as many times as you like. The system clipboard can hold only one thing at a time, so each time you cut text, you replace whatever was stored there before. The clipboard is cleared when you shut off your computer.

Activity Steps

 open EWLetter02.doc

1. Double-click the word **online** in the first sentence of the second paragraph within the body of the letter

2. Click the **Cut button** ✂

3. Click between the words **completed** and **that** in the second paragraph

4. Click the **Paste button** 📋

5. Scroll down until you can see the third paragraph

6. Click to position the insertion point before the word **Again** in the third paragraph, press and hold the mouse button, drag to highlight the entire first sentence including the space after the period, then release the mouse button

7. Point to the selected sentence and hold down the mouse button

8. Drag down so that the vertical indicator line attached to the pointer appears after the last sentence in the paragraph
   See Figure 1-6.

9. Release the mouse button to position the dragged sentence at the end of the paragraph
   See Figure 1-7.

 close EWLetter02.doc

tip

Click the Paste Options button that appears on the screen after you perform the Paste command or drag and drop text to choose options for changing the format of the pasted text.

extra!

Understanding the Office Clipboard

With Office XP you can use the standard system clipboard or the Office Clipboard. The system clipboard can store only the most recently cut or copied item. The Office Clipboard which opens as a task pane, can store up to 24 items. To activate it, click Office Clipboard on the Edit menu or perform several cut, copy, and paste commands in succession. To paste an item from the Office Clipboard, click the item in the Clipboard task pane. (When you use the Paste command, you paste only the last item placed on the system clipboard.)

Figure 1-6: Document with moved text and sentence being dragged and dropped

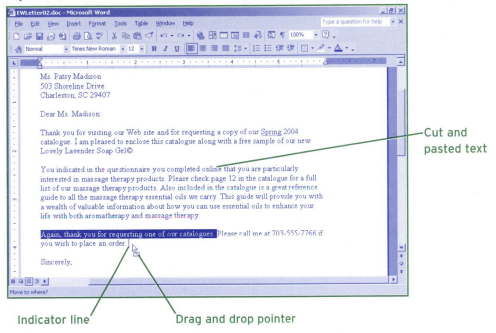

Cut and pasted text

Indicator line   Drag and drop pointer

Figure 1-7: Document after sentence is dropped in new location

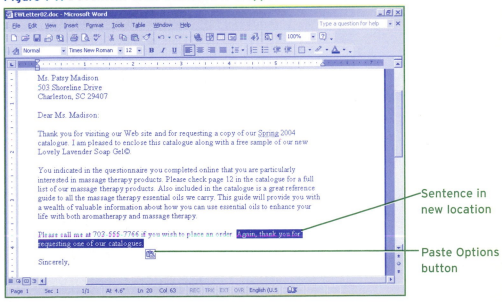

Sentence in new location

Paste Options button

Skill Set 1
Inserting and Modifying Text

Insert, Modify, and Move Text and Symbols
Copy and Paste Text

Copying is similar to cutting, but when you copy text, you don't remove it from its original location. As with cutting, whatever you copy is placed on the clipboard for you to paste as many times as you want, until you replace it with new cut or copied text.

Right-click selected text, then click Cut or Copy. Right-click where you want to paste the text, then click Paste.

Activity Steps

 open EWLetter03.doc

1. Select **Mr. Ng** in the salutation (do not select the colon)
2. Click the **Copy button**
3. Click immediately after **thank you** in the first line in the last paragraph, type **,** (a comma), then press the **[Spacebar]**
4. Click the **Paste button**, then type **,** (a comma)
   See Figure 1-8.
5. Double-click **catalogue** in the second line in the first paragraph
6. Press and hold **[Ctrl]**, then drag **catalogue** between **the** and **for** in the second line in the second paragraph
   See Figure 1-9.

close EWLetter03.doc

Figure 1-8: Text copied to new location

Copied text

Figure 1-9: Copied text being dragged and dropped

Indicator line

Drag and drop copy pointer

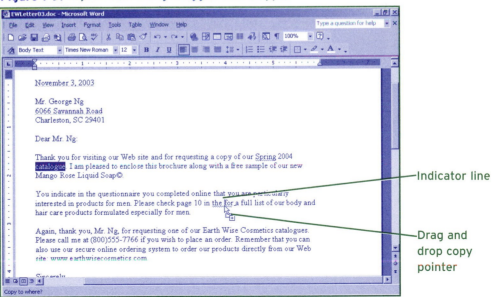

Skill Set 1
Inserting and Modifying Text

Insert, Modify, and Move Text and Symbols
Use the Paste Special Command

The Paste Special command allows you to control how information is pasted by giving you a variety of paste options. You can use it when you cut or copy something from one place in a Word document to another place in the same document, when you cut or copy between Word documents, or when you cut or copy from a file created in another program to a Word document. You can also use it to copy formatted text—text with a specific appearance—to another paragraph that is formatted differently, and have the pasted text pick up the formatting of its destination paragraph.

Activity Steps

 open EWBrochure01.doc
EWLetter04.doc

1. Click **Window** on the menu bar, then click **EWBrochure01.doc**

2. Select the entire paragraph under the heading **Lavender Soap Gel** (do not select the heading or the blank line below the paragraph) *See Figure 1-10.*

3. Click the **Copy button** 📋

4. Click **Window** on the menu bar, then click **EWLetter04.doc**

5. Click at the end of the first paragraph, after the period

6. Click **Edit** on the menu bar, click **Paste Special**, then click **Unformatted Text** in the list in the Paste Special dialog box

7. Click **OK** to paste the copied text so it picks up the formatting of the destination paragraph *See Figure 1-11.*

 close EWBrochure01.doc
EWLetter04.doc

tip

Another way to paste copied text so that it picks up the formatting of the destination paragraph is to use the Paste command, click the Paste Options button that appears on screen, then click Match Destination Formatting.

Using Paste Special to paste between files created in different programs
The Paste Special command is especially useful for inserting text or data copied from a file created in another program into a Word document. For example, you can paste a chart created in Microsoft Excel as an Excel **object**—an item that retains the format and characteristics of the original chart—as a picture or as text. If you paste it as an Excel object, you can double-click the object to automatically open Excel and edit the chart (as long as Excel is available on your computer).

Figure 1-10: Formatted text selected in a document

EWBrochure01 is the active file

Selected text

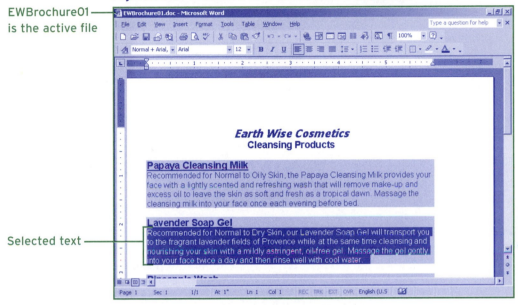

Figure 1-11: Pasted text with the formatting of the destination paragraph

EWLetter04 is the active file

Inserted text picks up formatting of this paragraph

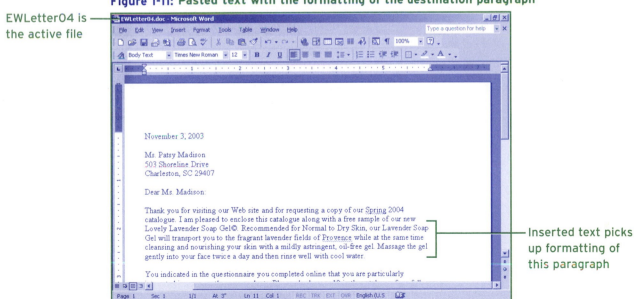

Skill Set 1
Inserting and Modifying Text

Insert, Modify, and Move Text and Symbols
Find and Replace Text

In a long document, you may need to locate a specific word or phrase. You may also want to replace that word or phrase with another. The Find and Replace commands in Word let you do this easily and quickly. Enter the word or words for which you are searching, and then tell Word to find them. If you want to replace the words you find, you can enter the new words and tell Word to replace the search terms.

Activity Steps

 open EWLetter05.doc

1. Click **Edit** on the menu bar, then click **Find** to open the Find and Replace dialog box

2. Type **massage therapy** in the Find what box

3. Click **Find Next**
   See Figure 1-12.

4. Click the **Replace tab** in the Find and Replace dialog box, click in the Replace with box, then type **aromatherapy**

5. Click **Replace** to replace the search term with the replacement term and to find the next instance of the search term in the document

6. Click **Replace** two more times to replace the next two instances of the search term
   See Figure 1-13.

7. Click **Find Next** to skip this instance of the search term and find the next one

8. Click **OK** in the dialog box that appears telling you that Word has finished searching the document, then click **Close** in the Find and Replace dialog box

 close EWLetter05.doc

If you are sure that you want to replace all instances of the text for which you are searching, click Replace All on the Replace tab in the Find and Replace dialog box.

Finding formatted text and special characters
You can search for text with specific formatting as well as special characters. Click More in the Find and Replace dialog box, then click Format or Special. For example, if you wanted to find all the words with bold formatting, click in the Find what box, click Format, click Font, click Bold, then click OK. When you click Find Next, Word searches for words with bold formatting. To remove formatting options from the search criteria, click No Formatting.

extra!

Figure 1-12: Using the Find command

Text found in document

Find what box

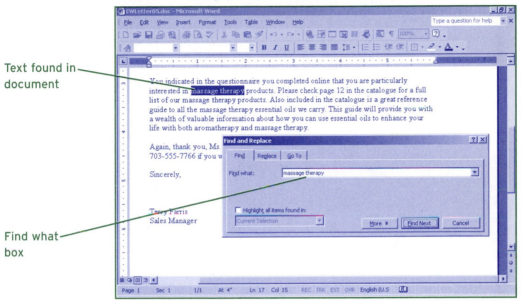

Figure 1-13: Replacing text

Replaced text

Don't replace this instance

Click to see more options

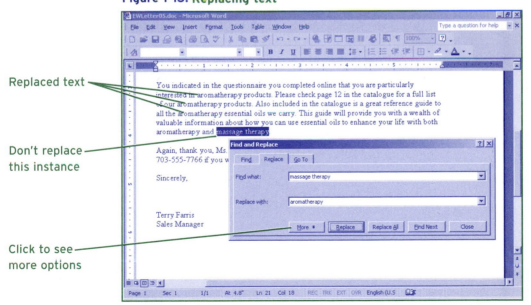

Skill Set 1

Inserting and Modifying Text

Insert, Modify, and Move Text and Symbols
Create AutoText Entries and Use AutoComplete

You can store frequently used words or phrases as AutoText, text that Word automatically enters. When you type the first few characters of an AutoText entry, a ScreenTip appears identifying it as AutoText. You can then use the AutoComplete feature by pressing [Enter] to insert the rest of the word or phrase automatically.

To see the predefined AutoText entries, click Tools on the menu bar, click AutoCorrect Options, then click the AutoText tab and scroll down the list.

Activity Steps

 open EWAnnouncement01.doc

1. Select **Earth Wise Cosmetics** in the first line in the document

2. Click **Insert** on the menu bar, point to **AutoText**, then click **New** to open the Create AutoText dialog box

3. Click **OK** to accept the suggested name for the AutoText entry

4. Click immediately before the word **Softball** in the last paragraph

5. Type **eart** to see the AutoComplete ScreenTip
   See Figure 1-14.

6 Press **[Enter]** to complete the AutoText entry
   See Figure 1-15.

7. Click **Insert** on the menu bar, point to **AutoText**, then click **AutoText** to open the AutoText tab in the AutoCorrect dialog box

8. Type **e** in the Enter AutoText Entries here box to jump to the entries beginning with **e** in the list, click **Earth Wise** in the list, click **Delete**, then click **OK** to close the dialog box

 close EWAnnouncement01.doc

Figure 1-14: AutoComplete ScreenTip

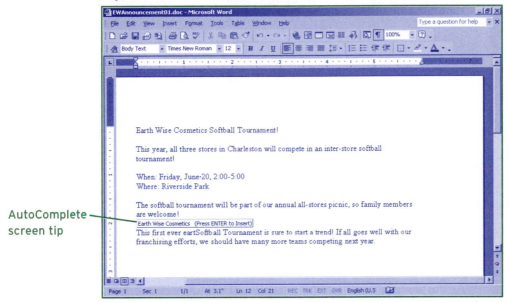

AutoComplete screen tip

Figure 1-15: Completed AutoText entry in document

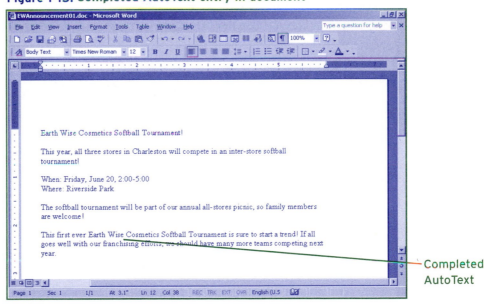

Completed AutoText

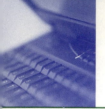

Skill Set 1

Inserting and Modifying Text

Insert, Modify, and Move Text and Symbols

Use AutoCorrect

AutoCorrect automatically detects and corrects frequently misspelled words, and it checks for and corrects incorrect capitalization. It also replaces text with symbols. For example, if you type *teh*, as soon as you press the [Spacebar] or [Enter], AutoCorrect replaces the mistyped word with *the*. You can add your own frequently typed words to the AutoCorrect list to cut down on the number of keystrokes you need to make.

To change the types of words automatically corrected, open the AutoCorrect tab in the AutoCorrect dialog box, and deselect any check boxes you wish.

Activity Steps

 open EWBrochure02.doc

1. Click below the **Lavender Soap Gel** heading, then type **We reccommend** with two *c*s exactly as shown

2. Press the **[Spacebar]**, watching the screen as you do to see AutoCorrect correct the spelling of **recommend**

3. Move the pointer over the word **recommend** to see the AutoCorrect Options button
   See Figure 1-16.

4. Move the pointer over the **AutoCorrect Options button** to change it to a button icon

5. Click the **AutoCorrect Options button**, click **Control AutoCorrect Options** in the drop-down menu to open the AutoCorrect tab in the AutoCorrect dialog box, scroll down the list to see the AutoCorrect entries, then click **OK**

6. Type **this gle for** and observe the red, squiggly line under **gle** that indicates the word is misspelled

7. Right-click the misspelled word **gle**, point to AutoCorrect on the shortcut menu, then click **gel** as shown in Figure 1-17 to add this misspelling to the AutoCorrect list and correct the word in the document

8. Click **Tools** on the menu bar, click **AutoCorrect Options**, type **gl** in the Replace box to scroll the list, click **gle** in the list, click **Delete**, then click **OK** to delete the word you added from the AutoCorrect list

 close EWBrochure02.doc

Figure 1-16: AutoCorrect box in document

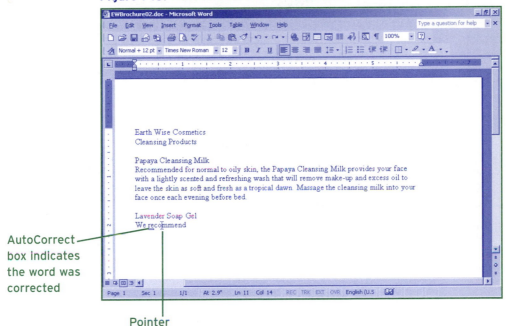

AutoCorrect box indicates the word was corrected

Pointer

Figure 1-17: Adding a word to the AutoCorrect list automatically

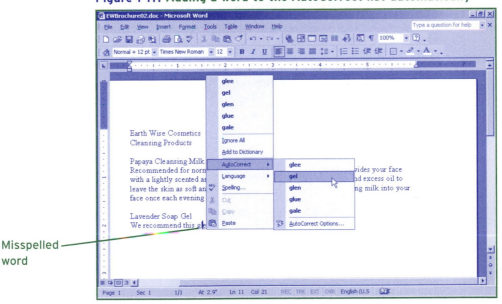

Misspelled word

Skill Set 1
Inserting and Modifying Text

Apply and Modify Text Formats
Apply Character Formats

Format refers to the way something looks. Specifically, you can add formatting to text by changing the **font** (the design of letters and numbers), the **font size**, and the **font style** (for example, adding boldface or italics). Judicious use of text formatting commands can make a document easier to read. Most text formatting can be accomplished using the buttons on the Formatting toolbar.

Activity Steps

open EWCoDescription01.doc

1. Select the first line of text, then click the **Bold button** B

2. Click the **Font box list arrow** , scroll, if necessary, then click **Arial**

3. Click the **Font Size box list arrow** 12 ▾, click **16**, then click in a blank area of the screen to deselect the text
   See Figure 1-18.

4. Select the second line of text, click the **Bold button** B, click the **Italic button** *I*, then change the font size to **14**

5. Click the **Bold button** B again to turn bold formatting off for the selected text

6. Select the third line of text, then click the **Underline button** U

7. Repeat step 6 for the **Company Background** line, then click in a blank area of the screen to deselect the text
   See Figure 1-19.

close EWCoDescription01.doc

tip

If unexpected changes occur as you type, click the AutoFormat As You Type tab in the AutoCorrect dialog box, then deselect the check boxes next to the items you want to stop formatting automatically.

---

extra!

Understanding points and picas

Points and picas are units of measurement for text. A **point** (pt) is approximately 1/72 of an inch, and a **pica** is equivalent to 12 points. Typically, fonts are measured in points, space between paragraphs is measured in points and picas, and margins and paragraph indents are measured in inches.

Figure 1-18: Document after formatting first line of text

Format of text changed —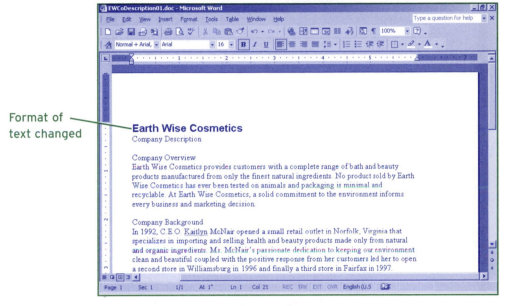

Figure 1-19: Document after formatting headings

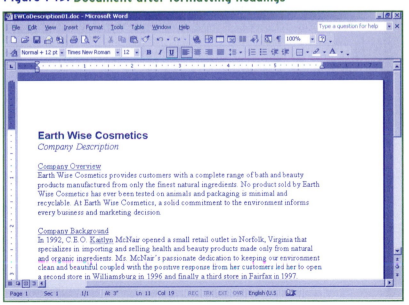

Skill Set 1
Inserting and Modifying Text

Apply and Modify Text Formats
Modify Character Formats

After you have applied formatting to characters, you can change it in any way you wish. Once you have formatted text the way you want, you can copy that formatting to other text in your document by using the Format Painter button.

To format text in different areas of the document with Format Painter, select the text whose format you want to copy, then double-click the Format Painter button. It will remain active until you click it again.

Activity Steps

 open EWAnnouncement02.doc

1. Select the first line of text
   See Figure 1-20.

2. Click the **Font size list arrow** 22 ▾, then click **18**

3. Click the **Font Color list arrow** **A**▾, then click the **Lavender color box** (last row, second to last column)

4. Select **When:**, click the **Bold button** **B** to turn the bold formatting off, then click the **Underline button** **U**

5. With **When:** still selected, click the **Format Painter button**

6. Drag across **Where:** to select it
   See Figure 1-21.

7. Click in a blank area of the screen to deselect the text

 close EWAnnouncement02.doc

Figure 1-20: Formatted text selected

Buttons reflect the formatting of the selected text

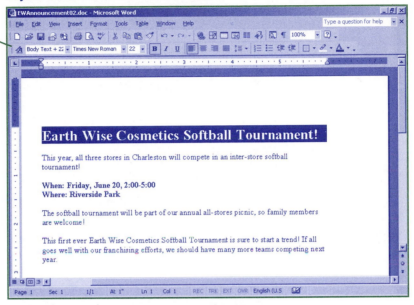

Figure 1-21: Reformatted text in document

Format Painter selected

Pointer

Skill Set 1

Inserting and Modifying Text

Correct Spelling and Grammar Usage

Correct Spelling Errors

When you click the Spelling command, Word scans the document and compares the words against its built-in dictionary. When it finds a word that isn't in its dictionary, it flags it as a possible misspelled word and offers a list of suggested corrections. You can choose one of the corrections from the list, correct the word yourself, or tell Word to ignore the word (in other words, that it is spelled correctly). If automatic spell checking is turned on, you will see red, squiggly lines under the words that Word is flagging as misspelled.

Right-click a word with a red, squiggly underline to open a shortcut menu containing a list of suggested corrections. Click a suggested correction or click Ignore All.

Activity Steps

 open EWLetter06.doc

1. Click the **Spelling and Grammar button**
   See Figure 1-22.

2. Click **catalog** in the Suggestions list, then click **Change All** to change all instances of the flagged word and search for the next possible misspelling

3. Click **Ignore All** to ignore all instances of the word **Provence** (a proper noun) and continue searching

4. Click **Change** to accept the selected entry **twice** in the Suggestions list and continue searching

5. Click **Change** to accept the selected entry **catalogs** in the Suggestions list and continue searching

6. Click **OK** in the dialog box that appears telling you that the spelling and grammar check is complete

 close EWLetter06.doc

Figure 1-22: Spelling dialog box

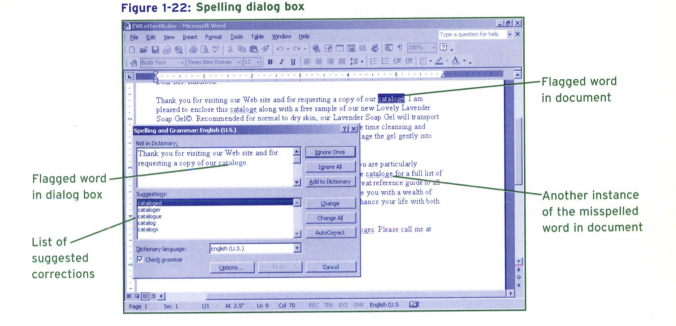

Flagged word in document

Another instance of the misspelled word in document

Flagged word in dialog box

List of suggested corrections

extra!

Changing Spelling and Grammar options

To change Spelling and Grammar checker options, click Options in the Spelling and Grammar dialog box or click Tools on the menu bar, click Options, then click the Spelling & Grammar tab. To hide the red and green squiggly lines in your document, deselect the check boxes next to Check spelling as you type and Check grammar as you type. To check style as well as grammar, click the arrow under Writing style and select Grammar and Style in the list. To change the Grammar checker rules, click Settings, then deselect the check boxes next to the items you don't want to check. If you have already checked the document for spelling and grammar errors but you want to recheck it, click Recheck Document to reset all of the items that you previously had told the Spelling and Grammar checker to ignore.

Skill Set 1

Inserting and Modifying Text

Correct Spelling and Grammar Usage

Correct Grammar Errors

The grammar checker is part of the spell checker. If the Check grammar check box in the Spelling and Grammar dialog box is selected, the grammar in your document will be checked at the same time as the spelling.

The grammar checker is not perfect. It compares sentences against a built-in set of rules, but it may miss errors or identify something that is correct as an error, so use your common sense.

Activity Steps

 open EWLetter07.doc

1. Click the **Spelling and Grammar button**
   See Figure 1-23.

2. Click **Explain**, then read the explanation that appears when the Office Assistant appears

3. Click **Ignore Once** to ignore this rule (*Spring* is a title in the document, not a season) and continue the search

4. Click in the document behind the Spelling and Grammar dialog box, position the insertion point immediately after the **e** in **guide** in the highlighted sentence, press the **[Spacebar]**, then type **will**
   See Figure 1-24.

5. Click **Resume** in the Spelling and Grammar dialog box

6. Click the second suggestion in the Suggestions list, then click **Change**

7. Click **OK** in the dialog box that appears telling you that the spelling and grammar check is complete

 close EWLetter07.doc

Figure 1-23: Grammar problem flagged by Spelling and Grammar checker

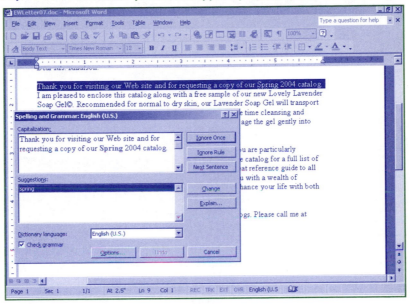

Figure 1-24: Fixing an error in the document

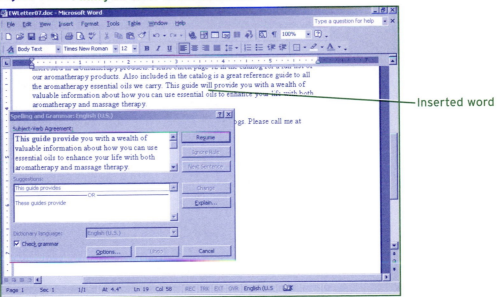

Inserted word

Skill Set 1

Inserting and Modifying Text

Correct Spelling and Grammar Usage

Use the Thesaurus

Word has a built-in thesaurus to help you when you need to find a synonym or an antonym for a word. You can access the thesaurus by right-clicking the word you want to replace or by using a command on the Tools menu.

If none of the Thesaurus suggestions is exactly the word you want, click Look Up in the dialog box to look up the synonym in the Replace with Synonym box to see more suggestions.

Activity Steps

 open EWLetter08.doc

1. Select **asking** in the first line in the body of the letter

2. Click **Tools** on the menu bar, point to **Language**, then click **Thesaurus**

3. Click **Look Up** to look up the infinitive form of the verb, which appears in the Replace with Related Word box
   See Figure 1-25.

4. Click **Replace** to replace the selected word in the document with the selected word in the Replace with Synonym box

5. Press **[Backspace]**, then type **ing**

6. Right-click **talk** in the last paragraph, point to **Synonyms** on the shortcut menu, then click **chat**, as shown in Figure 1-26

 close EWLetter08.doc

Figure 1-25: Thesaurus dialog box

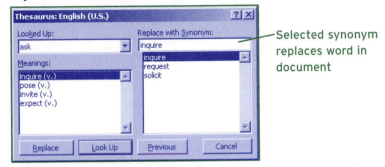

Selected synonym replaces word in document

Figure 1-26: Looking up synonyms

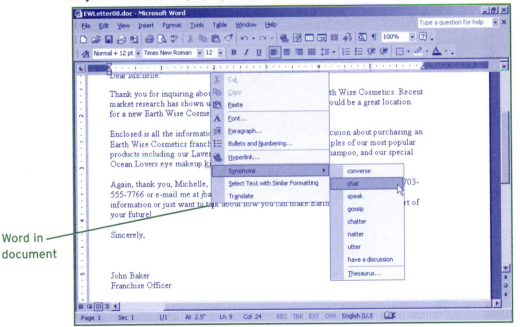

Word in document

Skill Set 1
Inserting and Modifying Text

Apply Font and Text Effects
Apply Character Effects

Formatting commands like Bold, Italic, and Underline are common and appear on the Formatting toolbar. You can apply additional formatting effects to your text if you use the Effects section in the Font dialog box. For example, you can add a line through text, shift text up or down for super- and subscripts, change text to all uppercase, and add interesting effects, such as a shadow, to text. In addition to the buttons on the Formatting toolbar, you can also open the Font dialog box and take advantage of a few additional formatting options.

Right-click selected text, then click Font on the shortcut menu to open the Font dialog box.

Activity Steps

 open EWCoDescription02.doc

1. Select **Earth Wise Cosmetics** in the first line

2. Click **Format** on the menu bar, then click **Font** to open the Font dialog box

3. Click the **Outline check box**, then click the **Small caps check box**
   See Figure 1-27.

4 Click **OK**

5. Select © in the fourth line in the paragraph under the heading **Company Background**

6. Open the Font dialog box, click the **Superscript check box**, click **OK**, then click in a blank area of the screen to deselect the text
   See Figure 1-28.

 close EWCoDescription02.doc

Figure 1-27: Font dialog box with text effects selected

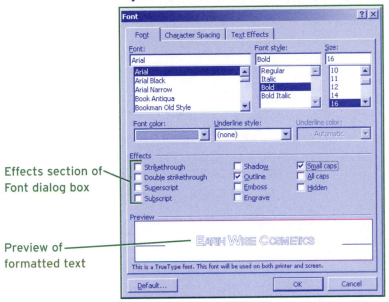

Effects section of Font dialog box

Preview of formatted text

Figure 1-28: Document with text effects applied

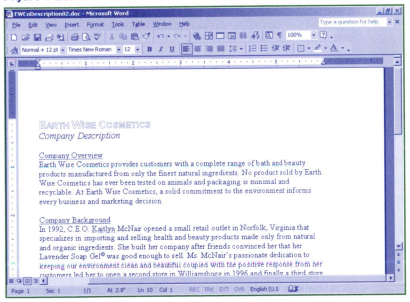

Skill Set 1

Inserting and Modifying Text

Apply Font and Text Effects

Apply Text Animation

If you create a document that is going to be read primarily onscreen rather than in printed form, you can add text animations. Animations are special text effects that move onscreen. You add animation effects in the Font dialog box.

Do not use too many text animations in a document because they can distract the reader from your message.

Activity Steps

 open EWAnnouncement03.doc

1. Select the first line in the document

2. Right-click the selected text, click **Font** on the shortcut menu, then click the **Text Effects tab**

3. Click **Sparkle Text** in the Animations list, then watch the Preview box
   See Figure 1-29.

4. Click **OK**

5. Click anywhere in the document to deselect the text
   See Figure 1-30.

 close EWAnnouncement03.doc

Figure 1-29: Text Effects tab in the Font dialog box

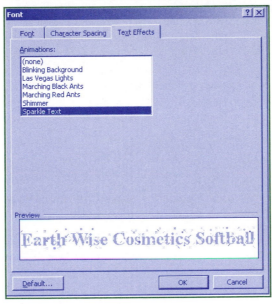

Figure 1-30: Text animation effect applied

Text with
Sparkle Text
animation

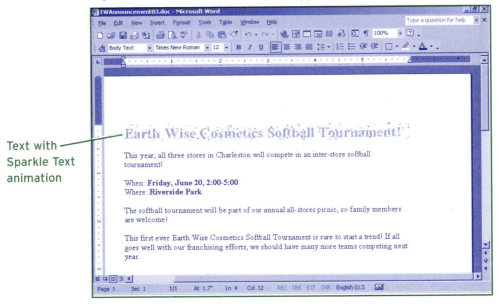

Skill Set 1

Inserting and Modifying Text

Apply Font and Text Effects

Apply Highlighting

Just as you would use a highlighting marker on paper documents, you can add highlighting to a Word document. Highlighting is easy to see when you are reading a document onscreen. If you want to print a document with highlighting, it's a good idea to use a light color for the highlight so that you can see the text underneath. To apply highlighting, you can select the text, then click the Highlight button list arrow and choose a highlight color, or you can click the Highlight button, and then drag it across the text you want to highlight.

Activity Steps

 open EWMemo02.doc

1. Select the phrase **wealth of valuable information** in the second paragraph in the body of the memo

2. Click the **Highlight button list arrow**

3. Click the **Yellow color box** to highlight the selected text

4. Click the **Highlight button** to activate it, then drag to highlight the phrase **you can use _____ to enhance your life** in the last line of the second paragraph
   See Figure 1-31.

5. Click the **Highlight button list arrow**, click **None**, then drag to remove the highlighting from the words **you can use _____ to** in the last line of the second paragraph

6. Click the **Highlight button** to deselect it
   See Figure 1-32.

 close EWMemo02.doc

Step 6
You can also press [Esc] to turn the Highlighter off.

Figure 1-31: Highlighted text

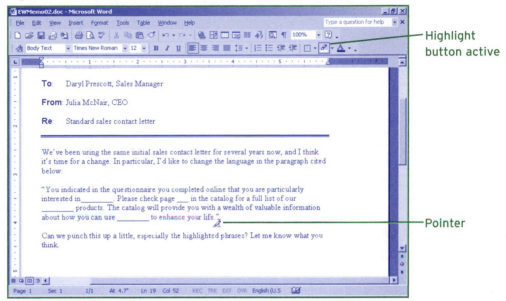

Highlight button active

Pointer

Figure 1-32: Highlight button deselected

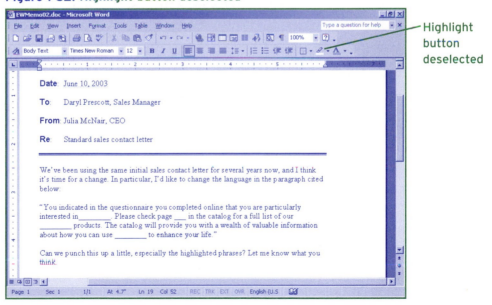

Highlight button deselected

Skill Set 1

Inserting and Modifying Text

Enter and Format Date and Time
Insert the Current Date and Time

Word makes it easy to insert the current date and time. You can insert them in two ways: either as static text that will not change, or as a date and time field that updates every time you open the document. A **field** is a placeholder for something that might change in a document. Fields are usually updated as the document changes.

Activity Steps

 open EWCoDescription03.doc

1. Click after **on:** in the third line (make sure there is a space between the colon and the insertion point)

2. Click **Insert** on the menu bar, click **Date and Time** to open the Date and Time dialog box, then click the third format in the list of Available formats
   See Figure 1-33.

3. If the **Update automatically check box** is selected, click it to deselect it so that the date in the document will not change, then click **OK**

4. Click after **Updated:** at the end of the third paragraph, immediately before the close parenthesis (make sure there is a space between the colon and the insertion point)

5. Click **Insert** on the menu bar, click **Date and Time**, then click the first format in the list of Available formats that shows the date and time (12th in the list)

6. Click the **Update automatically check box** to select it, then click **OK**
   See Figure 1-34.

 close EWCoDescription03.doc

To insert the current date using AutoText, type the first four characters of the current month, press [Enter], press the [Spacebar], then press [Enter] again.

Figure 1-33: Date and Time dialog box

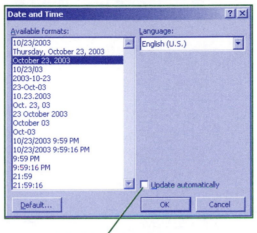

Select to update field
when file is opened

Figure 1-34: Date and time field in document

Date
inserted
as static
text

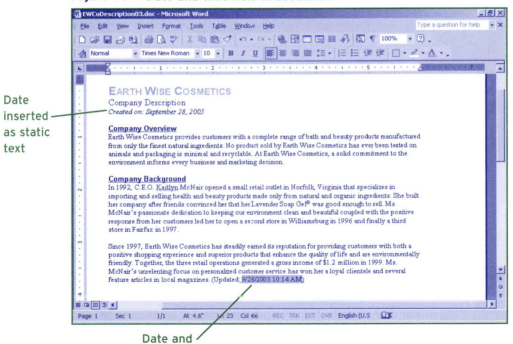

Date and
Time field

Skill Set 1

Inserting and Modifying Text

Enter and Format Date and Time
Modify Date and Time Field Formats

Once you've inserted a date or time, you can change it to a different format. For instance, if you inserted the date to be displayed in the format mm/dd/yy (for example, 06/04/03), you can change it to be displayed as text (for example, June 4, 2003).

Activity Steps

 open EWCoDescription04.doc

1. Position the insertion point so that it is immediately before the first number in the date at the end of the document

2. Press and hold **[Shift]**, then press **[➡]** to select the entire field
   See Figure 1-35.

3. Click **Insert** on the menu bar, then click **Date and Time**

4. Click the fourth format in the list of Available formats

5. If the **Update automatically check box** is not selected, click it to select it

6. Click **OK** to update the field with the new format

 close EWCoDescription04.doc

Once you've inserted the date and time, you can format it as you would any other text.

Figure 1-35: Selecting an entire field

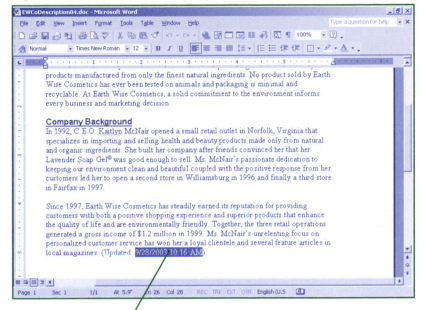

Entire field selected

extra!

Changing the date and time field codes

When the Date and Time is inserted into a document as a field instead of just simple text, you can modify the field codes to change how the date is displayed. Right-click the field, then click Toggle Field Codes to view the field codes instead of the result. Click anywhere in the code and make your changes. For example, if the date code contains the code M, the month number will display without a leading zero for single digit months (for example, 6 for June). You could change this to MM to display two digits for the month (06 for June), MMM to display a three letter abbreviation for the month (Jun), or MMMM to display the entire month name. Once you've made your changes, right-click the field again, then click Update Field to update the field and toggle back to the results.

Skill Set 1

Inserting and Modifying Text

Apply Character Styles

A **style** is a defined set of formats that is applied to text. If you want all the headings in your document to be 24 point, bold Arial, instead of selecting all of the text and then applying each of these formatting changes one at a time, you can apply a heading style that sets all three of these formats at once. Styles can be applied to characters and to paragraphs. When you apply a style, it overrides any formatting that was there previously. Word provides pre-defined styles from which you can choose.

Don't forget that to apply a character style, you must first select all the text to which you want to apply it.

Activity Steps

 open EWAnnouncement04.doc

1. Select the text **Earth Wise Cosmetics Softball Tournament** in the last paragraph

2. Click the **Style button list arrow** `Normal ▼`, then click **More** to open the Styles and Formatting task pane
   See Figure 1-36.

3. Click the **Show box list arrow** `Available formatting ▼` at the bottom of the Styles and Formatting task pane, then click **All styles** in the list

4. Scroll down the **Pick formatting to apply list** in the task pane, then click **Strong**

5. Select the text **first ever** in the last paragraph, scroll up the **Pick formatting to apply list**, then click **Emphasis**
   See Figure 1-37.

6. Click the **Styles and Formatting button** 🗐 to close the Styles and Formatting task pane

 close EWAnnouncement04.doc

Figure 1-36: Styles and Formatting task pane open

Click to open and close Styles and Formatting task pane

Style button arrow

Task pane

Format for selected text

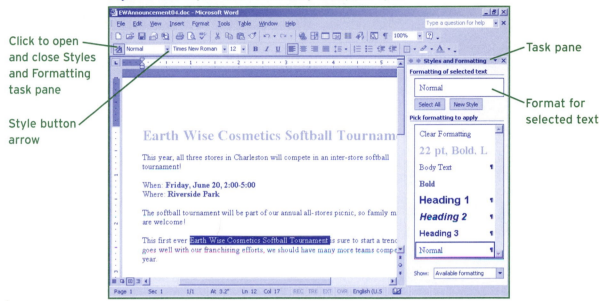

Figure 1-37: Applying a character style

"a" indicates this is a character style

Skill Set 1

Inserting and Modifying Text

Target Your Skills

1 Use Figure 1-38 as a guide to create a new letter. Make sure you insert the current date as a field that will be updated each time the file is opened. Use the [Backspace] and [Delete] keys if you make any typing errors. Remember, don't worry if the lines don't wrap exactly as in the figure.

Figure 1-38

Replace with your name   British pound symbol

 EWBrochure03.doc

2 Use Figure 1-39 as a guide to create a final document. Use the spelling and grammar checker to get rid of any errors in the document. Note that the pargraph order is changed. Also note that you need to move, copy, or find a synonym for some of the words.

Figure 1-39

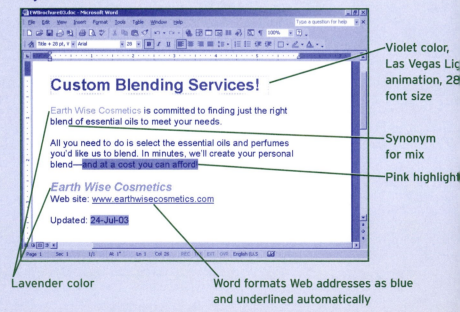

Violet color, Las Vegas Lig animation, 28 font size

Synonym for mix

Pink highlight

Lavender color   Word formats Web addresses as blue and underlined automatically

Skill List

1. Modify paragraph formats
2. Set and modify tabs
3. Apply bullet, outline, and numbering format to paragraphs
4. Apply paragraph styles

In Skill Set 2, you learn how to work with paragraphs. Word provides many commands to format paragraphs. Most of the paragraph formatting commands are available on the toolbars, although a few can be accessed only from within dialog boxes. Using good paragraph formatting results in neat, professional-looking documents.

Once you've formatted a paragraph, the formatting remains even if you make modifications to the paragraph text. Using paragraph formatting allows you to avoid a lot of tedious adjusting with the [Spacebar] every time you change the text.

Skill Set 2

Creating and Modifying Paragraphs

Modify Paragraph Formats
Apply Paragraph Formats

To select a paragraph, place the insertion point anywhere within the paragraph. If you want to apply a format to more than one paragraph, you must select each paragraph. Once you have set a paragraph format, that format is applied to subsequent paragraphs when you press [Enter].

To insert blank space above and below individual paragraphs without pressing [Enter] twice, select the paragraphs, click Format on the menu bar, click Paragraph, then adjust the numbers in the Before and After boxes.

Activity Steps

file open EWMemo03.doc

1. Position the insertion point anywhere in the second paragraph in the body of the memo

2. Click the **Line Spacing (1) button list arrow** ⬚
   See Figure 2-1.

3. Click **2.0** in the Line Spacing button drop-down list to set the line spacing in the current paragraph to double-space

4. Position the insertion point after the period at the end of the second paragraph, then press **[Enter]** twice to start a new paragraph with the same formatting as the previous one

5. Type **The essential oils used in our new line of aromatherapy products will bring pleasure to your senses while nourishing and revitalizing your skin.**

6. Drag to select the second and third paragraphs, click the **Line Spacing button list arrow** ⬚, then click **1.5** in the drop-down list

7. Click anywhere in the document to deselect the text
   See Figure 2-2.

file close EWMemo03.doc

Figure 2-1: Setting paragraph line spacing

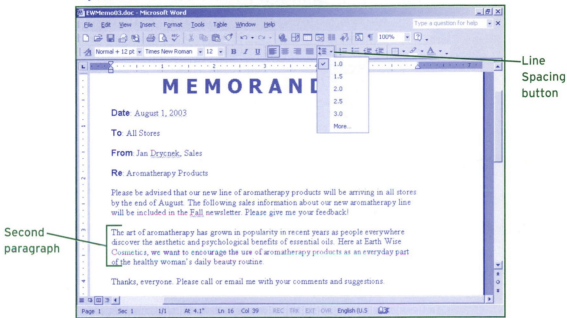

Line Spacing button

Second paragraph

Figure 2-2: Paragraphs formatted differently

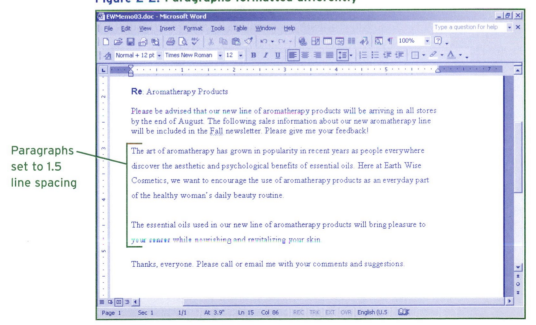

Paragraphs set to 1.5 line spacing

Skill Set 2
Creating and Modifying Paragraphs

Modify Paragraph Formats
Modify Paragraph Alignment

Paragraphs can be **left-aligned** (aligned along the left margin), **right-aligned** (aligned along the right margin), **centered**, or **justified** (aligned along both the left and right margins). Left-aligned paragraphs are the easiest to read. Justified paragraphs are often used in books and newspapers because they look neater.

Activity Steps

 open EWNewsletter01.doc

1. Make sure that the Insertion point is in the title line, **Earth Wise Cosmetics**, then note that the Align Left button ▤ is selected

2. Click the **Center button** ▤ to center the paragraph

3. Click anywhere in the second line on the page, **Fall 2003 Newsletter**, then click the **Align Right button** ▤

4. Select the two paragraphs below the heading **Aromatherapy Products**, press and hold [Ctrl], then drag to select the paragraphs below **Franchise Opportunities** and below **Online Ordering**

5. Click the **Justify button** ▤ to justify all of the selected paragraphs
See Figure 2-3.

6. Click anywhere in the document to deselect the text

 close EWNewsletter01.doc

A paragraph that is left-aligned is sometimes called ragged right, because the right side of the paragraph is not aligned.

Figure 2-3: Paragraphs justified in document

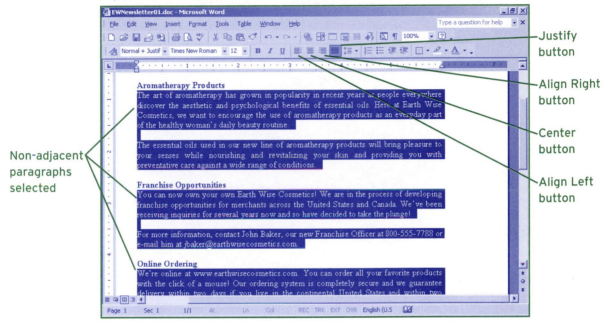

Non-adjacent paragraphs selected

Justify button

Align Right button

Center button

Align Left button

extra!

Using the Paragraph dialog box

To open the Paragraph dialog box click Paragraph on the Format menu (see Figure 2-4). The Paragraph dialog box contains the paragraph formatting commands available on the Formatting toolbar, as well as additional commands for formatting paragraphs. For example, to set the alignment from within the Paragraph dialog box, click the Alignment list arrow, then select an alignment option from the list.

Figure 2-4: Paragraph dialog box

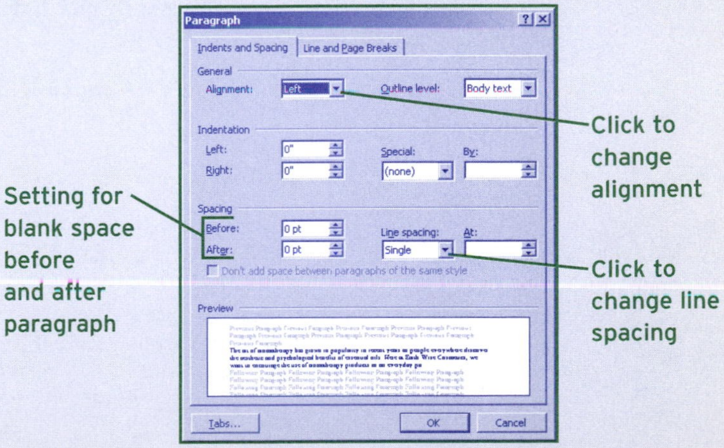

Setting for blank space before and after paragraph

Click to change alignment

Click to change line spacing

Skill Set 2

Creating and Modifying Paragraphs

Modify Paragraph Formats

Add Paragraph Borders and Shading

You may want to make a paragraph stand out from the rest of the paragraphs on the page. You can do this by adding a border or shading. You can also add borders to blank paragraphs to separate sections of a document visually.

Activity Steps

 open EWAnnouncement04.doc

1. With the insertion point positioned anywhere in the first line of text, click **Format** on the menu bar, click **Borders and Shading**, then click the **Borders tab**, if necessary

2. Click the **down scroll arrow** in the Style list six times, then click the line style that shows a thick line with a thin line above and below it

3. Click the **Color list arrow**, then click the **Dark Teal square** (first row, fifth box)

4. Click the **left, right,** and **top lines** in the Preview box so they disappear and the only remaining line is the bottom line
See Figure 2-5.

5. Click **OK**

6. Scroll to the bottom of the page, select the paragraph that starts with **For more information**, click **Format** on the menu bar, click **Borders and Shading**, click the **Shading tab**, then click the **last gray square** in the top row below No Fill so that the indicator box to the right displays **Gray-30%**

7. Click **OK**, click anywhere in the document to deselect the text, click the **Zoom box list arrow** 100% ▾, then click **75%**
See Figure 2-6.

 close EWAnnouncement04.doc

tip

You can click the Outside Border button list arrow to apply a border.

Figure 2-5: Borders tab in the Borders and Shading dialog box

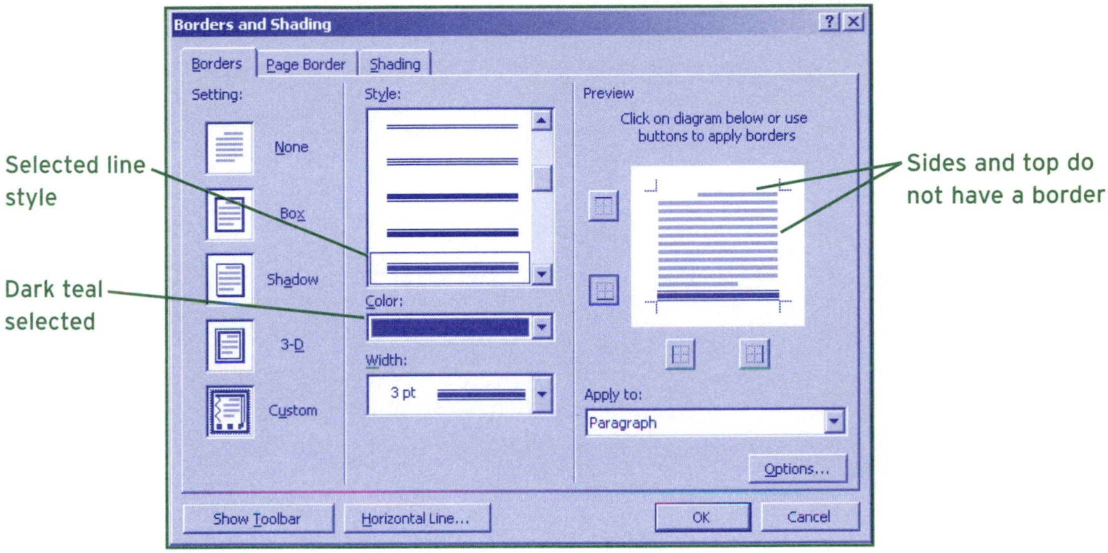

Selected line style

Dark teal selected

Sides and top do not have a border

Figure 2-6: Paragraphs with a border and shading

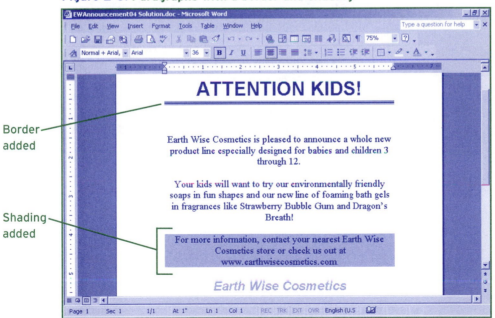

Border added

Shading added

Skill Set 2
Creating and Modifying Paragraphs

Modify Paragraph Formats
Set First-line Indents

To visually indicate a new paragraph, you typically press [Enter] twice or set the line space after a paragraph so that there is a blank line between paragraphs. You can, of course, also indicate a new paragraph by indenting the first line. (Note: It's not good practice to both skip a line between paragraphs and indent the first line; do one or the other.)

Activity Steps

 open EWNewsletter02.doc

1. If the ruler is not displayed on your screen, click **View** on the menu bar, then click **Ruler**

2. Select the two paragraphs below the heading **Aromatherapy Products**

3. Click the **square** to the left of the ruler as many times as necessary to cycle through the selections until you see the **First Line Indent icon** ▽
   See Figure 2-7.

4. Click the **¼" mark** on the ruler to place the First Line Indent marker at that point

5. Select the two paragraphs below the heading **Franchise Opportunities**, press and hold **[Ctrl]**, then select the two paragraphs below **Online Ordering**

6. Click the **¼" mark** on the ruler to indent the first line of these selected paragraphs to ¼" as well
   See Figure 2-8.

7. Click anywhere in the document to deselect the text

 close EWNewsletter02.doc

Step 5
You may need to click the ¼" mark on the ruler a second time to format all of the selected text.

Figure 2-7: Selecting a different ruler icon

First Line Indent icon

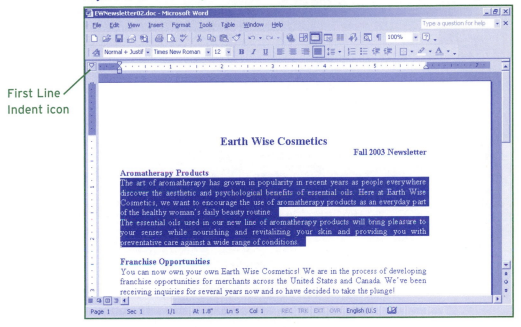

Figure 2-8: Document with first-line indents set

First Line Indent marker at ¹/₄" mark

First lines indented

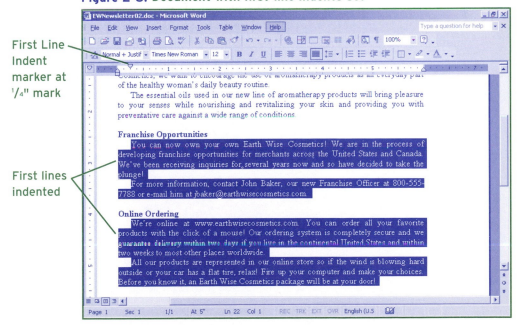

Skill Set 2
Creating and Modifying Paragraphs

Modify Paragraph Formats
Indent Entire Paragraphs

There may be times when you want to indent an entire paragraph in a document. You can click the Increase Indent button, or you can drag the Left and Right Indent Markers on the ruler.

Activity Steps

 open EWMemo04.doc

Step 2
Click the Decrease Indent button to decrease the left indent by $1/2$".

1. Select the three paragraphs in the body of the memo listing the promotion dates

2. Click the **Increase Indent button** 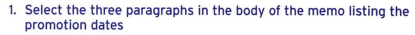 to increase the indent by $1/2$"
   See Figure 2-9.

3. Position the pointer over the **Right Indent marker** △ on the right side of the ruler so that the ScreenTip appears

4. Drag the **Right Indent marker** △ to the left to the $51/2$" mark on the ruler as shown in Figure 2-10

5. Click anywhere in the document to deselect the text

 close EWMemo04.doc

Figure 2-9: Paragraphs indented ¹/₂"

Selected paragraphs indented to ¹/₂" mark

Increase Indent button

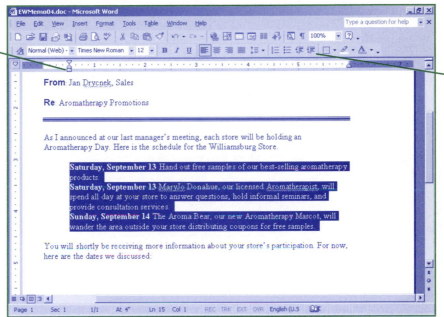

Figure 2-10: Dragging Right Indent marker to the 5¹/₂" mark

Right Indent marker

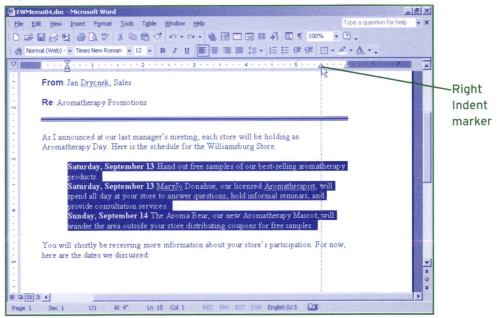

Skill Set 2
Creating and Modifying Paragraphs

Modify Paragraph Formats
Set Hanging Indents

A paragraph with a **hanging indent** is formatted so that all of the lines after the first line are indented more than the first line. You can set up a hanging indent by using the ruler or the Paragraph dialog box. Avoid trying to set up a hanging indent using the [Spacebar] and [Enter]. Any subsequent changes that you make to the document or to its format will alter the spacing you created by using the [Spacebar].

tip

If you accidentally drag the Left Indent marker, either drag it back to the 0" mark on the ruler or click the Undo button.

Activity Steps

 open EWMemo05.doc

1. Select the three paragraphs in the body of the memo listing the promotion dates

2. Point to the **Hanging Indent marker** on left side of the ruler so that the ScreenTip appears
See Figure 2-11.

3. Drag the **Hanging Indent marker** to the 2$^{1}/_{4}$" mark on the ruler
See Figure 2-12.

4. Click anywhere in the document to deselect the text

close EWMemo05.doc

Figure 2-11: Finding the hanging indent marker

Hanging Indent marker

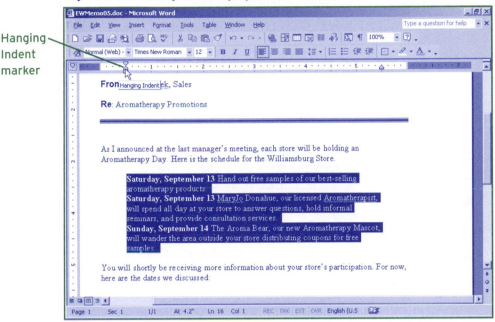

Figure 2-12: Paragraphs with hanging indents set

Hanging Indent set at 2¹/₄" mark

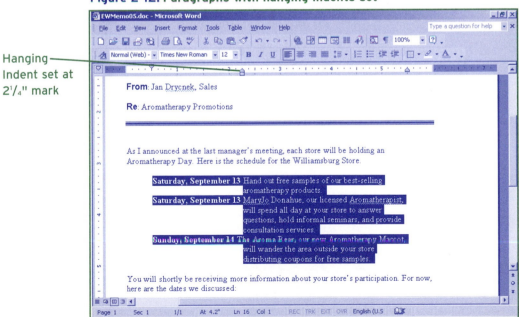

Skill Set 2
Creating and Modifying Paragraphs

Set and Modify Tabs
Set Tabs

You use tabs to align text to the same point in different paragraphs. Default **tab stops**, the location on the ruler where the text moves when you press [Tab], are set every half-inch across the page.

Activity Steps

 open EWMemo06.doc

1. Click immediately before **August** in the Date line, then press **[Backspace]** to delete the space after the colon

2. Press **[Tab]** to move the text over to the default tab stop at $1/2$"

3. Replace the spaces after the colons in the next three memo header lines with tabs
   See Figure 2-13.

4. Click the **square** to the left of the ruler as many times as necessary to cycle through the selections until you see the **Left Tab icon**

5. Select the four memo header lines, starting with the Date line

6. Click the $3/4$" **mark** on the ruler to place a Left Tab stop and override the default tab setting in the selected paragraphs
   See Figure 2-14.

7. Click anywhere in the document to deselect the text

 close EWMemo06.doc

tip

If you accidentally click the ruler and place a new tab stop on it, just drag it off the ruler.

Figure 2-13: Tabs inserted in memo header paragraphs

Text aligned at default tab stop of ¹/₂"

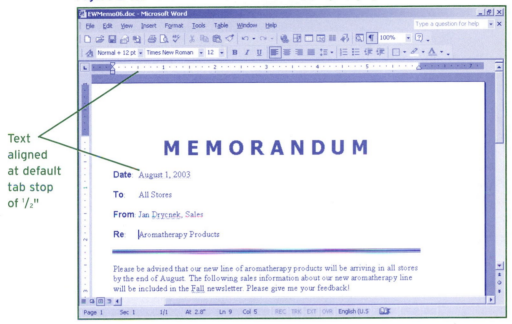

Figure 2-14: New tab stops set in memo header paragraphs

Inserted Left Tab stop overrides the default tab stop at ¹/₂"

Text aligned at new tab stop

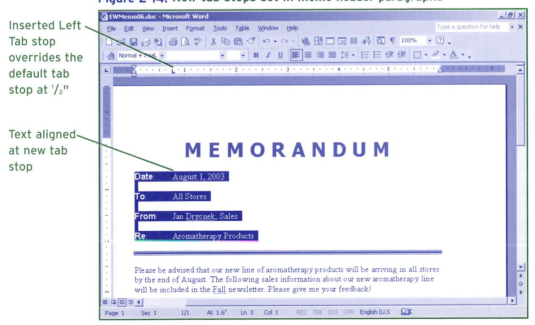

Skill Set 2
Creating and Modifying Paragraphs

Set and Modify Tabs
Modify Tabs

Once you have set tab stops, you can change them or delete them. You can also change the type of tab you set. For example, you can change from a left tab stop to a right tab stop.

Step 1
If tab markers don't appear when you click the Show/Hide ¶ button, click Options on the Tools menu, then click the Tab characters check box or the All check box to select it.

Activity Steps

 open EWAnnouncement05.doc

1. Click the **Show/Hide ¶ button** ¶ if necessary to display paragraph symbols and tab markers, then select the last four lines in the document

2. Drag the **Left Tab stop** ⌊ at the 3½" mark on the ruler off the ruler to delete it

3. Click the **square** to the left of the ruler as many times as necessary to cycle through the selections until you see the **Decimal Tab icon**

4. Click the 3³/₄" **mark** on the ruler to place a Decimal Tab stop

5. Drag the **Left Tab stop** ⌊ at the 4³/₄" mark off the ruler, then click the 5¹/₄" **mark** on the ruler to place a Decimal Tab stop

6. Click anywhere in the first line of text, then click the **square** to the left of the ruler as many times as necessary to cycle through the selections until you see the **Right Tab icon**

7. Click just to the left of the **Right Indent marker** △ on the ruler to place the Right Tab stop, then drag the **Right Tab stop** to the right so it is directly on top of the Right Indent marker *See Figure 2-15.*

8. Click the **Show/Hide ¶ button** ¶ to turn off paragraph symbols and tab markers

 close EWAnnouncement05.doc

Figure 2-15: Tabs modified

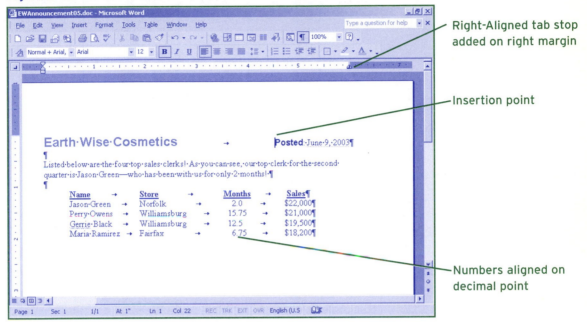

Right-Aligned tab stop added on right margin

Insertion point

Numbers aligned on decimal point

extra!

Using tab leaders

You can set a tab leader, a dotted, dashed, or solid line before a tab stop, by using the Tabs dialog box. Select the paragraphs in which you want to set the tab leaders, click Format on the menu bar, then click Tabs (see Figure 2-16). In the Tab stop position list, select the tab stop for which you want to set a leader, then click the leader style you want to use.

Figure 2-16: Tabs dialog box

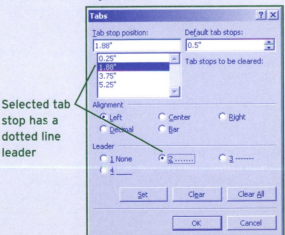

Selected tab stop has a dotted line leader

Skill Set 2
Creating and Modifying Paragraphs

Apply Bullet, Outline, and Numbering Format to Paragraphs
Create a Bulleted List

You can use bulleted lists for lists in which the order is not important, and no one item in the list is any more important than another. To create a bulleted list in Word, you can type the items in the list and then click the Bullets button, or you can click the Bullets button first, then start typing your list. A new bullet will be created every time you press [Enter] until you click the Bullets button again to turn the feature off.

Activity Steps

 open EWNewsletter03.doc

1. Select the five lines listing products, above the heading **Franchise Opportunities**

2. Click the **Bullets button** ▤

3. Right-click the selected list, then click **Bullets and Numbering** on the shortcut menu

4. Click **Customize**, then click **Character** to open the Symbol dialog box

5. Click the **Font list arrow**, scroll down the list, then click **Wingdings**

6. Scroll through the list, then click the bullet style shown in Figure 2-17

7. Click **OK**, click **OK** in the Customize Bulleted List dialog box, then click anywhere in the document to deselect the list
   See Figure 2-18.

 close EWNewsletter03.doc

tip

Step 3
You can also click Bullets and Numbering on the Format menu to open the Bullets and Numbering dialog box.

Figure 2-17: Symbol dialog box

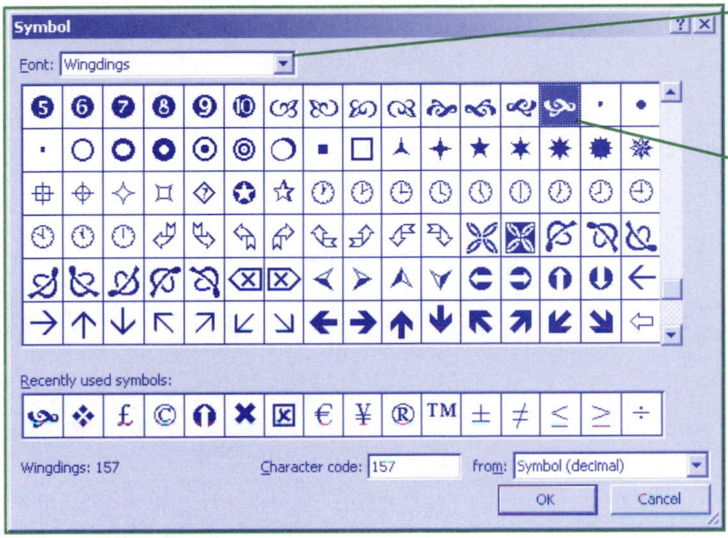

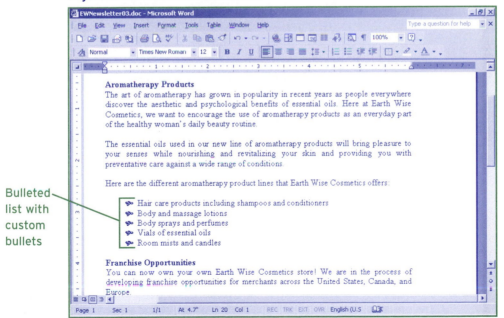

Font list arrow

Select this bullet

Figure 2-18: Bullets added to list

Bulleted list with custom bullets

Skill Set 2
Creating and Modifying Paragraphs

Apply Bullet, Outline, and Numbering Format to Paragraphs
Create a Numbered List

If you are working with a list in which the order is important or you need to be able to identify the items by a number, a numbered list is a better choice than a bulleted list.

Click the Number style list arrow in the Customize Numbered List dialog box to select another style of numbering, such as A, B, C or I, II, III.

Activity Steps

 open EWNewsletter04.doc

1. Scroll down to the bottom of the document, then select the last seven lines in the document
2. Click the **Numbering button**
3. Right-click the **selected list**, then click **Bullets and Numbering** on the shortcut menu
4. Click **Customize**, click to the right of the entry in the **Number format box**, then press **[Backspace]** to delete the period after the number 1
   See Figure 2-19.
5. Click **Font**, click **Bold** in the Font style list, then click **OK** in the Font dialog box
6. Click **OK** in the Customize Numbered List dialog box, then click anywhere in the document to deselect the list
   See Figure 2-20.

 close EWNewsletter04.doc

Figure 2-19: Customize Numbered List dialog box

Period deleted

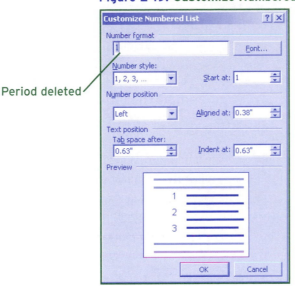

Figure 2-20: Numbers added to list

Formatted numbered list

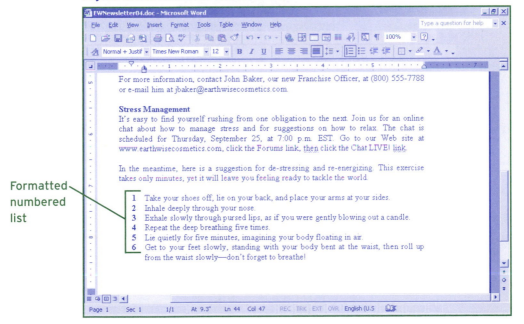

Skill Set 2

Creating and Modifying Paragraphs

Apply Bullet, Outline, and Numbering Format to Paragraphs

Create a Numbered List in Outline Style

A numbered list can be set up in standard outline style: a list of topics and sub-topics with each topic numbered according to its position in the outline and its level. You can create an automatically numbered outline using the Numbering command.

Activity Steps

 open EWProposal01.doc

1. Select all of the text except the two title lines

2. Click **Format** on the menu bar, click **Bullets and Numbering**, then click the **Outline Numbered tab**

3. Click the second style in the first row
   See Figure 2-21.

4. Click **OK**

5. Click anywhere in the **Benefits** line in the middle of the list, then click the **Increase Indent button** to move it down a level

6. Click anywhere in the **Financial Considerations** line in the last line, then click the **Decrease Indent button** to move it up a level

7. Click after the word **Considerations** in the last line, press **[Enter]**, press **[Tab]**, type **Projected Revenues**, press **[Enter]**, then type **Liabilities**

8. Press **[Enter]**, press **[Shift][Tab]**, then type **Conclusion**
   See Figure 2-22.

 close EWProposal01.doc

You can press [Tab] to increase the indent of an existing outline item and indent it to the next level, or you can press [Shift][Tab] to decrease the indent level of an existing outline item.

Figure 2-21: Outline Numbered tab in the Bullets and Numbering dialog box

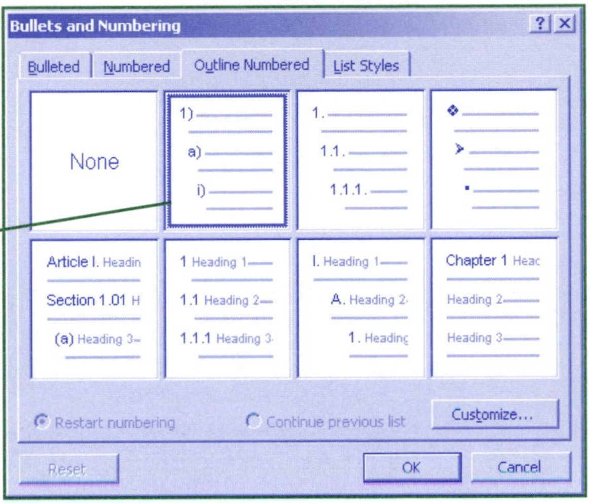

Select this style (it may be in a different spot on your screen)

Figure 2-22: Numbered outline

Skill Set 2
Creating and Modifying Paragraphs

Apply Paragraph Styles

To make it easier to apply consistent formatting throughout a document, you can use paragraph styles. Remember, a style is a defined set of formats. Just as character styles are applied to selected text, paragraph styles are applied to entire paragraphs.

Activity Steps

 open EWNewsletter05.doc

1. Click anywhere in the **Aromatherapy Products** line, then click the **Style list arrow**

2. Click **Heading 1** in the Style list as shown in Figure 2-23 to apply the Heading 1 style to the paragraph

3. Apply the Heading 1 style to the lines **Franchise Opportunities** and **Stress Management**

4. Click anywhere in the first line of the document, then click the **Styles and Formatting button** to open the Styles and Formatting task pane

5. Click the **Show list arrow** at the bottom of the task pane, click **All Styles**, scroll to the bottom of the **Pick formatting to apply list** in the task pane, then click **Title**

6. Click anywhere in the **Fall 2003 Newsletter** line, then apply the **Heading 3 style** using either the task pane or the toolbar

7. With the Fall 2003 Newsletter line still selected, click the **Align Right button**
   See Figure 2-24.

8. Click the **Close button** in the Styles and Formatting task pane title bar

 close EWNewsletter05.doc

Step 7
When you modify a style with manual formatting, the formats you add are listed after the style name in the Style list box.

Figure 2-23: Style list on the Formatting toolbar

Style list arrow

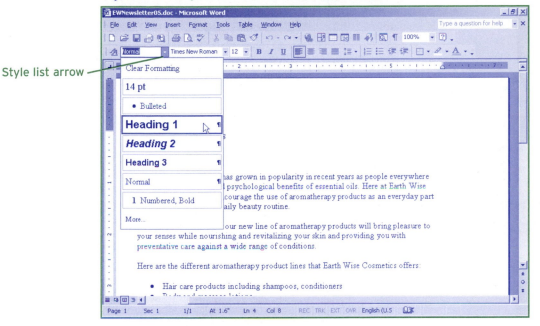

Figure 2-24: Document with styles applied

Styles and Formatting button

Current paragraph style

Insertion point

Style of selected paragraph with modified formatting

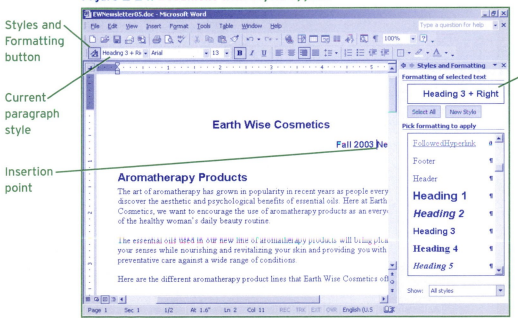

Skill Set 2
Creating and Modifying Paragraphs

Target Your Skills

 EWAnnouncement06.doc

Figure 2-25

1 Modify the file **EWAnnouncement06** to create the document shown in Figure 2-25. Paragraph marks are turned on to help you format the document correctly.

1.5 line spacing

Double-spaced

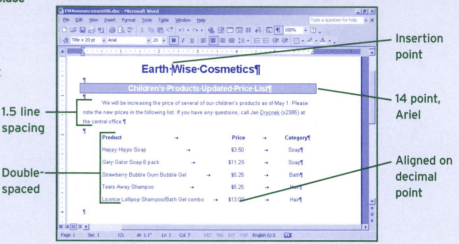

Insertion point

14 point, Ariel

Aligned on decimal point

 EWBrochure04.doc

Figure 2-26

2 Revise the **EWBrochure04** file to create the document shown in Figure 2-26. Paragraph marks are turned on to help you format the document correctly.

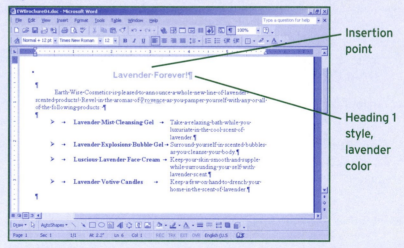

Insertion point

Heading 1 style, lavender color

Skill List

1. Create and modify a header and footer
2. Apply and modify column settings
3. Modify document layout and page setup options
4. Create and modify tables
5. Preview and print documents, envelopes, and labels

Once you've formatted the words and paragraphs in a document, you can think about the document as a whole. Adding headers and footers to a document can help the reader keep printed documents organized. You will learn how to add the filename, date, page numbers, and custom text to the header or footer. Sometimes a document is best laid out in more than one column, as in a newsletter. You will also learn how to set up a document with more than one column.

If you have quite a bit of information that would look better in multiple rows and columns, a table might be the best way to present it. You will learn how to insert a table into your document and modify it to fit your needs. Finally, you will learn to preview and print your document, as well as envelopes and labels.

Skill Set 3
Formatting Documents

Create and Modify a Header and Footer
Create a Header

A **header** is text that appears at the top of every page in a document. Headers can be very useful in a multiple-page document. You can insert **fields**, place-holders that will update automatically to match specific information like a page number or a date, or you can insert text that you type directly. Text in a header can be formatted just as any other text in a document.

Activity Steps

 open GCMemo01.doc

1. Click **View** on the menu bar, then click **Header and Footer**

2. Type **Draft Copy**, then click the **Align Right button**

3. Press **[Enter]**

You must be in Print Layout view or Print Preview to see headers and footers on the page.

4. Click the **Insert Date button** on the Header and Footer toolbar
   See Figure 3-1.

5. Select the two lines of text you entered, click the **Bold button** **B**, then click anywhere in the header area to deselect the text

6. Click the **Close button** on the Header and Footer toolbar
   See Figure 3-2.

 close GCMemo01.doc

Figure 3-1: Creating a header and using the Header and Footer toolbar

Header area

Align Right button

Date field (the format of the date on your screen may differ)

Insert Date button

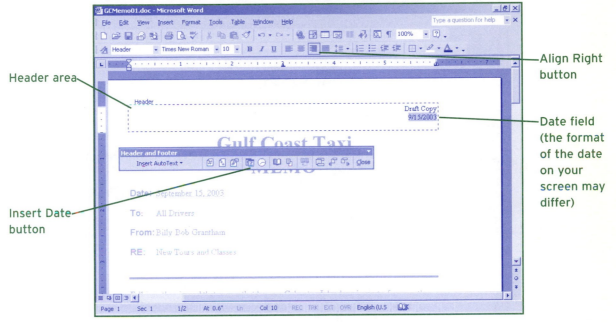

Figure 3-2: Header displays in Print Layout view

Header in Print Layout view

Print Layout view selected

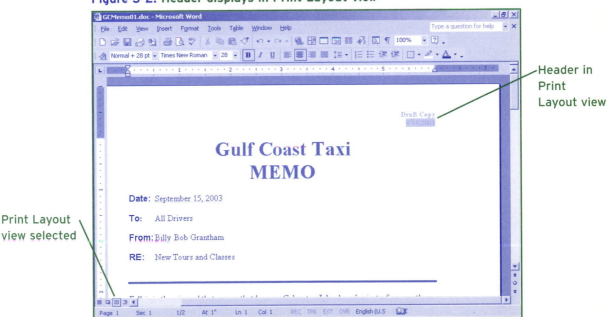

Skill Set 3
Formatting Documents

Create and Modify a Header and Footer
Create a Footer

A **footer** is text that appears at the bottom of every page in a document. Footers are identical to headers, except that they appear at the bottom of a page instead of the top.

To insert the current page number and the total number of pages quickly, click the Insert AutoText button on the Header and Footer toolbar, then click Page X of Y.

Activity Steps

 open GCMemo02.doc

1. Click **View** on the menu bar, then click **Header and Footer**

2. Click the **Switch Between Header and Footer button** 🔳 on the Header and Footer toolbar to jump to the Footer area

3. Click the **Insert AutoText button** `Insert AutoText ▾` on the Header and Footer toolbar

4. Click **Filename** to insert the filename in the footer

5. Press **[Tab]** twice, then type **Gulf Coast Taxi Company Memo**
   See Figure 3-3.

6. Click the **Close button** on the Header and Footer toolbar, then scroll down to see the footer on the page
   See Figure 3-4.

    close GCMemo02.doc

extra!

Skipping a header or footer on the first page
Sometimes you may not want a header or footer to appear on the first page of a document, for example, when you create a report with a title page. To suppress headers or footers on the first page of a document, click the Page Setup button 📄 on the Header and Footer toolbar, or click File on the menu bar, click Page Setup, then make sure the Layout tab is on top. Click the Different first page check box to select it.

Figure 3-3: Inserting the Filename field in a footer

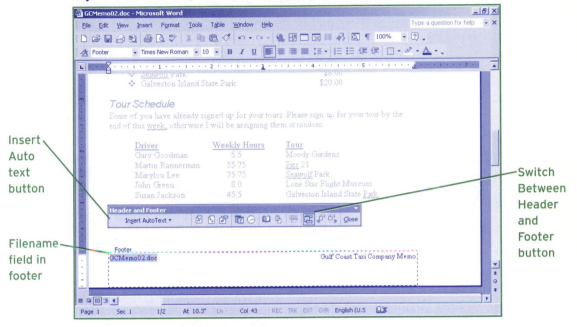

Insert Auto text button

Switch Between Header and Footer button

Filename field in footer

Figure 3-4: Viewing headers and footers on two pages in Print Layout view

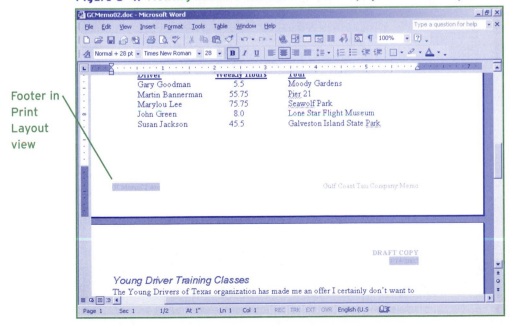

Footer in Print Layout view

Skill Set 3
Formatting Documents

Apply and Modify Column Settings
Create Columns for Existing Text

Text in a document normally appears in one column. You may decide that the text would be easier to read or that you could fit more text if you used two or more columns. Newsletters are frequently set up in this way. The easiest way to create columns is to enter your text, then use the Columns command. You can choose to apply as many columns as you want.

Activity Steps

 open GCBrochure01.doc

1. Select all of the text below the line **Spring 2003**
2. Click the **Columns button**
3. Point to the **second column icon** in the drop-down list so that **2 Columns** appears below the icons
   See Figure 3-5.
4. Click the **second column icon** in the Columns button drop-down list
5. Click anywhere in the document to deselect the text
6. Click the **Zoom button list arrow**  then click **Whole Page** to see the columns on the page
   See Figure 3-6.

 close GCBrochure01.doc

If you want to format the entire document with multiple columns, click Select All on the Edit menu before you click the Columns button.

Understanding sections
When you apply the Columns command to selected text, you created a second section in the GCBrochure01 document. **Sections** are parts of a document with separate page formatting options. If you turn on paragraph marks, you can see a double-dotted line labeled **Section Break (Continuous)** next to the heading line **Spring 2003**. Everything after that break—everything in the second section of the document—has a different page format from the text in the first section in the document. You can have as many sections as you want in a document.

extra!

Figure 3-5: Using the Columns button

Columns button

Figure 3-6: Document formatted with two columns

Formatted as single column

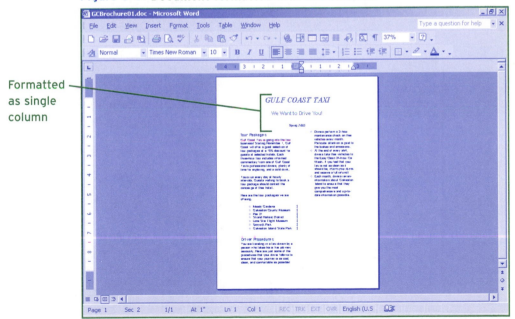

Skill Set 3
Formatting Documents

Apply and Modify Column Settings
Modify Text Alignment in Columns

Once you have created columns, you need to adjust them so that they look balanced on the page; in other words, so that you don't have one column that fills the length of the page and a second column that contains only a few lines.

To insert a vertical line between columns, make sure the insertion point is anywhere within the columns, click Columns on the Format menu, then click the Line between check box to select it.

Activity Steps

 open GCBrochure02.doc

1. Click the **Zoom button list arrow** `100%` on the menu bar, then click **Whole Page** to see the columns

2. Click below the text in the second column (the insertion point will seem to appear between the columns)

3. Click **Insert** on the menu bar, then click **Break** to open the Break dialog box

4. Click the **Continuous option button**

5. Click **OK** to balance the columns on the page
   See Figure 3-7.

 close GCBrochure02.doc

extra!

Using the Columns dialog box
In addition to using the Columns button, you can click Columns on the Format menu to open and use the Columns dialog box to set and modify columns. See Figure 3-8. If you want to format the document with one column in one section and two columns in another, position the insertion point in the document at the point where you want to start the new column layout, open the Columns dialog box, select the number of columns you want, then click the Apply to list arrow at the bottom of the dialog box and select This point forward. You can also precisely adjust the column width and space between each column by typing measurements (in inches) in the Width and Spacing boxes. Deselect the Equal column width check box if you want columns of different widths.

Figure 3-7: Balanced newsletter columns

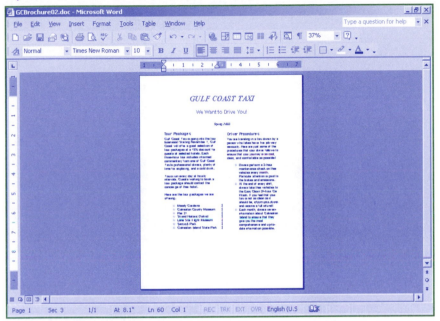

Figure 3-8: Columns dialog box

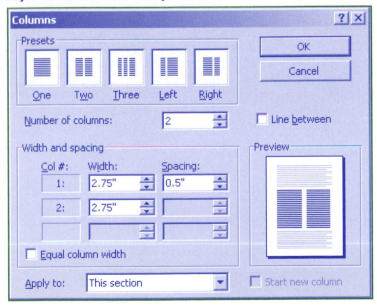

Skill Set 3
Formatting Documents

Apply and Modify Column Settings
Create Columns before Entering Text

If you know before you enter text that you want it to appear in two or more columns, you can use the Columns command before you enter the text. Note that if you start with a blank document, choosing the Columns command applies to all of the text in the document, even if you type a few lines first for a headline. So after you finish typing the text for your columns, you need to select the headline and format it with one-column layout.

Activity Steps

To force a new column to start, position the insertion point at the point in the document where you want to start the new column, click Break on the Insert menu, then click the Column break option button.

1. Open a new, blank document, change the zoom to 100% if necessary, click the **Style list arrow** [Normal ▾], click **Heading 1**, type **Gulf Coast Taxi Newsletter**, then press **[Enter]**

2. Click the **Style list arrow** [Normal ▾], click **Heading 3**, type **Summer 2003**, then press **[Enter]**

3. Click the **Columns button** , then click the **second column icon** to format the text in two columns

4. Click the **Style list arrow** [Normal ▾], click **Heading 1**, type **Employee News**, then press **[Enter]**

5. Type **Elisa Newcomb was married last weekend to Frank Jessup. Believe it or not, the happy couple met in Elisa's cab!** *See Figure 3-9.*

6. Select the first two paragraphs (everything above **Employee News**), click the **Columns button**, then click the **first column icon** to format the selected text in one column

7. Click the **Center button** to center the title over the two columns

8. Click anywhere in the document to deselect the text *See Figure 3-10.*

   close file

Figure 3-9: Text filling in first column in two-column format

Second column not yet filled

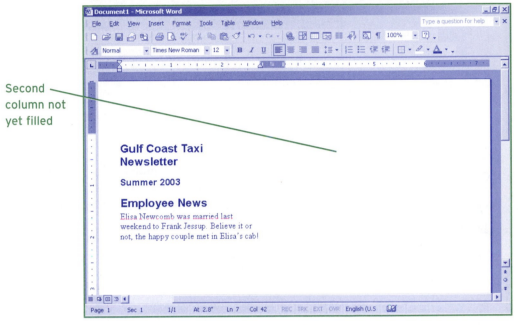

Figure 3-10: Headline spanning two columns

Paragraphs formatted as single column

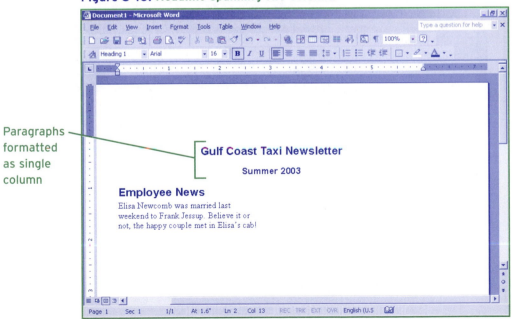

Skill Set 3
Formatting Documents

Apply and Modify Column Settings
Revise Column Layout

The default space between columns in a Word document is $^1/_2$". The column widths change depending on how many columns are on a page. You can adjust both the column width and the space between columns. If you want to see the columns as you change the width, drag the Move Column markers on the ruler. To adjust columns precisely, you should use the Columns dialog box.

tip

To create two columns quickly with one of the columns twice as wide as the other, select the text, click Columns on the Format menu, then click Left or Right at the top of the dialog box.

Activity Steps

 open GCBrochure03.doc

1. Scroll down until you can see the bulleted list of tour packages in the first column, then click anywhere in the first column

2. Position the pointer over the **Move Column dotted box marker** between the 2" and 3" markers on the ruler so that the pointer changes to ↔

3. Drag the **Move Column dotted box marker** to the right until it's approximately over the 3.25" mark on the ruler and the list of tours and the fees charged in the first column appears with each fee on the same line as the tour name
   See Figure 3-11.

4. Click **Format** on the menu bar, then click **Columns** to open the Columns dialog box

5. Drag to select all of the text in the **Col # 2 Width box**, then type **1.6**

6. Press **[Tab]**, type **.3** to decrease the space between the second and third columns, then press **[Tab]** to adjust the width in the Col # 3 Width box automatically

7. Click **OK** to close the Columns dialog box

8. Click the **Zoom button list arrow** [100% ▾], then click **Whole Page**
   See Figure 3-12.

 close GCBrochure03.doc

Figure 3-11: Widening a column using the ruler

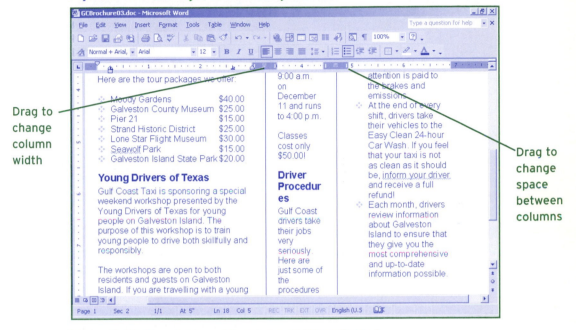

Drag to change column width

Drag to change space between columns

Figure 3-12: Newsletter with column widths adjusted

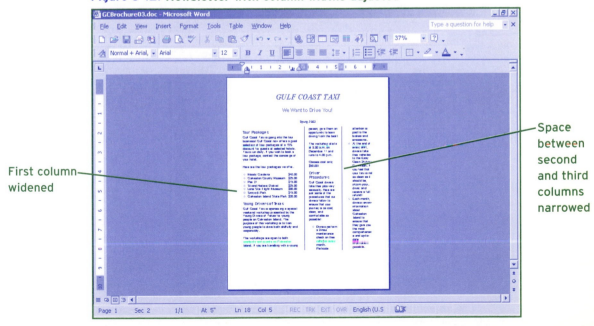

First column widened

Space between second and third columns narrowed

Skill Set 3

Formatting Documents

Modify Document Layout and Page Setup Options

Insert Page Breaks

Word automatically inserts page breaks in a document when the text will no longer fit on one page. You can insert page breaks manually if you want to start the next page at a different point in the document. In Print Layout view, manual page breaks look the same as automatic page breaks unless you turn on paragraph marks.

Activity Steps

 open GCProposal01.doc

1. Click the **Show/Hide ¶ button** ¶ to display paragraph marks, if necessary

2. Scroll down so that you can see the heading **Introduction**

3. Click at the beginning of the **Introduction** line to position the insertion point at the top of the new page you want to create

4. Click **Insert** on the menu bar, then click **Break** to open the Break dialog box

5. Make sure that the **Page break option button** is selected, then click **OK** to insert a manual page break
   See Figure 3-13.

6. Scroll down until you see the heading **Conclusion**

7. Click at the beginning of the **Conclusion** line, then press **[Ctrl][Enter]** to insert a manual page break

 close GCProposal01.doc

To delete a manually inserted page break, turn on paragraph marks, select the dotted line page break indicator, then press [Delete].

Figure 3-13: Manual page break

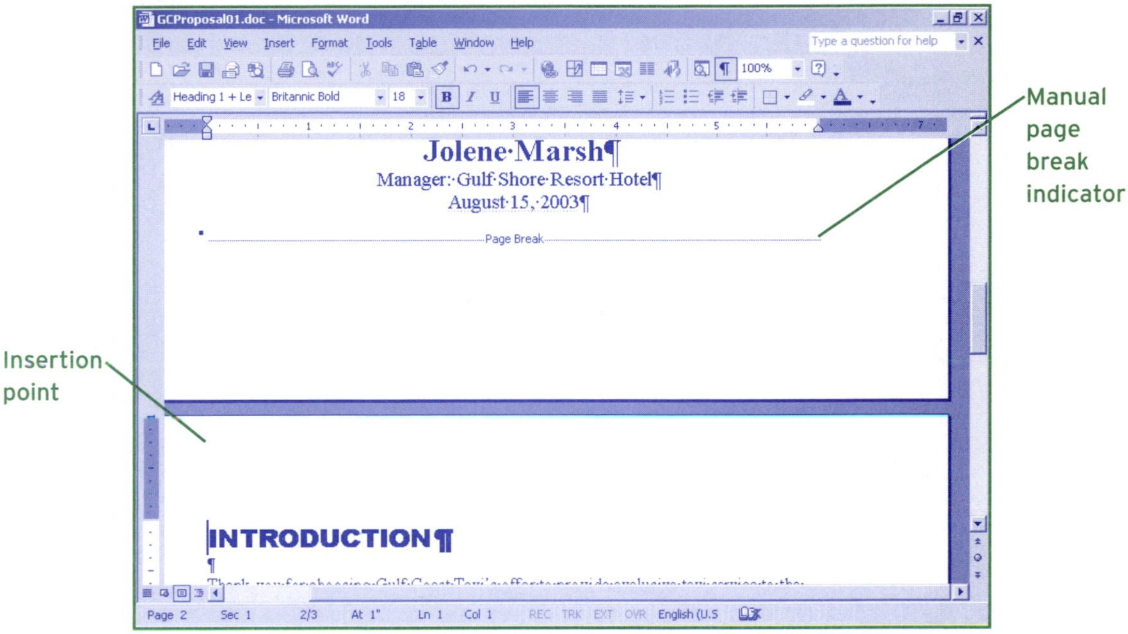

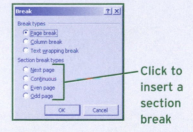

Manual page break indicator

Insertion point

---

extra!

Inserting section breaks

To create manual section breaks, click Break on the Insert menu, then select one of the option buttons under Section break types in the Break dialog box. See Figure 3-14. Clicking the Next page option button forces the new section to start on a new page. Clicking the Continuous option button creates a new section but keeps it on the same page. Clicking the Even and Odd page option buttons creates a new section that begins on the next even or odd-numbered page.

Figure 3-14: Break dialog box

Click to insert a section break

Skill Set 3
Formatting Documents

Modify Document Layout and Page Setup Options
Insert Page Numbers

When you work with multiple-page documents, it's a good idea to add page numbers so that you don't mix up the pages when you print the document. To insert page numbers, you insert a field, and Word automatically updates the field to reflect the correct page number. You can insert page numbers using the Insert Page Number button on the Header and Footer toolbar or you can use the Page Numbers command on the Insert menu.

Activity Steps

 open GCProposal02.doc

1. Click **Insert** on the menu bar, then click **Page Numbers** to open the Page Numbers dialog box

2. Make sure that **Bottom of page (Footer)** is selected in the Position list box

3. Click the **Alignment list arrow**, then click **Left**

4. Click the **Show number on first page check box** to deselect it
See Figure 3-15.

5. Click **OK**

6. Scroll down to the bottom of the first page to see that there is no page number in the footer

7. Scroll down to the bottom of the second page to see the page number in the footer
See Figure 3-16.

 close GCProposal02.doc

To format the page number, make the footer area active, then select the page number field and format it as you like.

Figure 3-15: Page Numbers dialog box

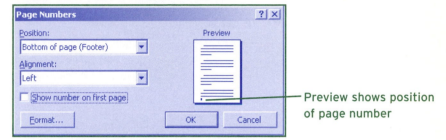

Preview shows position
of page number

Figure 3-16: Page number in footer of page 2

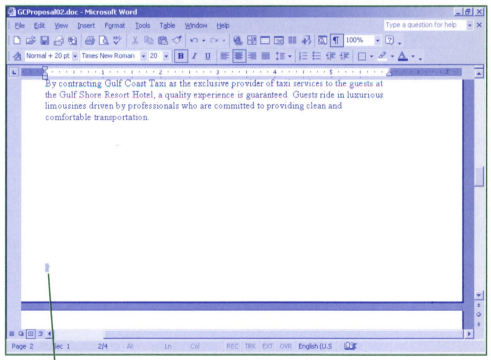

Page number in
footer of page 2

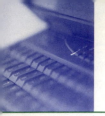

Modify Document Layout and Page Setup Options

Modify Page Margins

The default page margins in a Word document are 1" at the top and bottom of the page and 1¹/₄" at the right and left of the page. Headers and footers print ¹/₂" from the top and bottom of the page. You can change the default page margins to suit your needs.

To adjust text to fit on a page quickly, click the Print Preview button, then click the Shrink to Fit button on the Print Preview toolbar.

Activity Steps

 open GCLetter01.doc

1. Click **File** on the menu bar, then click **Page Setup**
2. Click the **Margins tab**, if necessary
3. Type **1.25** in the Top box
4. Press **[Tab]** twice to select the text in the Left box, then type **1.5**
5. Click the **Right box down arrow** three times to change the right margin to 1"
   See Figure 3-17.
6. Click **OK**
   See Figure 3-18.

 close GCLetter01.doc

Understanding gutter and mirror margins
You can set up **mirror margins** for odd and even pages as if the pages were in a book. That means that instead of setting margins for the left and right, you set margins for the inside and outside. The inside margin is the right margin on even pages and the left margin on odd pages. You can also set up a gutter margin for material that is going to be bound on one side. When you set a **gutter margin**, you add extra space to the side that will be bound. You set both of these options on the Margins tab in the Page Setup dialog box.

Figure 3-17: Margins tab of the Page Setup dialog box

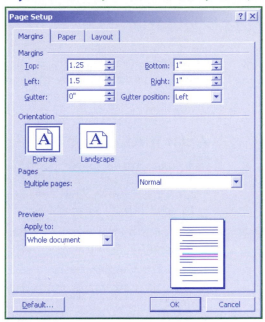

Figure 3-18: Margins changed in document

Top margin increased to 1.25"

Left margin increased to 1.5"

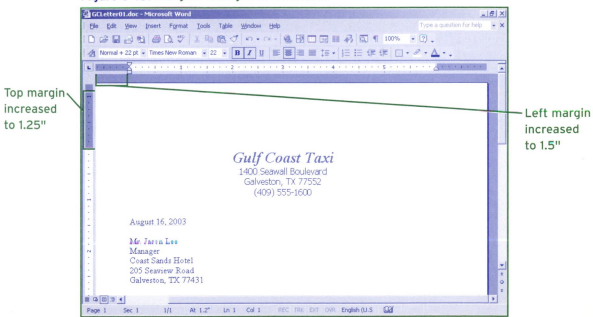

Skill Set 3
Formatting Documents

Modify Document Layout and Page Setup Options
Modify Page Orientation

Most documents are meant to be printed lengthwise on a page. This is called **portrait** orientation. Some documents look best if they are printed sideways on the page. This is called **landscape** orientation. The default for Word documents is portrait, but you can change the orientation to landscape in the Page Setup dialog box.

To set different orientations in a document, select the text to which you want to apply the new orientation, open the Margins tab in the Page Setup dialog box, select the orientation, then click Selected text in the Apply to list.

Activity Steps

 open GCAnnouncement01.doc

1. Click the **Zoom button list arrow** 100%, then click **Whole Page** to see the entire page in portrait orientation

2. Click **File** on the menu bar, then click **Page Setup** to open the Page Setup dialog box

3. Click the **Margins tab**, if necessary

4. Click the **Landscape orientation box**
   See Figure 3-19.

5. Click **OK**
   See Figure 3-20.

 close GCAnnouncement01.doc

Figure 3-19: Margins tab in Page Setup dialog box

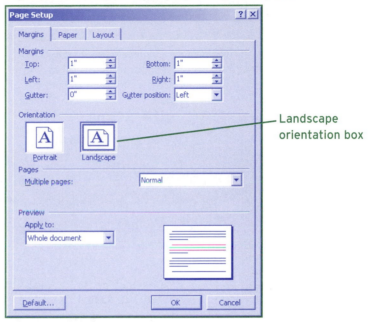

Landscape orientation box

Figure 3-20: Document in landscape orientation

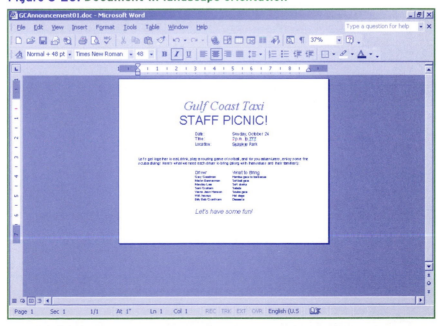

Skill Set 3

Formatting Documents

Create and Modify Tables
Create Tables

You can use tabs to arrange text in rows and columns, but when you have a lot of information to present in that format, a table is usually a better choice. A table sets up a grid of rows and columns. Each intersection of a row and column is called a **cell**. To move from one cell to another, you press [Tab] or an arrow key.

Activity Steps

 open GCBrochure04.doc

Step 6
If you press [Tab] after the last entry and accidentally insert a new row, click the Undo button.

1. Press **[Ctrl][End]** to position the insertion point at the end of the document, then press **[Enter]**

2. Click the **Insert Table button**

3. Move the pointer over the grid to create a **4 × 3 Table**
   See Figure 3-21.

4. Click to create the table

5. Type **Destination**, press **[Tab]**, type **Average Time**, press **[Tab]**, type **Average Fare**, then press **[Tab]**

6. Type the rest of the information in the table as shown in Figure 3-22 in the same manner

 close GCBrochure04.doc

Figure 3-21: Using the Table button

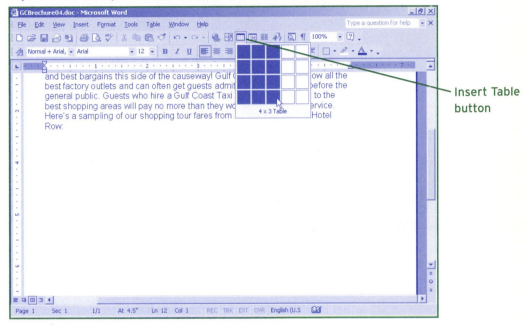

Insert Table button

Figure 3-22: Completed table

Tables and Borders toolbar may not appear on your screen

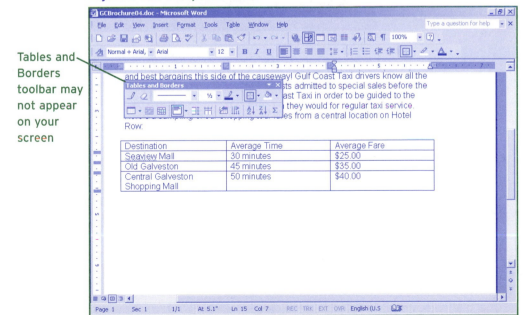

Skill Set 3

Formatting Documents

Create and Modify Tables

Modify Tables

Once you have created a table, you can modify it in several ways. You can resize the table to fit better on the page. You can merge several cells to form one cell, or you can split one cell to form several cells. You can also rotate text in a cell. These are only a few of the changes you can make to a table.

To make several columns or rows the same size, select them, then click the Distribute Columns Evenly button or the Distribute Rows Evenly button on the Tables and Borders toolbar.

Activity Steps

 open GCBrochure05.doc

1. Scroll down until you can see the table, then move the pointer anywhere over the table to see the table move and resize handles *See Figure 3-23*.

2. Position the pointer over the **table resize handle** ⊞ so that the pointer changes to ⊞, then drag the resize handle to the left until the dotted outline indicates that the table is approximately 4.5" wide

3. Drag the **table move handle** ⊞ to center the table horizontally on the page

4. If the Tables and Borders toolbar is not open, right-click any toolbar, then click **Tables and Borders**

5. Position the pointer over the first column so that the pointer changes to ↓, then click to select the entire first column

6. Click the **Merge Cells button** ▦ on the Tables and Borders toolbar

7. With the first column still selected, click the **Change Text Direction button** ▥ twice to rotate the text to read vertically up the page, then click anywhere in the table to deselect the text *See Figure 3-24*.

8. Click the **Close button** ✕ on the Tables and Borders toolbar

 close GCBrochure05.doc

Figure 3-23: Table handles

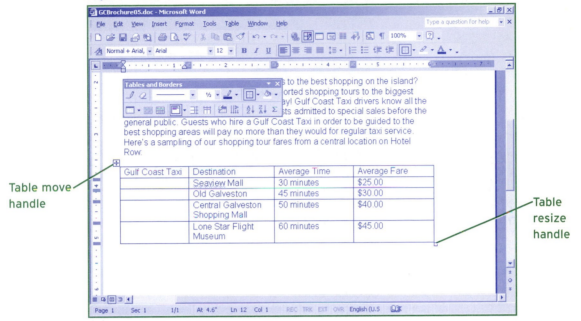

Table move handle

Table resize handle

Figure 3-24: Modified table

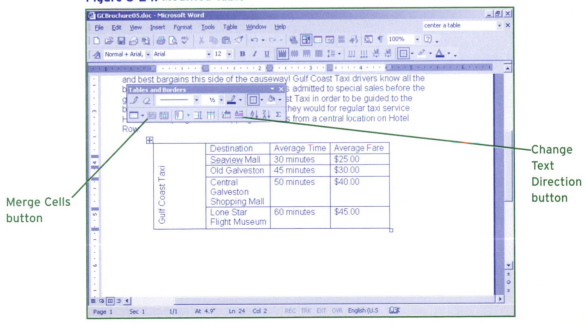

Change Text Direction button

Merge Cells button

Skill Set 3
Formatting Documents

Create and Modify Tables
Apply AutoFormat to Tables

After you create a table, you can format it to make it look better. The quickest way to format a table is to use the Table AutoFormat command on the Table menu.

Activity Steps

 open GCMemo03.doc

1. Scroll down until you can see the table, then click anywhere within the table

2. Right-click any toolbar, then click **Tables and Borders** to open the Tables and Borders toolbar, if necessary

3. Click the **Table AutoFormat button** on the Tables and Borders toolbar to open the Table AutoFormat dialog box

4. Scroll up the Table styles list, then click **Table Classic 3**

5. Click the **Last row** and **Last column check boxes** to deselect them
   See Figure 3-25.

6. Click **Apply**

7. Click the **table move handle** ⊞ to select the entire table, click the **Center button** ▥ to center the table on the page, then click anywhere in the document to deselect the table
   See Figure 3-26.

8. Click the **Close button** ☒ on the Tables and Borders toolbar

 close GCMemo03.doc

Step 7
You can drag the table move handle to position the table anywhere you like.

Figure 3-25: Table AutoFormat dialog box

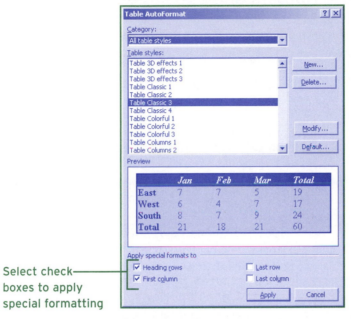

Select check boxes to apply special formatting

Figure 3-26: Table with AutoFormat applied

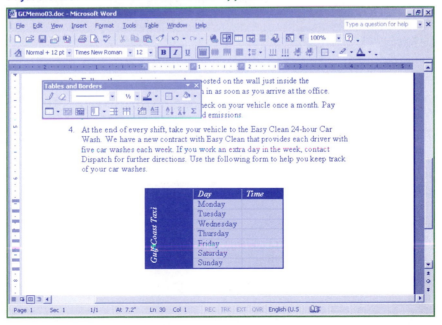

Create and Modify Tables
Modify Table Borders and Shading

You can manually change table borders and the shading in cells by changing the options in the Borders and Shading dialog box. You can make changes to these properties even after you've applied a table AutoFormat.

Activity Steps

 open GCBrochure06.doc

1. Scroll down until you can see the table, right-click any toolbar, then click **Tables and Borders** to open the Tables and Borders toolbar, if necessary

2. Move the pointer into the left margin to the left of the top row of the table so that it changes to ◿, then click to select the top row *See Figure 3-27.*

3. Click the **Shading Color button list arrow** on the Tables and Borders toolbar, then click the **Blue box**

4. Select the bottom four rows in the table, click the **Shading color button list arrow** on the Tables and Borders toolbar, then click the **Light Turquoise box**

5. Click the **Outside Border button list arrow** on the Tables and Borders toolbar, click the **All Borders button**, then click anywhere in the table to deselect the text

6. Click the **Line Style button list arrow** on the Tables and Borders toolbar, then click the thick line with thin lines above and below it

7. Drag the pointer, which changes to ✐, across the line below the top row, then click the **Draw Table button** on the Tables and Borders toolbar to deselect it *See Figure 3-28.*

8. Click the **Close button** on the Tables and Borders toolbar

 close GCBrochure06.doc

Make sure the Line Style button displays the line style you want before you click one of the Borders buttons or draw a border.

Figure 3-27: Selecting a row in a table

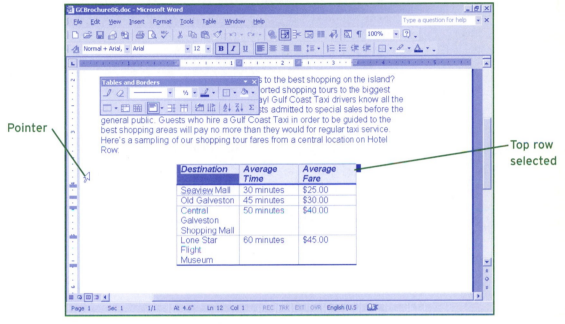

Pointer

Top row selected

Figure 3-28: Table with modified borders and shading

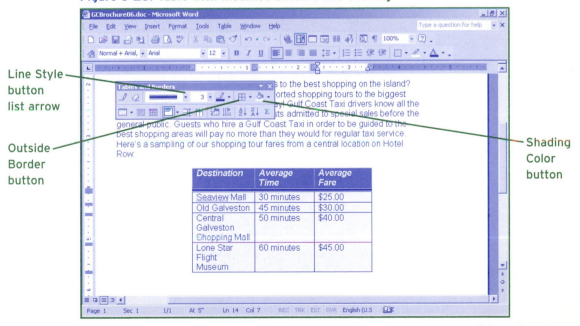

Line Style button list arrow

Outside Border button

Shading Color button

Skill Set 3
Formatting Documents

Create and Modify Tables
Insert and Delete Columns and Rows in a Table

You can add additional columns and rows to a table by using the Insert command on the Table menu. You can delete extra columns and rows from a table by using the Delete command on the Table menu.

tip

If you want to prevent a table that flows onto a second page from breaking in the middle of a row, position the insertion point in the table, click Table Properties on the Table menu, click the Row tab, then click the Allow row to break across pages check box to deselect it.

Activity Steps

 open GCMemo04.doc

1. Scroll down so you can see the entire table, then click anywhere in the **Weekly Hours column**

2. Click **Table** on the menu bar, point to **Insert**, then click **Columns to the Right** to insert a new column to the right of the current column

3. Select the row with **Gary Goodman** in the **Driver column**

4. Click **Table** on the menu bar, point to **Insert**, then click **Rows Above** to insert a row above the selected row
See Figure 3-29.

5. Select the row with **Verna Graham** in the **Driver column**

6. Right-click the selected row, then click **Delete Rows** on the shortcut menu
See Figure 3-30.

 close GCMemo04.doc

Figure 3-29: Column and row inserted in table

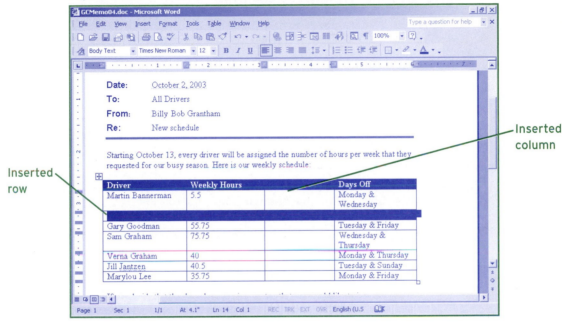

Inserted row

Inserted column

Figure 3-30: Table with row deleted

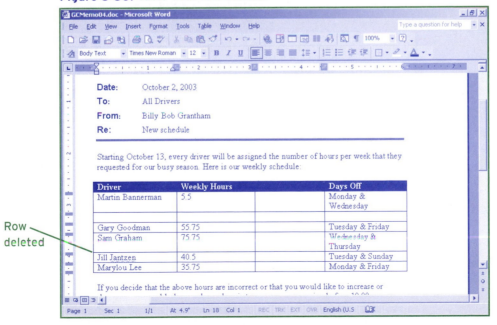

Row deleted

Skill Set 3

Formatting Documents

Create and Modify Tables

Modify Cell Format in a Table

You can format the text in cells just as you format regular text. For example, you can change the alignment of text within a cell, or you can add additional blank space around the entry in a cell.

Activity Steps

 open GCMemo05.doc

1. Scroll down until you can see the table, right-click any toolbar, then click **Tables and Borders** to open the Tables and Borders toolbar, if necessary

2. Drag to select all of the cells except those in the top row, then click the **Align Top Left button list arrow** on the Tables and Borders toolbar

3. Click the **Align Center Left button**

4. Click **Table** on the menu bar, click **Table Properties**, then click the **Table tab**, if necessary

5. Click **Options** on the Table tab to open the Table Options dialog box

6. Click the **Top up arrow** six times to change the Top cell margin to **0.06"**, then change the Bottom cell margin to **0.06"**
   See Figure 3-31.

7. Click **OK**, click **OK** in the Table Properties dialog box, then click anywhere on the screen to deselect the cells
   See Figure 3-32.

8. Click the **Close button** on the Tables and Borders toolbar

 close GCMemo05.doc

To repeat the heading rows of a table automatically if a table occupies more than one page, select the header row (or rows), click Table, then click Heading Rows Repeat.

Figure 3-31: Table Options dialog box

Cell margins ——

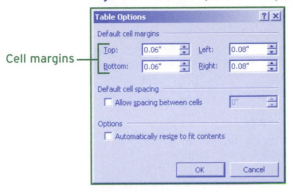

Figure 3-32: Table with modified cell formats

Increased
space above
and below
text in cells

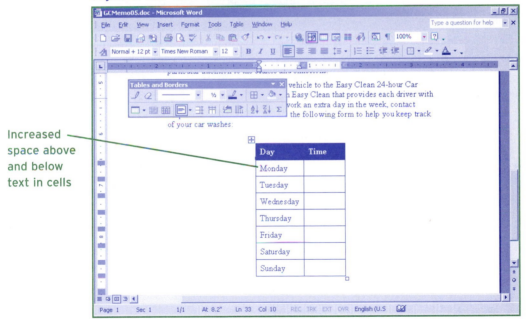

Skill Set 3

Formatting Documents

Preview and Print Documents, Envelopes, and Labels

Preview a Document

Before you print a document, you should look at it in Print Preview to make sure that it will print the way you expect it to.

 open GCLetter02.doc

Activity Steps

1. Click the **Print Preview button**

2. Click below the scroll box in the vertical scroll bar to move to the second page

3. Position the pointer over the page so that it changes to ⊕, click the line of text on page 2 to zoom in, and observe that the pointer changes to ⊖
   See Figure 3-33.

4. Click the screen again to zoom back out

5. Click the **Shrink to Fit button**  on the Print Preview toolbar
   See Figure 3-34.

6. Click the **Close button** on the Print Preview toolbar

 close GCLetter02.doc

> **tip**
>
> You can print from Print Preview by clicking the Print button or using the Print command on the File menu.

---

extra!

Adjusting text in Print Preview
You can enter and edit text in Print Preview. Click the Magnifier button 🔍 on the Print Preview toolbar to deselect it and change the pointer to Ⅰ. Click the screen at the point where you want to insert or edit text, then start typing. When you are finished editing, click the Magnifier button again, and the pointer changes back to ⊕ or ⊖.

Figure 3-33: Document magnified in Print Preview

Pointer

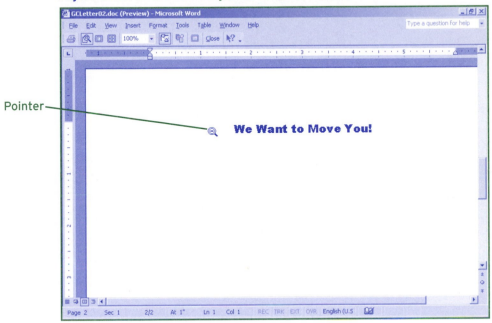

Figure 3-34: Text shrunk to fit on one page in Print Preview

Shrink to
Fit button

Pointer

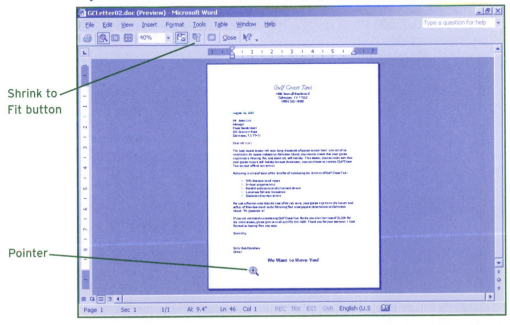

Skill Set 3
Formatting Documents

Preview and Print Documents, Envelopes, and Labels
Print a Document

Once you've created a document, you usually want to print it. To print a document, you can click the Print command on the File menu to change print settings (like the number of copies to print), or you can click the Print button to print your document with the current print settings.

Activity Steps

 open GCProposal03.doc

1. Click **File** on the menu bar, then click **Print** to open the Print dialog box
2. Click the **Pages option button**, then type **2-3** to print only the last two pages
3. Click the **Number of copies up arrow** to change the number of copies to **2**
4. Make sure the **Collate check box** is selected
   See Figure 3-35.
5. Click **OK**

 close GCProposal03.doc

When you click the Print button, the Print dialog box does not open, and the document prints using the current print settings.

Figure 3-35: Print dialog box

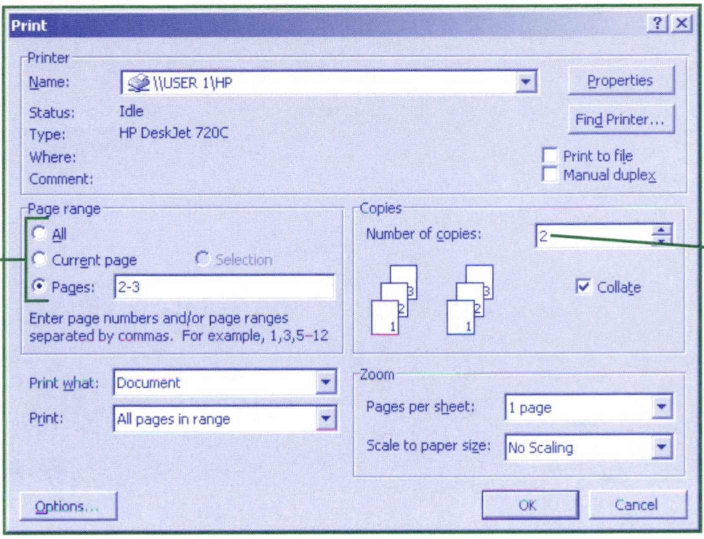

Select pages to print

Select number of copies

extra!

Print dialog box options

To change your printer's options, click Properties at the top of the Print dialog box. To print several document pages on one piece of paper, select one of the options from the Pages per sheet list in the Print dialog box. To scale the document to fit on a specific paper size, click the Scale to paper size list arrow in the Print dialog box.

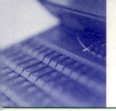

Skill Set 3

Formatting Documents

Preview and Print Documents, Envelopes, and Labels

Print Envelopes

You can set up a document to print as an envelope. With the Envelopes and Labels command, you simply type the address, tell Word what size envelope you are using, and Word formats the address to fit in the proper position on the envelope. After you create your envelope, you can print it directly from the Envelopes and Labels dialog box, or you can click Add to Document to add it to the current document as a new section.

Step 2
You can change the Delivery address from the one suggested by typing a different one or by clicking the Insert Address button to insert a name and address from your electronic address book.

Activity Steps

 open GCLetter03.doc

1. Click **Tools** on the menu bar, point to **Letters and Mailings**, click **Envelopes and Labels**, then click the **Envelopes tab**, if necessary

2. Make sure that the Delivery address is the address for **Anna Perkins**, as shown in the letter
   See Figure 3-36.

3. Click in the **Return address box**, type **Gulf Coast Taxi**, press **[Enter]**, type **1400 Seawall Blvd.**, press **[Enter]**, then type **Galveston, TX 77552**

4. Click the **Feed box** to open the Printing Options tab in the Envelope Options dialog box, note the selected direction to feed the envelope into the printer, then click **OK**

5. Click the **Preview box** to open the Envelope Options tab in the Envelope Options dialog box, click the **Envelope size list arrow**, read through the list of envelope sizes, make sure that **Size 10** (the standard business size envelope) is selected in the list, then click **OK**

6. Click **Add to Document** to add the envelope as a new section in the current document, then if necessary, click **No** in the dialog box that opens asking if you want to save the return address as the default return address

7. Click the **Print Preview button** 🔍
   See Figure 3-37.

8. Click below the scroll box in the vertical scroll bar to move to the second page

9. Click **File** on the menu bar, click **Print**, click the **Pages option button**, type **1**, insert your envelope into the printer, then click **OK**

 close GCLetter03.doc

Figure 3-36: Envelopes tab in the Envelopes and Labels dialog box

Delivery address picked up from inside address in letter

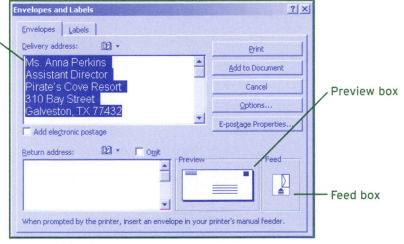

Preview box

Feed box

Figure 3-37: Envelope in Print Preview

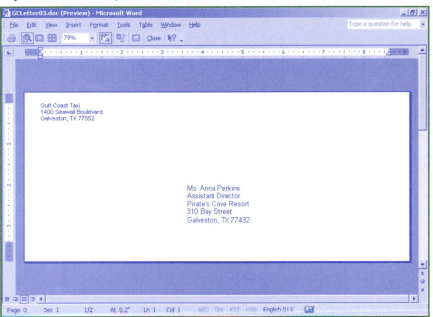

Skill Set 3
Formatting Documents

Preview and Print Documents, Envelopes, and Labels
Printing Labels

Labels are as easy to print as envelopes. Click the Labels tab in the Envelopes and Labels dialog box and select the options for the size of labels you are using. Word automatically formats the address to fit on the labels. After you create your label, you can print it directly from the Envelopes and Labels dialog box, or you can click New Document to create a new document so you can see how the labels will print.

Step 5
If your label is not in the Product number list in the Label Options dialog box, click New Label and specify the dimensions of your label.

Activity Steps

1. Open a new, blank document
2. Click **Tools** on the menu bar, point to **Letters and Mailings**, click **Envelopes and Labels**, then click the **Labels tab** if necessary
3. Click in the **Address box**, type **Mr. Jason Lee**, press **[Enter]**, then continue typing the address in the Address box, as shown in Figure 3-38
4. Click the **Label box** to open the Label Options dialog box, then examine the list of labels in the Product number list
5. Click the label that you are using in the Product number list (if you do not have a label, choose any label in the list), then click **OK**
6. Click **New Document**, click the **Zoom button list arrow** , then click **Whole Page**
   See Figure 3-39.
7. Click the **Print button**

   file close file

Figure 3-38: Labels tab in Envelopes and Labels dialog box

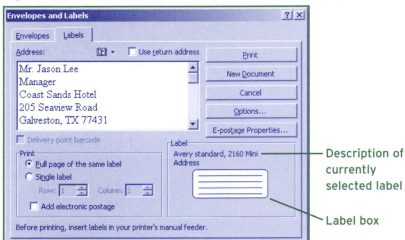

Description of currently selected label

Label box

Figure 3-39: Labels in document

Temporary filename

Your layout may look different depending on the label you chose

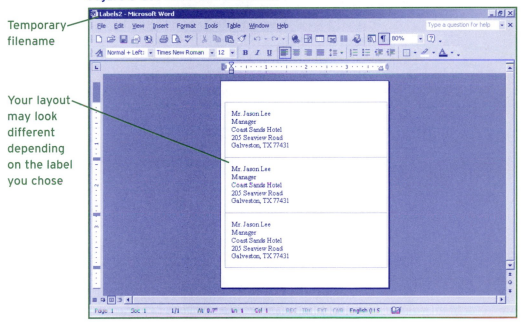

Skill Set 3

Formatting Documents

Targeting Your Skills

 GCNewsletter01.doc

1 Create the document shown in Figure 3-40. Insert a footer that identifies the page number and the total number of pages. Position this text so it is on the right side of the footer. Finally, make sure the columns are balanced. Preview your completed document and print it.

Figure 3-40

Header says "GCT News"

Date field

 GCAnnouncement02.doc

2 Create the document shown in Figure 3-41. Note that you need to insert page numbers and change the margins. Preview your completed document and print it.

Figure 3-41

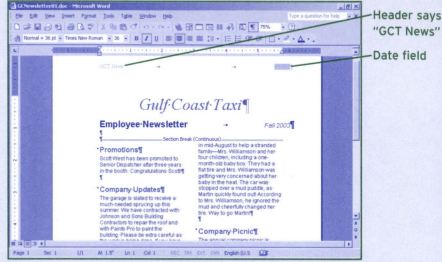

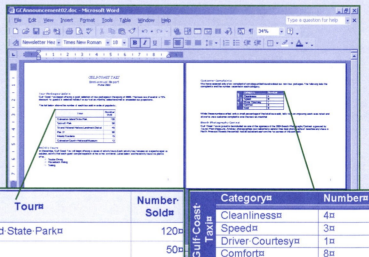

Tour¤	Number·Sold¤
Galveston·Island·State·Park¤	120¤
Seawolf·Park¤	50¤
Strand·National·Historic·Landmark·District¤	45¤
Pier·21¤	30¤
Moody·Gardens¤	15¤
Galveston·County·Historical·Museum·¤	12¤

	Category¤	Number¤
Gulf·Coast·Taxi¤	Cleanliness¤	4¤
	Speed¤	3¤
	Driver·Courtesy¤	1¤
	Comfort¤	8¤
	Cost¤	3¤

Skill List

1. Manage files and folders for documents
2. Create documents using templates
3. Save documents using different names and file formats

In Skill Set 4, you will learn about managing documents. First, you will learn how to create folders within Word. Folders make it easy to organize your files so that you can quickly locate them when you want them. Then you will learn how to create a document from a template, which is a pre-designed document. Finally, you will learn how to save your documents with different names and in different file formats.

Learning how to manage your documents will save you time. If you master these skills, you will always be able to locate, organize, and store your documents quickly.

Skill Set 4

Managing Documents

Manage Files and Folders for Documents

Using the Open and Save As dialog boxes in Word, you can create new folders. To create a new folder, you click the Create New Folder button in the dialog box, then type a name for the folder. The folder is created as a new folder within the current folder, and the new folder becomes the current folder. Specifically, the Look in box at the top of the Open dialog box or the Save in box at the top of the Save As dialog box changes to display the new folder name.

Activity Steps

Step 3
The Create New Folder button is also available on the toolbar at the top of the Open dialog box.

1. Create a new, blank document

2. Click **File** on the menu bar, then click **Save As** to open the Save As dialog box

3. Click the **Create New Folder button**  on the toolbar at the top of the Open dialog box

4. Type **My New Folder** in the Name box

5. Click **OK**
   See Figure 4-1.

6. Click the **Up One Level button** 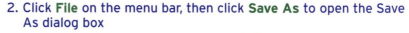 on the toolbar at the top of the Save As dialog box to see your new folder in the folder list
   See Figure 4-2.

7. Click **Cancel** to close the Save As dialog box without saving the file

 close file

Figure 4-1: New folder created in Save As dialog box

Current folder

Create New Folder button

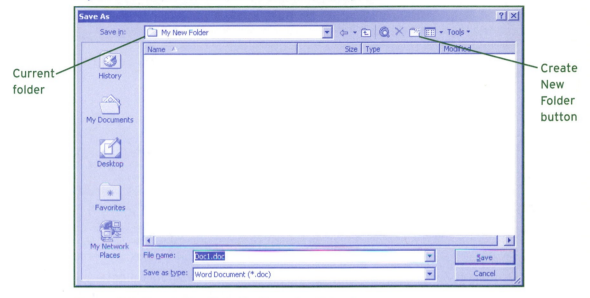

Figure 4-2: New folder listed in Save As dialog box

Folders in the current folder

Up One Level button

New folder listed in file list (your list may differ)

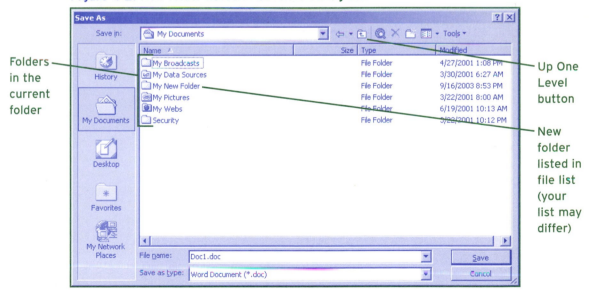

Create Documents Using Templates

A **template** is a set of styles and formats that determines how a document will look. Every document is based on the Normal template, a template that is available to all documents. Word provides additional templates to make it easier for you to create specially formatted documents, like memos and resumes. Most templates provided with Word include **placeholders**, items you click once to select all of the existing text, then type to substitute your replacement text. When you save a document created from a template, it is saved as an ordinary Word document.

Activity Steps

tip

To use any existing document as a template for a new document, click the Choose document link in the New Document task pane to open a copy of the document.

1. If the task pane is not open, click **View** on the menu bar, then click **Task Pane**

2. If the New Document task pane is not visible, click the **Other Task Panes list arrow** ▼ in the task pane title bar, then click **New Document**

3. Click the **General Templates link** in the New Document task pane to open the Templates dialog box

4. Click the **Other Documents tab**, click **Contemporary Resume**, then make sure that the **Document option button** is selected under Create New
   See Figure 4-3.

5. Click **OK**

6. Click the **[Click here and type address] placeholder**, type **4598 Main Street**, press **[Enter]**, then type **Charleston, SC 29407**

7. Drag to select the name **Deborah Greer**, then type **Mark Rodriguez**
   See Figure 4-4.

 close file

---

extra!

Using wizards
Word provides several wizards that customize templates for you by asking a series of questions. For example, you could start the Resume Wizard by clicking it in the Templates dialog box. After you read each dialog box and fill in any requested information or make a selection, click the Next button at the bottom of the dialog box to move to the next screen. When you are finished answering questions, click the Finish button. A formatted resume appears on screen with much of your personal information already filled in.

Figure 4-3: Templates dialog box

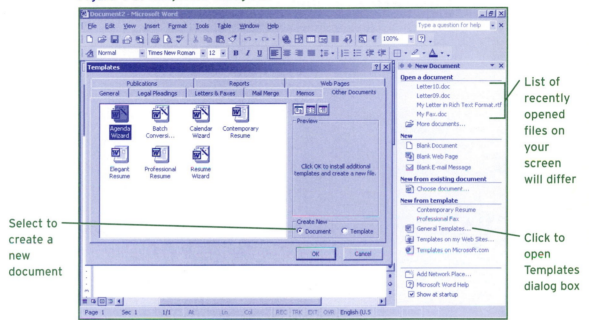

Select to create a new document

List of recently opened files on your screen will differ

Click to open Templates dialog box

Figure 4-4: Resume template with text selected

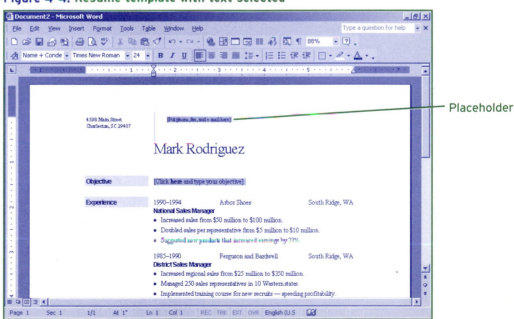

Placeholder

Skill Set 4
Managing Documents

Save Documents Using Different Names and File Formats
Save a Document

When you create a new document, you will probably need to save it. When you save a new document for the first time, you use the Save As dialog box, where you can change the drive and folder to which you are saving the file and specify the filename. If you want to save a copy of the document with a new name, you use the Save As command. If you make changes to a document and then want to save the changes without creating a new copy of the document, you use the Save command.

Step 3
If you want to save your document to the My Documents folder, you can click My Documents in the Places bar on the left in the Save As dialog box.

Activity Steps

 open EWLetter09.doc

1. Click **File** on the menu bar, then click **Save As**

2. Type **My Saved Letter** in the File name box

3. Click the **Save in list arrow**, then select the folder or drive to which you want to save your document

4. Double-click the folder name in which you want to save your document
   See Figure 4-5.

5. Click **Save** in the Save As dialog box
   See Figure 4-6.

6. Select **August 15** in the first paragraph in the body of the letter, then type **September 8**

7. Click the **Save button** 🖫 to save the change to the document

 close My Saved Letter.doc

Figure 4-5: Save As dialog box

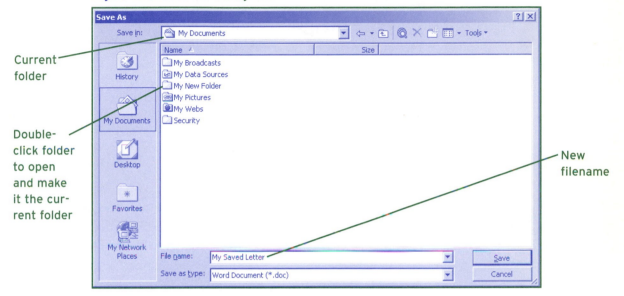

Current folder

Double-click folder to open and make it the current folder

New filename

Figure 4-6: File saved with a new name

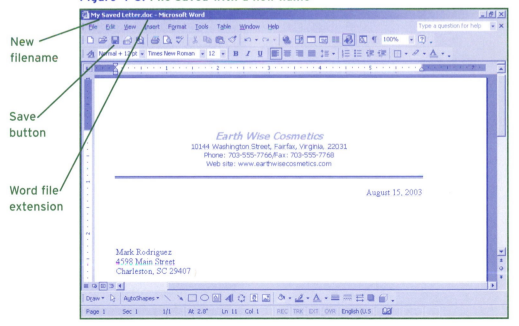

New filename

Save button

Word file extension

Skill Set 4
Managing Documents

Save Documents Using Different Names and File Formats
Save a Document with a Different File Format

When you save a document, you save it in the default Word file format. The file extension is .doc. If you are sending the file to someone who doesn't have Word, you can save the file with a different file format. For example, rich text format is a format that most word processors can read and will allow you to save most of your formatting. To save a document with a different file format, you need to use the Save As command.

Step 3
Select the file type Document Templates (*.dot) to save the file as a Word template that appears on the General tab in the Templates dialog box.

Activity Steps

 open EWMemo07.doc

1. Click **File** on the menu bar, then click **Save As** to open the Save As dialog box

2. Type **My Memo in Rich Text Format** in the File name box

3. Click the **Save as type list arrow**, then click **Rich Text Format (*.rtf)**

4. Click the **Save in list arrow**, then select the folder or drive to which you want to save your document
   See Figure 4-7.

5. Click **Save** in the Save As dialog box
   See Figure 4-8.

 close My Memo in Rich Text Format.rtf

Figure 4-7: Save As dialog box with Rich Text Format selected

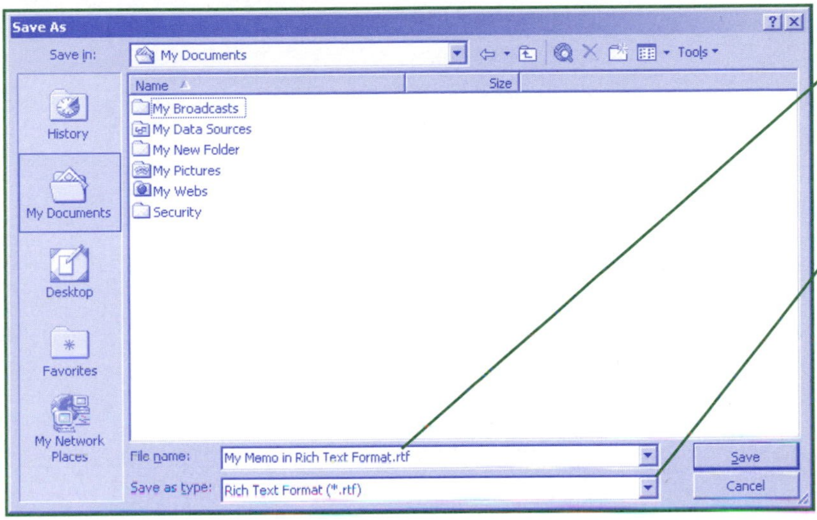

Rich text format file extension

Save as type list arrow

Rich text format file extension

Figure 4-8: File saved in rich text format

Skill Set 4
Managing Documents

Target Your Skills

1 Use Figure 4-9 as a guide to save the EWNewsletter06 file with a new name as a template. Make sure you save it in the folder indicated (you'll need to create the folder first).

Figure 4-9

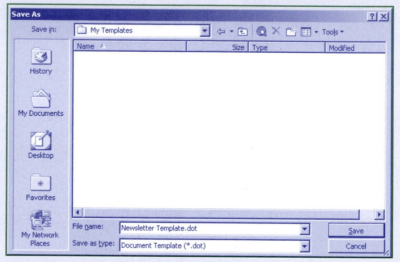

2 Use Figure 4-10 as a guide for creating a fax cover sheet from the Professional Fax template. (*Hint*: To insert a checkmark in a box, double-click the box. To delete the **Company Name Here** box, position the pointer above it so that it looks like a downward-pointing arrow, click to select the entire box, then click the Cut button.) Save the file as **My Fax**.

Figure 4-10

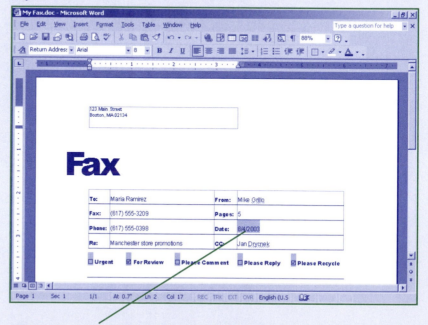

Current date will appear here

Skill List

1. Insert images and graphics
2. Create and modify diagrams and charts

Pictures, diagrams, and charts can make your documents more interesting and informative. For example, you might want to insert a company logo or an image into a newsletter. You can insert clip art or other pictures stored on your hard drive or on the Web.

You can use the Insert Diagram command to insert a variety of diagrams, including an organizational chart diagram or a pyramid diagram. Diagrams can help get your point across visually. You can also use a program built into Word called Microsoft Graph to insert a graph of numerical data.

Skill Set 5

Working with Graphics

Insert Images and Graphics

Insert Clips Using the Clip Organizer

A **clip**, sometimes called **clip art**, is a drawing, photograph, sound, or movie that you can insert into a document. Clips are organized in the Clip Organizer in collections, or groups on the basis of keywords stored with the file. You can find clips appropriate to your subject by searching for a keyword you type in the Insert Clip Art task pane.

To add your own clips to the Clip Organizer, on the File menu in the Clip Organizer, point to Add Clips to Gallery, click On My Own, click the clip you want to add, click Add to, click the collection in which you want to store the clip, then click Add.

Activity Steps

 open GCAnnouncement03.doc

1. If the Drawing toolbar is not visible, click the **Drawing button** 🔲, then position the insertion point between the headline and the paragraph

2. Click the **Insert Clip Art button** 🔲 on the Drawing toolbar to open the Insert Clip Art task pane

3. If a dialog box appears asking if you want to catalog your clips, click **Later**

4. Click in the **Search text box** in the task pane, if necessary delete any text that is already there (from a previous search), type **wedding**, then click **Search**

5. Click the **clip** indicated in Figure 5-1 (if you don't have this clip, select another), then click the **Close button** ☒ in the Insert Clip Art task pane

6. Click the clip to select it, then drag the **lower-right sizing handle** down and to the right until the dotted outline indicates that the clip extends to the right margin of the paragraph as shown in Figure 5-2

7. Click anywhere in a blank area of the document to deselect the clip

close GCAnnouncement03.doc

Figure 5-1: Insert Clip Art task pane

Select this clip

Figure 5-2: Resizing a clip

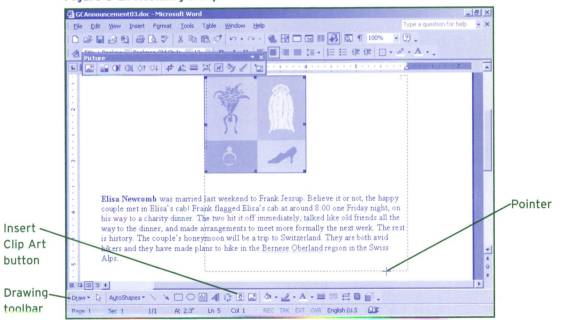

Insert Clip Art button

Drawing toolbar

Pointer

Skill Set 5
Working with Graphics

Insert Images and Graphics
Insert Images Not Stored in the Clip Organizer

In addition to clips from the Clip Organizer, you can insert graphic images stored on your hard drive, another disk, or on the Web. Graphic images are saved in many file formats. Common file formats for graphics include .bmp, .tif, .jgp (also called JPEG), and .wmf.

To insert a picture directly from a scanner or a digital camera, point to Picture on the Insert menu, then click From Scanner or Camera.

Activity Steps

 open GCProposal04.doc

1. If the Drawing toolbar is not visible, click the **Drawing button** , click the **Zoom button list arrow** 100% , then click **Whole Page**

2. With the insertion point at the beginning of the document, click the **Insert Picture button** on the Drawing toolbar to open the Insert Picture dialog box

3. Locate the **GCTaxiLogo01.bmp** project file, then click it to select it
   See Figure 5-3.

4. Click **Insert** to insert the image at the insertion point

5. Click the image to select it, then drag the **bottom-right sizing handle** down and to the right until the dotted line indicates that the right edge of the image will be aligned with the **T** in **Taxi**

6. With the image still selected, click the **Center button**

7. Click anywhere in the document to deselect the image
   See Figure 5-4.

 close GCProposal04.doc

Figure 5-3: Logo selected in the Insert Picture dialog box

Figure 5-4: Picture resized and centered in document

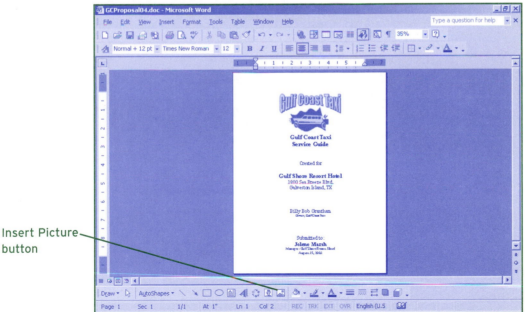

Insert Picture button

Skill Set 5
Working with Graphics

Create and Modify Diagrams and Charts
Create an Organizational Chart

Sometimes diagrams can convey information more clearly than a written description. You can insert a variety of diagrams into a Word document using the Insert Diagram or Organization Chart button. An **organizational chart** is a graphical representation of a hierarchical structure.

Right-click the edge of a chart box to see commands you can use to format or change the organizational chart.

Activity Steps

1. Open a new, blank document, then, if the Drawing toolbar is not visible, click the **Drawing button**

2. Click the **Insert Diagram or Organization Chart button** on the Drawing toolbar to open the Diagram Gallery dialog box

3. Make sure the **Organization Chart button** is selected
   See Figure 5-5.

4. Click **OK** to insert an organizational chart into the document

5. Click in the top box in the chart, type **Billy Bob Grantham**, press **[Enter]**, type **Owner**, then click outside the box but inside the drawing canvas to automatically resize the box

6. Click in the first box on the left in the second row, type **Scott West**, press **[Enter]**, then continue filling in the boxes as shown in Figure 5-6

 close file

Figure 5-5: Diagram Gallery dialog box

Thick blue square indicates button is selected

Description of selected diagram type

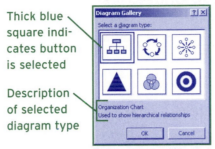

Figure 5-6: Completed organizational chart

Organization Chart toolbar

Drawing canvas

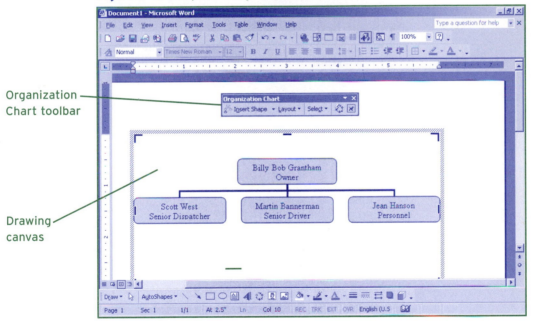

Skill Set 5

Working with Graphics

Create and Modify Diagrams and Charts

Modify an Organizational Chart

Once you have created a diagram or organizational chart, you can add elements to it and change their formatting. You can also rearrange the layout of the parts of the diagram.

Click the Layout button on the Organization Chart toolbar to change the arrangement of the boxes in the organizational chart.

Activity Steps

 open GCOrgChart01.doc

1. Click the **Jean Hanson box**, click the **Insert Shape button list arrow** `Insert Shape` on the Organization Chart toolbar, click **Assistant**, click in the new Assistant box, then type **Mary Lou Lee**

2. Click the **Martin Bannerman box**, click the **Insert Shape button list arrow** `Insert Shape`, click **Subordinate**, then with the Martin Bannerman box still selected, add another Subordinate box

3. Click the edge of the **Mary Lou Lee box** with 🖱, then drag the box on top of the Scott West box

4. Click the edge of the **Subordinate box** on the left under the Martin Bannerman box, then press **[Delete]**
   See Figure 5-7.

5. Click the **Autoformat button** 🔄 on the Organization Chart toolbar, click **Beveled** in the list in the Organization Chart Style Gallery dialog box, then click **Apply**

6. Right-click the edge of one of the boxes, then click **Use AutoFormat** to turn off the AutoFormat option so you can add manual formats

7. If the Drawing toolbar is not visible, click the **Drawing button** 🔷, click the edge of the **Scott West box**, click the **Select button** `Select` on the Organization Chart toolbar, click **Level**, click the **Fill Color button list arrow** 🎨 on the Drawing toolbar, then click the **Turquoise box**

8. Click the edge of the **Billy Bob Grantham box**, click the **Fill Color button list arrow** 🎨 on the Drawing toolbar, click the **Blue box**, click the **Font Color button list arrow** 🔤, click the **White box**, click the **Bold button** 🅱, then click in a blank area of the document to deselect the chart and the drawing canvas (you may need to click twice)
   See Figure 5-8.

 close GCOrgChart01.doc

Figure 5-7: Moving a box in an organizational chart

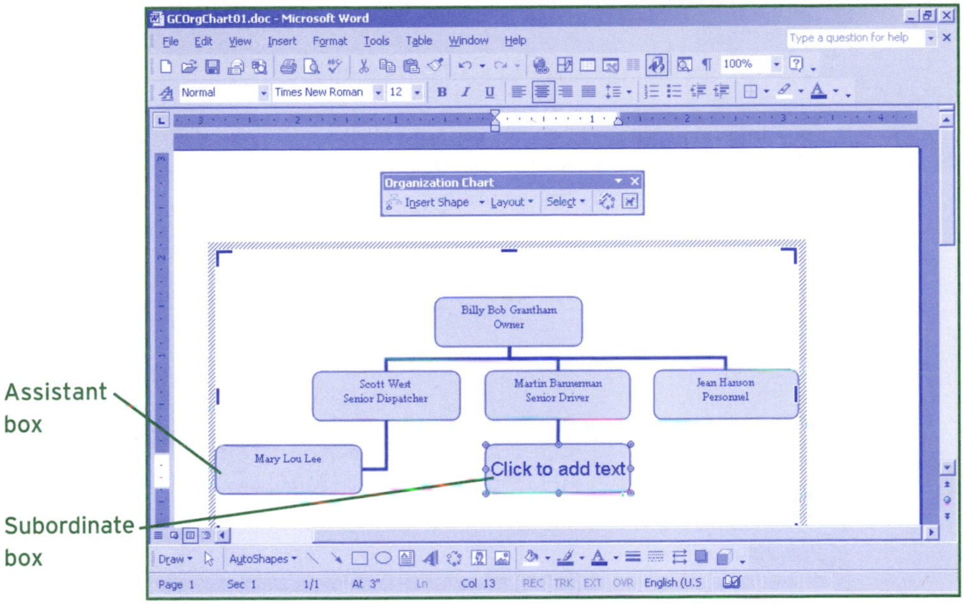

Assistant box

Subordinate box

Figure 5-8: Formatted organizational chart

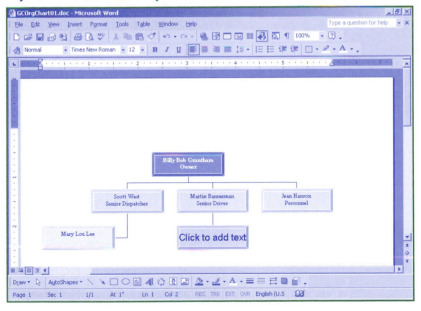

extra!

Understanding diagram types

In addition to organizational charts, you can create cycle, radial, pyramid, Venn, and target diagrams and flowcharts. Each diagram conveys information in a particular way by illustrating how a process works or by showing the relationship between parts of something larger. To create any of these diagrams except the flowchart, select the digram type in the Diagram Gallery dialog box. To create a flowchart, click the AutoShapes button on the Drawing toolbar, point to Flowchart, select the shape you want to insert, then drag to draw it in the document. Connect the flowchart shapes with lines from the Connectors or Lines categories on the AutoShapes menu.

Skill Set 5
Working with Graphics

Create and Modify Diagrams and Charts
Create a Chart

Graphs are a good way to communicate numerical information visually; for example, they can show at a glance how much sales have increased or whether one item is selling significantly more than another. You can add a graph to a document by using the built-in program Microsoft Graph. A graph consists of two parts: a **datasheet**, similar to a table or a spreadsheet, in which you enter the data you want to graph, and a **chart**, in which the data from the datasheet is graphed. When you start Microsoft Graph, the Word menu bar and toolbars are replaced with the Graph menu bar and toolbars.

Activity Steps

 open GCReport01.doc

1. Press **[Ctrl][End]** to position the insertion point at the end of the document, click **Insert** on the menu bar, then click **Object** to open the Object dialog box

2. Scroll down and click **Microsoft Graph Chart** in the Object type list, then click **OK**
   See Figure 5-9.

3. Click the **1st Qtr cell**, type **Airport**, press **[Tab]**, type **Tours**, press **[Tab]**, then type **Shopping**

4. Double-click the **column D header** to eliminate this column from the chart

5. Click the **East cell**, type **October**, press **[Enter]**, type **November**, then double-click the **row 3 header** to eliminate this row from the chart

6. Click in the first cell below the Airport column heading, type **140**, then continue filling in the datasheet as shown in Figure 5-10

7. Drag the datasheet by its title bar so you can see the chart, then click anywhere in the document to exit Microsoft Graph

 close GCReport01.doc

If the labels on an axis in the chart do not all appear, drag a sizing handle on the chart to enlarge the chart object while Microsoft Graph is still active.

Understanding charts
Charts are made up of data markers grouped in series and data labels. A **data marker** represents a single piece of data—a number from the datasheet—in the chart. In this activity, the shorter bar over the Airport label in the chart is the data marker for the data in the first cell under the Airport column. A **data series** is the collection of all the data markers in a row or column in the datasheet. In this activity, the dark purple data markers make up the data series for the November data. A **data label** is text that identifies any part of the chart.

Figure 5-9: Graph and datasheet inserted into a document

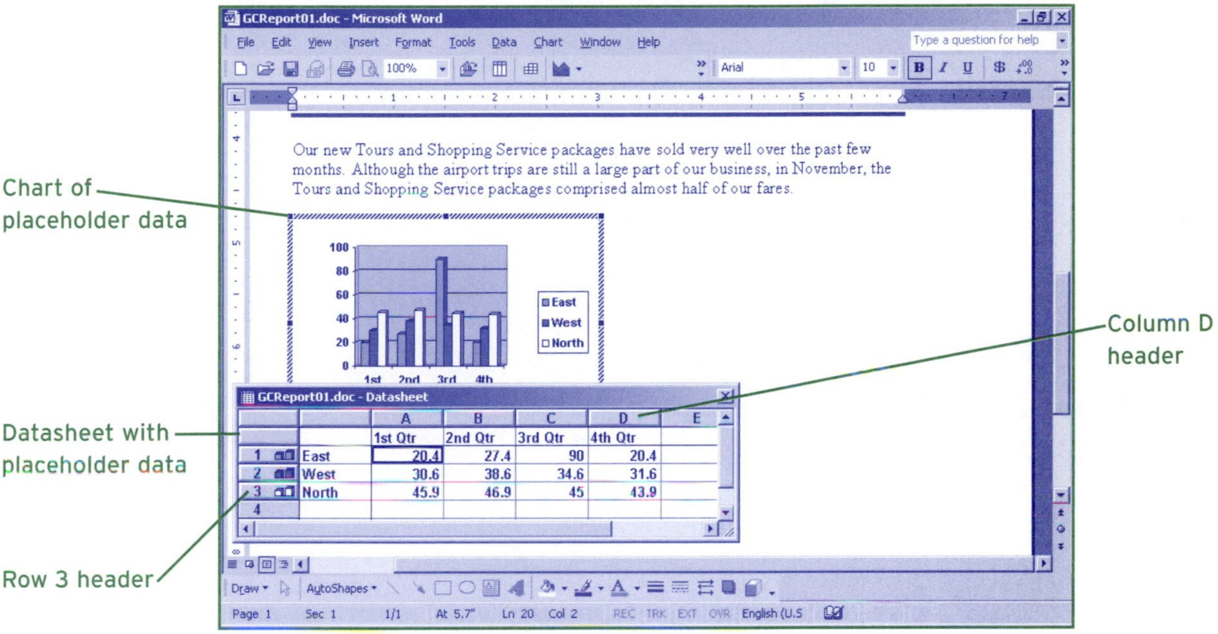

Chart of placeholder data

Column D header

Datasheet with placeholder data

Row 3 header

Figure 5-10: Completed datasheet

Airport data marker for October

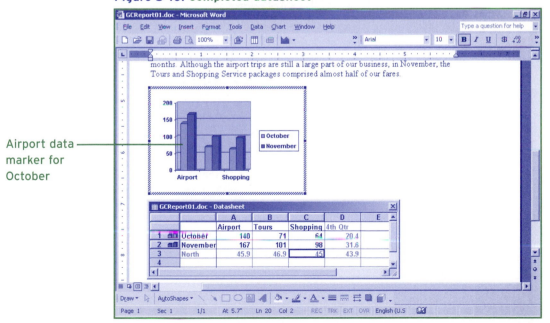

Skill Set 5
Working with Graphics

Create and Modify Diagrams and Charts
Modify a Chart

Once you have inserted a chart, you can modify it in several ways. For example, you can change the chart type, add labels, and resize the objects that make up the chart object. To format an object within a chart, make sure Microsoft Graph is open, click the chart to select it, then click the object in the chart that you want to format.

Activity Steps

 open GCReport02.doc

1. Scroll down to see the chart, then double-click the **chart** to open Microsoft Graph

2. Click the **Chart Type button list arrow** , then click the **Pie Chart button**

3. Double-click the **row 1 header** in the datasheet to exclude the October data and use only the November data in the pie chart *See Figure 5-11.*

4. Click **Chart** on the menu bar, then click **Chart Options** to open the Chart Options dialog box

5. Click the **Titles tab** if necessary, click in the **Chart title box**, type **November Fares**, click the **Data Labels tab**, click the **Percentage check box**, then click **OK**

6. Click anywhere in the chart area, position the pointer over the area just around the pie chart so that the ScreenTip says **Plot Area**, click to select the **Plot Area**, then drag the **sizing handles** to resize the pie chart so that it fills the left side of the chart object

7. Right-click the **Plot Area**, click **Format Plot Area** on the shortcut menu, click the **None option button** in the Border section to remove the border around the Plot Area, then click **OK**

8. Click outside of the **chart object** to close Microsoft Graph, click the chart object to select it, click the **Center button** , then click anywhere outside the chart to deselect the object *See Figure 5-12.*

 close GCReport02.doc

You can close the datasheet by clicking its Close button and reopen it by clicking Datasheet on the View menu.

Figure 5-11: Changing which data series is plotted in the pie chart

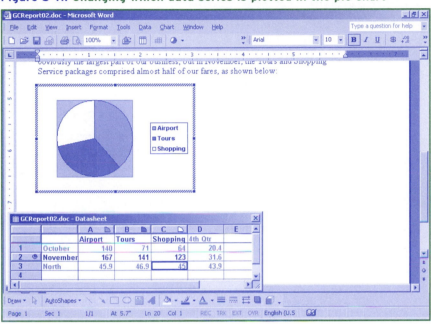

Figure 5-12: Modified chart

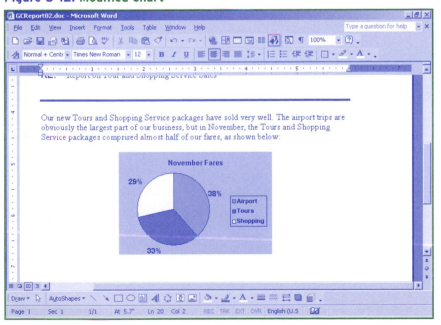

Skill Set 5
Working with Graphics

Create and Modify Diagrams and Charts
Add and Format Objects in a Chart

You can format almost any object in a chart individually. You can add labels to the axes, change the font of labels, add formatting to numbers on the chart, and add objects to your chart to enhance it.

Activity Steps

 open GCMemo06.doc

1. Scroll down to see the chart, double-click the chart to open Microsoft Graph, then click the **Close button** ⊠ in the datasheet title bar

2. Right-click any label on the vertical axis, click **Format Axis** on the shortcut menu, then click the **Number tab**

3. Click **Currency** in the Category list, click the **Decimal places down arrow** twice to change it to **0**, then click **OK**

4. Click **Chart** on the menu bar, click **Chart Options**, click the **Titles tab** if necessary, click in the **Value (Z) axis box**, type **Total Sales**, click the **Legend tab**, click the **Show legend check box** to deselect it, then click **OK**

5. Right-click **Total Sales**, click **Format Axis Title**, click the **Alignment tab**, double-click in the Degrees box, type **90**, then click **OK**

6. If the Drawing toolbar is not visible, click the **Drawing button** , click the **Arrow button** ◥ on the Drawing toolbar, then drag down to draw an arrow pointing to the top of the **Apr** data point as shown in Figure 5-13

7. Click the **Text Box button** on the Drawing toolbar, click above the **Apr** data point, click the **Font size list arrow** 11 ▾, click **9**, then type **Easter sales increase**

8. Click anywhere in the document to close Microsoft Graph
   See Figure 5-14.

 close GCMemo06.doc

Step 7
If the text box you inserted is in the wrong place, drag it by its edge. If the text box is not large enough, drag a sizing handle.

Figure 5-13: Adding an arrow object to a chart

Arrow object

Formatted axis label

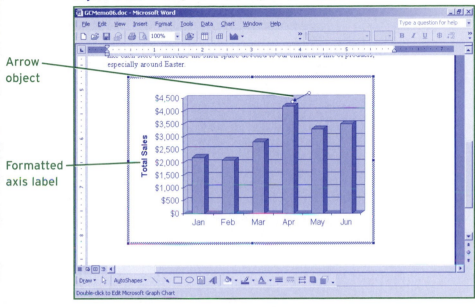

Figure 5-14: Chart with formatted objects

Text box

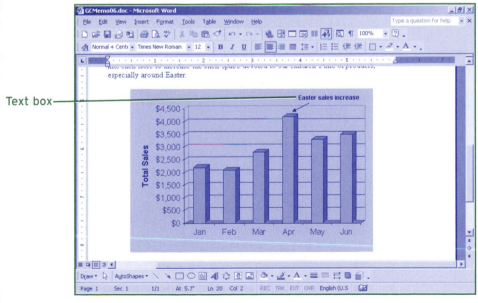

extra!

Understanding objects

An object is anything that can be manipulated—resized, dragged, recolored—as a unit. In this activity, once the chart was inserted into the document, it became a chart object, and Word treats it as one element. You can right-click the object, then use the Format Object command to change characteristics about the object, such as its fill color. Also, it's important to understand that many objects are made up of smaller objects. When you work with the chart in Microsoft Graph, you can manipulate individual components of the chart, such as the legend or the axis labels. Each of these components is an object.

Skill Set 5

Working with Graphics

Target Your Skills

1 Modify the **GCMemo07** file to create the final document shown in Figure 5-15. To format the organizational chart, first choose a diagram style, then modify individual components as needed. (*Hint*: To format the connecting lines, click the Select button on the Organization Chart toolbar, then click All Connecting Lines.)

Blue line color

Figure 5-15

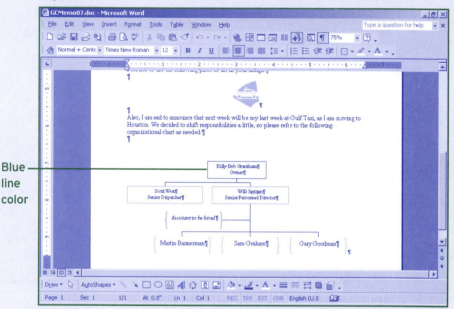

GCAnnouncement04.doc

2 Modify the **GCAnnouncement04** file to create the document shown in Figure 5-16. The image at the top of the document is in the **GCTaxiLogo02.bmp** file. Create the chart with the following tours and numbers of tours sold: **Galveston State Park, 120; Seawolf Park, 50; Moody Gardens, 45;** and **Pier 21, 30.**

Figure 5-16

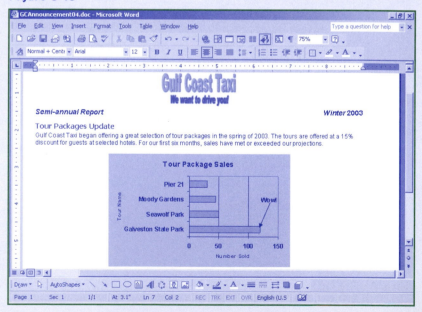

Skill List

1. Compare and merge documents
2. Insert, view, and edit comments
3. Convert documents into Web pages

Word has several features and commands that make it easy to share information with others. For example, when you create a document, you might want to make changes based on someone else's input. In Skill Set 6, you will learn how to compare and merge two versions of the same document. You will also learn how to insert, view, and edit comments in your documents.

Posting a document on the Web is an easy way to make it available to others. You can do this easily by saving a Word document as a Web page. You will learn how to do this and how to preview the Web page before you save it.

Compare and Merge Documents

Sometimes you need to get another person's opinion on a document you create. Someone else can open your document and make changes, then you can use the Compare and Merge command to see all the changes clearly shown on the screen. See Table 6-1 for a list of the three ways you can merge documents. Once you've created the merged document, you can display or print it with the changes showing or with all the changes made but hidden. You can also display or print the original document with the changes showing (which looks slightly different than the merged document, but the results are the same) or without any changes made at all.

Activity Steps

 open EWProductInfo01.doc, EWProductInfo02.doc

1. Make sure the **EWProductInfo02** project file, the edited document, is the current document, click **Tools** on the menu bar, then click **Compare and Merge Documents**

2. Locate and click the **EWProductInfo01** project file, then click the **Merge list arrow**
   See Figure 6-1.

3. Click **Merge into new document**

4. Click in the **Zoom box**, type **90**, press **[Enter]**, then scroll down, if necessary, so that all of the changes are visible on your screen

5. Position the insertion point over the word **Peppermint** in the first header to see the ScreenTip that identifies the person who made the change
   See Figure 6-2.

6. Click the **Display for Review list arrow** `Final Showing Markup ▼` on the Reviewing toolbar that opened, then click **Final** to see the result of all the changes

7. Click the **Display for Review list arrow** `Final Showing Markup ▼` on the Reviewing toolbar, then click **Original Showing Markup** to revert to the original marked-up document

8. Right-click any toolbar, then click **Reviewing** to close the Reviewing toolbar

 close EWProductInfo01.doc, EWProductInfo02.doc

Step 3
Another way to merge the documents into a new document is to click the Legal blackline check box in the Compare and Merge dialog box, then click Compare.

Figure 6-1: Compare and Merge Documents dialog box

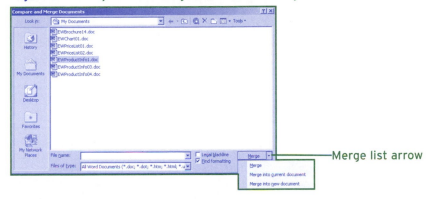

Merge list arrow

Figure 6-2: New document created by merging documents

Name of person
who made changes
and date and time
edits were made

Pointer

Text inserted into
original document

Identifies deletion
to original document

Identifies formatting
change to original
document

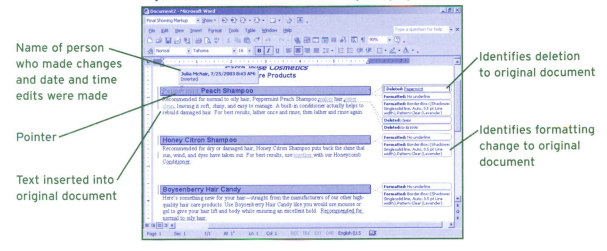

TABLE 6-1: Three ways to merge documents

command	best used for
Merge	Merges the changes into the original document and opens the original document if it's not already open
Merge into current document	Merges the changes into the edited (current) document
Merge into new document	Merges the changes into a new document and leaves the original and edited documents unchanged; clicking the Legal blackline check box and then clicking Compare produces the same result

Skill Set 6
Workgroup Collaboration

Insert, View, and Edit Comments
Insert and View Comments

Comments are notes that you add to a document. They are not printed with the document unless you specifically want them to be, but they are easily displayed on screen. In Print Layout and Web Layout view, comments are visible in Comment balloons, but you can hide them if you wish. You can also view comments in the Reviewing pane, a pane that you can open at the bottom of the window.

Activity Steps

 open EWBrochure05.doc

1. Position the insertion point immediately before **and chemicals** in the first line under the first heading

2. Click **Insert** on the menu bar, then click **Comment** to open a Comment balloon and the Reviewing toolbar
See Figure 6-3.

3. Type **Mention UV rays** in the Comment balloon

4. Drag the horizontal scroll bar to the left if necessary, position the insertion point after **over-worked** in the first paragraph, click the **New Comment button** on the Reviewing toolbar, then type **Delete "over-worked"** in the Comment balloon
See Figure 6-4.

5. Click the **Show button** `Show ▼` on the Reviewing toolbar, then click **Comments** to hide the Comment balloons

6. Click the **Show button** `Show ▼` on the Reviewing toolbar, then click **Reviewing Pane** to display the Reviewing pane

7. Click the **Show button** `Show ▼` on the Reviewing toolbar, click **Comments** to display the Comment balloons again, click the **Show button** `Show ▼`, then click **Reviewing Pane** to close the Reviewing pane

8. Right-click any toolbar, then click **Reviewing** to close the Reviewing toolbar

 close EWBrochure05.doc

tip

To see the names of all the people who have inserted comments in a document, click the Show button on the Reviewing toolbar, then point to Reviewers.

Figure 6-3: Comment balloon and Reviewing toolbar opened

Reviewing toolbar may be in a different position on your screen

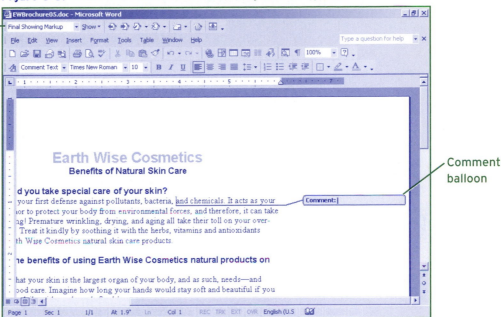

Comment balloon

Figure 6-4: Comments entered in document

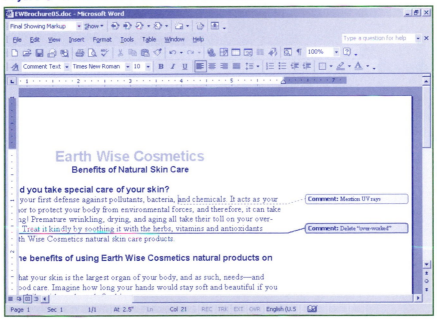

Skill Set 6
Workgroup Collaboration

Insert, View, and Edit Comments
Edit Comments

Once you've entered comments into a document, you can edit or delete them just like regular text. You can do this in each Comment balloon or in the Reviewing pane.

Activity Steps

open EWPriceList01.doc

1. Click **View** on the menu bar, point to **Toolbars**, then click **Reviewing** to open the Reviewing toolbar, if necessary

2. Click the **Next button** on the Reviewing toolbar to move to the next comment in the document

3. Double-click **deluxe** in the selected comment, then type **luxury**

4. Click the **Next button** on the Reviewing toolbar

5. Click the **Reject Change/Delete Comment button** on the Reviewing toolbar
   See Figure 6-5.

6. Right-click any toolbar, then click **Reviewing** to close the Reviewing toolbar

close EWPriceList01.doc

tip

To print comments in a document, select Document showing markup in the Print what list in the Print dialog box. To print only comments, select List of markup in the Print what list.

Figure 6-5: Document with edited comments

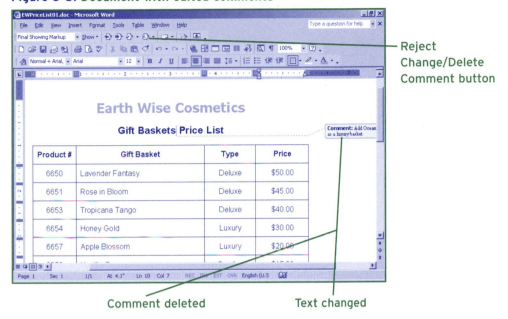

Reject Change/Delete Comment button

Comment deleted   Text changed

extra!

Changing the size and appearance of comments

You can change the way tracked comments look in the Comment balloons and in the Reviewing pane. To change the size of the text in the Comment balloons and in the Reviewing pane, click the Next button on the Reviewing toolbar to select a Comment balloon, open the Styles and Formatting task pane, click the list arrow next to Comment Text under Formatting of selected text, click Modify, then change the options in the dialog box. To change the size of the Comment balloons, click Options on the Tools menu, then click the Track Changes tab. Change the width in the Preferred width box under Use balloons in Print and Web Layout.

Skill Set 6
Workgroup Collaboration

Convert Documents into Web Pages
Preview and Save Documents as Web Pages

Publishing a document on the Web or a company intranet is an easy way to make it accessible to a wide audience. Before you save a document as a Web page, you should preview it to make sure that it looks the way you expect it to. After previewing the Web page, you use the Save as Web Page command to automatically save a copy of the document in the HTML file format, a file format that Web browsers use to display pages.

Step 5
The Web page title appears in the title bar of the browser window when the page is being viewed. It also appears in the browser's history list and would appear on a favorite or bookmark list if someone saves the link to the page.

Activity Steps

 open EWChart01.doc

1. Click **File** on the menu bar, then click **Web Page Preview**

2. Click the **Maximize button** in your Web browser window, if necessary

3. Click the **Close button** ☒ in your Web browser window

4. Click **File** on the menu bar, then click **Save as Web Page** to open the Save As dialog box

5. Click **Change Title**, press [➡], press the **[Spacebar]**, type **Aromatherapy Best Sellers**, then click **OK**

6. Select all of the text in the File name box, then type **My Web Page**
   See Figure 6-6.

7. Click **Save** to close the Save As dialog box, and view the HTML document in Web Layout view
   See Figure 6-7.

 close EWChart01.doc

Figure 6-6: Save As dialog box for saving a document as a Web page

Web page title

File type changes to HTML when Save as Web Page command is selected

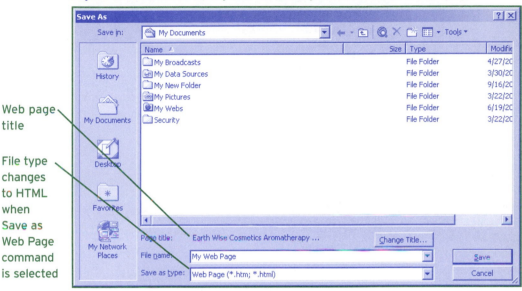

Figure 6-7: Document converted to a Web page in Web Layout view

File extension indicates document is saved as a Web page

Web Layout view selected

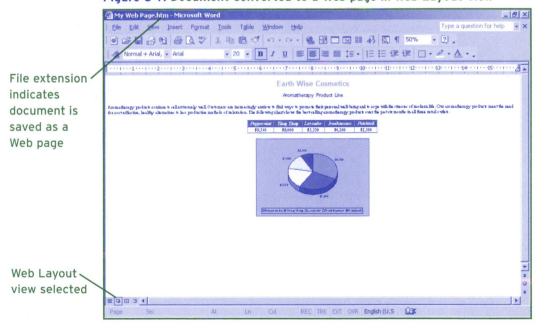

Skill Set 6

Workgroup Collaboration

Target Your Skills

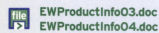 **EWProductInfo03.doc**
EWProductInfo04.doc

1 Use Figure 6-8 as a guide for creating a new merged document. In addition to the changes in the figure, delete the comment **Will this be manufactured next year?** After you have created the final document, select Final in the Display for Review list. Close the Reviewing toolbar when you are finished.

Figure 6-8

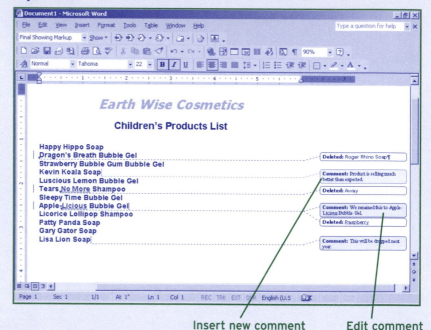

Insert new comment   Edit comment

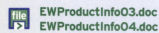 **EWPriceList02.doc**

2 Use Figure 6-9 as a guide to create the Web page shown. Note that the Web page in the figure is in a browser window, but you will end up with an HTML document displayed in Web Layout view in Word. Make sure you change the Web page title to match the one shown in the title bar in the figure.

Web page title

Filename

Figure 6-9

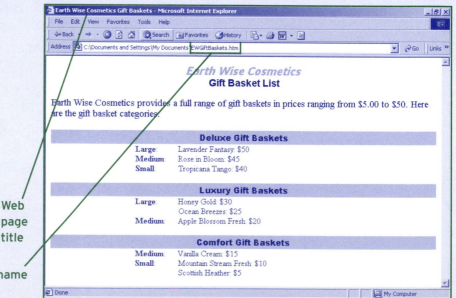

Skill List

1. Control pagination
2. Sort paragraphs in lists and tables

In Skill Set 7, you will learn more advanced commands for managing paragraphs. You will learn how to control pagination automatically. You can set paragraph formats so that page breaks occur only within a paragraph within certain parameters, do not occur within a paragraph at all, always occur after a paragraph, or never occur between two specific paragraphs.

You will also learn how to use Word's Sort feature. You can sort entries in a list or in a table. You can customize the sort in the Sort dialog box. Managing the pagination and sorting lists and paragraphs gives you more control of your documents so that you can achieve the look you want.

Skill Set 7
Customizing Paragraphs

Control Pagination
Control Page Breaks within Paragraphs

You can set options within paragraphs to make sure that a page break does not occur in an unexpected place. A **widow** is the last line of a paragraph printed at the top of a page or column. An **orphan** is the first line of a paragraph printed at the bottom of a page or column. It's generally considered to be bad page layout to have widows and orphans. The default in Word is for widow and orphan control to be turned on, preventing paragraphs from breaking with only one line of the paragraph printed on a page or in a column. You can also format a paragraph so that a page or column break does not occur in the middle of the paragraph at all.

Activity Steps

 open CCNewsletter02.doc

1. Scroll down, then select the three paragraphs below the heading **Head of the Penobscot**

2. Click **Format** on the menu bar, click **Paragraph** to open the Paragraph dialog box, then click the **Line and Page Breaks tab**

3. Notice that the **Widow/Orphan control check box** is selected by default

4. Click the **Keep lines together check box** to select it and prevent a page or column break from occurring within the selected paragraphs
   See Figure 7-1.

5. Click **OK**

6. Click anywhere in the document to deselect the paragraphs
   See Figure 7-2.

 close CCNewsletter02.doc

A manual page break overrides paragraph formatting.

Skill 1

Control Pagination

Figure 7-1: Line and Page Breaks tab in the Paragraph dialog box

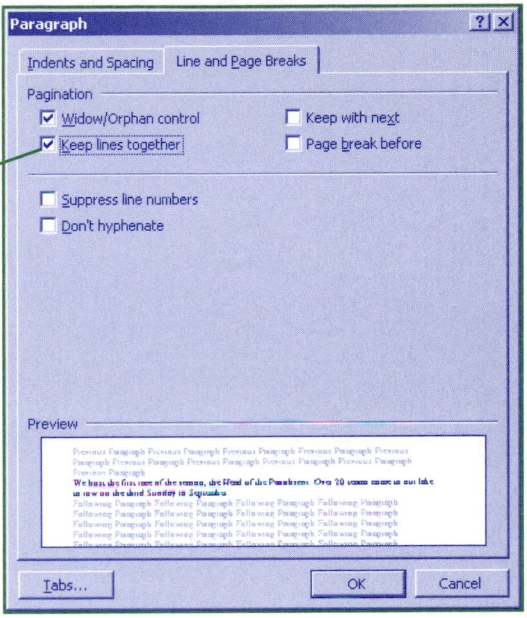

Select to prevent a page break in the middle of a paragraph

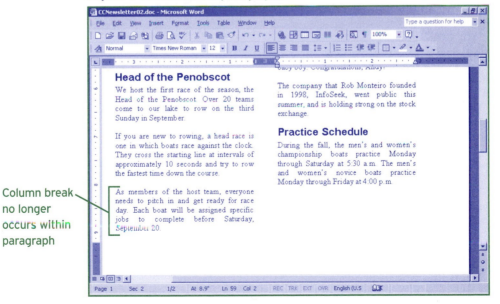

Figure 7-2: Formatted paragraphs

Column break no longer occurs within paragraph

Skill Set 7

Customizing Paragraphs

Control Pagination

Control Page Breaks between Paragraphs

You can format a paragraph so that it will always appear at the top of a page; in other words, so that a page break will always occur before it. You can also format a paragraph so that a page break never occurs after it and so it will always appear on the same page as the paragraph following it.

To prevent rows in a table from breaking across pages, click Table Properties on the Table menu, click the Row tab, then click the Allow row to break across pages check box to deselect it.

Activity Steps

 open CCHistory01.doc

1. Scroll down and right-click in the heading **The Beginning**, click **Paragraph** on the shortcut menu to open the Paragraph dialog box, then click the **Line and Page Breaks tab**

2. Click the **Page break before check box** to select it so that the heading will always appear at the top of a new page

3. Click **OK**
   See Figure 7-3.

4. Scroll down to the bottom of the second page so that you can see the heading **The Boathouse and Lake**

5. Right-click in the heading **The Boathouse and Lake**, then click **Paragraph** to open the **Line and Page Breaks tab** in the Paragraph dialog box

6. Click the **Keep with next check box** to select it so that the heading will never appear at the bottom of a page

7. Click **OK**
   See Figure 7-4.

 close CCHistory01.doc

Figure 7-3: Paragraph formatted to start at top of page

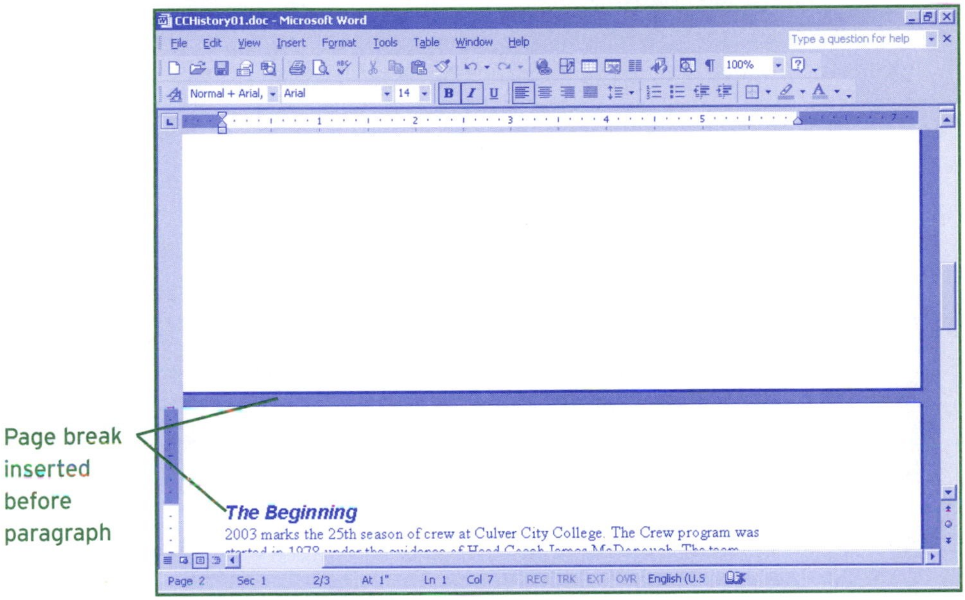

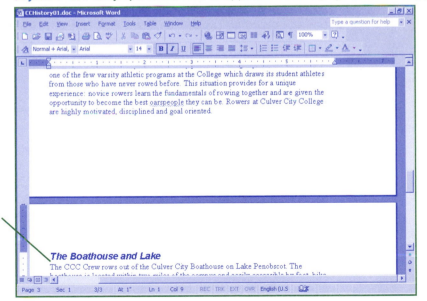

Page break inserted before paragraph

Figure 7-4: Paragraph formatted to appear on same page as following paragraph

Page break no longer occurs between pargraphs

Skill Set 7
Customizing Paragraphs

Control Pagination
Control Line Breaks

By default, Word does not hyphenate words at the ends of lines. You may decide that the text would look better if words were hyphenated; for example, justified paragraphs that have hyphenation turned off might have too much space added between words to force the justification. You can also manually force a line break without creating a new paragraph.

Activity Steps

 open CCNewsletter03.doc

1. Scroll down so you can see the paragraph above the heading **Head of the Penobscot** and the last paragraph in that column, click **Tools** on the menu bar, point to **Language**, then click **Hyphenation** to open the Hyphenation dialog box

2. Click the **Automatically hyphenate document check box**, then click **OK** to have Word hyphenate the document

3. Select the paragraph immediately above the heading **Head of the Penobscot**, click **Format** on the menu bar, click **Paragraph**, then click the **Line and Page Breaks tab**

4. Click the **Don't hyphenate check box** to select it and override the automatic hyphenation for the selected text, then click **OK**
   See Figure 7-5.

5. Click immediately before **September** in the last paragraph in the first column, then press **[Shift][Enter]** to insert a manual line break without creating a new paragraph

6. Drag to select the entire paragraph above the heading **Practice Schedule**, click **Tools** on the menu bar, point to **Language**, click **Hyphenation**, then click **Manual**

7. Press **[◄]** three times to reposition the insertion point at the first suggested hyphenation location (between the **s** and the **t**), then click **Yes**

8. Click **No** in the dialog box that appears asking if you want to continue checking the rest of the document, then click **OK** in the dialog box that appears telling you that hyphenation is complete
   See Figure 7-6.

 close CCNewsletter03.doc

If you do not want a word that has a hyphen in it to break at the end of a line (for example, a phone number), press [Ctrl][Shift][-] to insert the hyphen, and the entire word will shift to the next line if necessary.

Figure 7-5: Hyphenated document

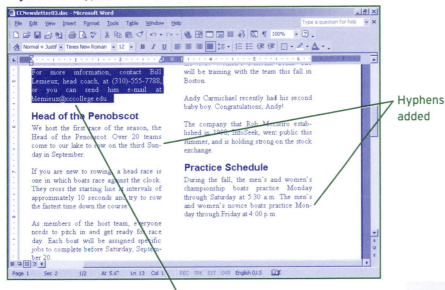

Hyphens added

Hyphens removed from paragraph

Figure 7-6: Document with some paragraphs manually hyphenated

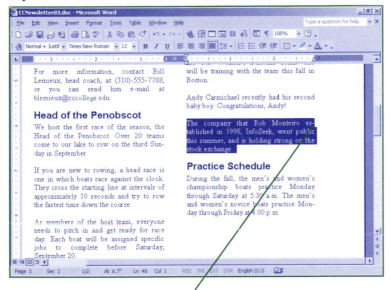

Hyphen repositioned in word

extra!

Using manual hyphenation

If you want to approve each suggested hyphenation, click Manual in the Hyphenation dialog box. The Manual Hyphenation dialog box then appears with the first suggestion for a hyphenated word, and the word appears in the document with the hyphen already inserted. Click Yes to accept the suggested hyphen, click No to reject it, or reposition the insertion point to another position in the word, and then click Yes to accept the changed hyphenation.

Skill Set 7
Customizing Paragraphs

Sort Paragraphs in Lists and Tables

A long list of data can be easier to interpret if it is sorted in some order. You can sort a list or a column in a table using the Sort command. Word can sort data as text, numbers, or dates. When the data is text, Word sorts words that begin with punctuation marks or symbols first, then numbers, then letters.

Activity Steps

 open CCLists01.doc

1. Select the list under the heading **Team List** (do not select the **Team List heading** or the three **column headings**), stopping before the page break above **GPA List**
   See Figure 7-7.

2. Click **Table** on the menu bar, then click **Sort** to open the Sort Text dialog box

3. Click the **Sort by list arrow**, click **Field 1** or **Word 1**, then make sure that the **Ascending option button** is selected

4. Make sure that the **No header row option button** is selected, then click **OK** to sort the list of names in alphabetical order

5. Scroll down and click in the **GPA List table**, click **Table** on the menu bar, then click **Sort** to open the Sort dialog box

6. Click the **Sort by list arrow**, click **GPA**, then click the **Descending option button**

7. Click the **Then by list arrow** in the middle of the dialog box, then click **Name**
   See Figure 7-8.

8. Make sure that the **Header row option button** is selected, then click **OK** to sort the table first in descending order by GPA then in ascending order by Name

 close CCLists01.doc

To sort only one column in a table, select the column, open the Sort dialog box, click Options, then click the Sort column only check box.

Figure 7-7: List to be sorted

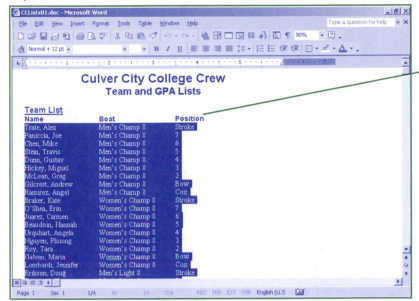

Header row not selected

Figure 7-8: Sort dialog box

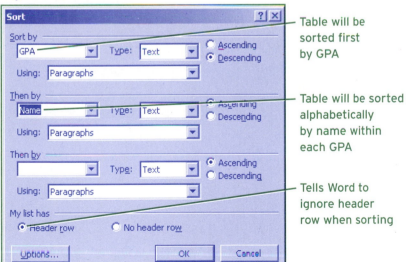

Table will be sorted first by GPA

Table will be sorted alphabetically by name within each GPA

Tells Word to ignore header row when sorting

extra!

Sorting a column with more than one word in each cell

If a column in a table contains items consisting of more than one word, for example a list of first and last names, you can sort by any word in the column. Select the column, then open the Sort dialog box and click Options. If the words are separated by something other than a comma or a tab, click the Other option button, then type the character that separates the words in the column (you can type a space). Click OK to close the Sort Options dialog box, then click the Using list arrow and select the word or field that you want to sort on.

Skill Set 7
Customizing Paragraphs

Target Your Skills

 CCPressRelease01.doc

1 Use Figure 7-9 as a guide for formatting the project file **CCPressRelease01.** First, hyphenate the document. After formatting the document as directed by the callouts, format the heading **From points south** so that there is no page break between it and the directions under it, then format the paragraph containing the directions from points south so that a page break does not occur in the middle of that paragraph.

 CCBrochure01.doc

2 Use Figure 7-10 as a guide for formatting the project file **CCBrochure01.** Hyphenate the document then format any paragraphs as needed to ensure that page 2 automatically starts with the Senior Program heading.

Figure 7-9

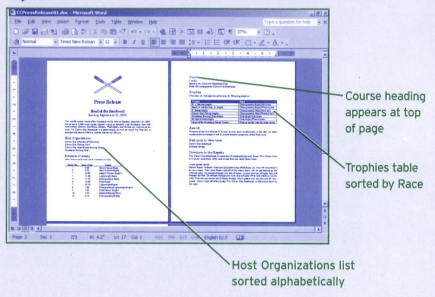

Course heading appears at top of page

Trophies table sorted by Race

Host Organizations list sorted alphabetically

Figure 7-10

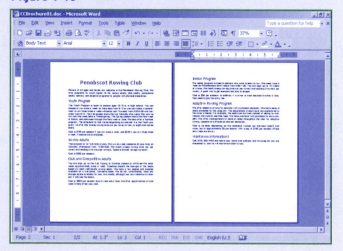

Skill List

1. Create and format document sections
2. Create and apply character and paragraph styles
3. Create and update document indexes and tables of contents, figures, and authorities
4. Create cross-references
5. Add and revise endnotes and footnotes
6. Create and manage master documents and subdocuments
7. Move within documents
8. Create and modify forms using various form controls
9. Create forms and prepare forms for distribution

As you work with longer documents, you can take advantage of Word's many formatting commands to make managing your documents easier. Working with document sections allows you to format parts of a document separately. You can create indexes, tables of contents, tables of figures, cross-references, and footnotes with little effort. You can create a master document and subdocuments to make working with a long document easier. You'll also find navigating in a long document becomes much easier when you use bookmarks or the Document Map.

You can also use Word to create and format electronic and printed forms. You can then prepare the forms for electronic distribution. If you learn to take advantage of the many advanced formatting capabilities in Word, you will find it easier to manage and work with longer, more complicated documents.

Skill Set 8
Formatting Documents

Create and Format Document Sections
Use Page Setup Options to Format Sections

Sections are parts of a document with separate page formatting options. For example, when you select some of the text in a document and format it with multiple columns, you actually create a new section. You can have as many sections as you want in a document. You can also decide where you want the new section to begin. If a section break is labeled as continuous, the new section will start on the same page as the paragraph before it. A section break labeled as next, even or odd page means that the new section starts at the top of a new page. When a section starts on a new page, it can have different page setup options (orientation, margins, etc.) applied to it than to other sections in the document.

Step 5
To apply the page setup options to the entire document, click the Apply to list arrow in the Page Setup dialog box, then select Whole document.

Activity Steps

 open EWMemo08.doc

1. Click the **Print Preview button** 🔍, click the **down scroll arrow** if necessary to view the second page, then click 🔍 on the right side of the table to zoom in and see that the table is cut off on the right

2. Click the **Close button** `Close` on the Print Preview toolbar, scroll down and click to position the insertion point immediately before the heading **Earth Wise Cosmetics**, then click the **Show/Hide ¶ button** ¶ to display paragraph marks, if necessary

3. Click **Insert** on the menu bar, click **Break** to open the Break dialog box, click the **Next page option button** under Section break types, then click **OK** to insert a section break and start a new page
   See Figure 8-1.

4. Click the **Show/Hide ¶ button** ¶ to hide paragraph marks, make sure the insertion point is still positioned in the new section, click **File** on the menu bar, click **Page Setup**, then click the **Margins tab**

5. Click the **Landscape orientation box**, then make sure that **This section** appears in the Apply to list

6. Click the **Layout tab**, click the **Vertical alignment list arrow**, click **Center**, then make sure that **This section** appears in the Apply to list

7. Click **OK**, click the **Print Preview button** 🔍, click the **Multiple Pages button** ⊞, then click the second icon in the top row to display **1 x 2 Pages**, if necessary
   See Figure 8-2.

 close EWMemo08.doc

Figure 8-1: Section break inserted

Next page
section break

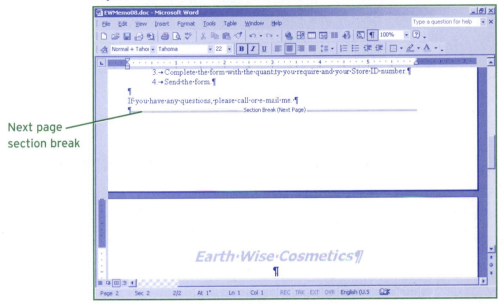

Figure 8-2: Sections formatted differently in document

First section
formatted
with portrait
orientation

Second
section
formatted
with
landscape
orientation

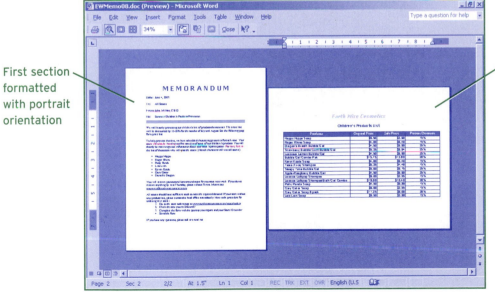

Skill Set 8
Formatting Documents

Create and Format Document Sections
Verify Paragraph and Character Formats

Sometimes it can be helpful to know exactly what formatting is applied to text in a document. To see the formatting of selected text, you can use the Reveal Formatting task pane. When you open this task pane, the font and paragraph formats of the selected text are listed. You can click the links above each format description to open a dialog box to modify that format.

To check for formatting inconsistencies as you type, click Options on the Tools menu, click the Edit tab, then select the Keep track of formatting and Mark formatting inconsistencies check boxes.

Activity Steps

 open EWBrochure06.doc

1. Select the first line of text, click **Format** on the menu bar, then click **Reveal Formatting** to open the Reveal Formatting task pane

2. Click the **Font link** in the Reveal Formatting task pane to open the Font dialog box, click **Arial Black** in the Font list as shown in Figure 8-3, then click **OK**

3. Click anywhere in the paragraph beginning with **Earth Wise Cosmetics**, and note the styles for the selected text in the Reveal Formatting task pane

4. Click the **Distinguish style source check box** at the bottom of the Reveal Formatting task pane to select it and see on which style the current paragraph format is based

5. Point to the box under **Selected text** at the top of the Reveal Formatting task pane, click the **list arrow** that appears, then click **Select All Text With Similar Formatting**

6. Click the **Alignment link** under Paragraph in the Reveal Formatting task pane to open the Paragraph dialog box, click the **Indents and Spacing tab**, click the **Alignment list arrow**, click **Centered**, then click **OK**
   See Figure 8-4.

7. Click the **Distinguish style source check box** to deselect it, click the **Close button** ⊠ in the task pane title bar to close the task pane, then click anywhere in the document to deselect the text

 close EWBrochure06.doc

Figure 8-3: Using the Reveal Formatting task pane

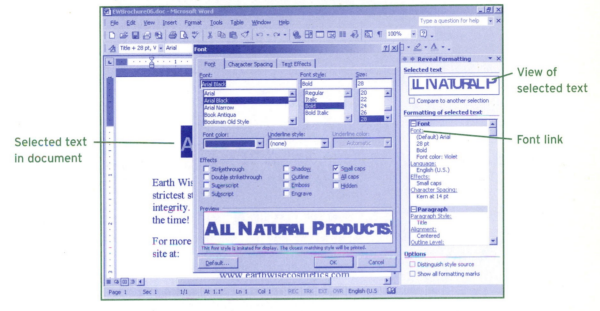

Selected text in document

View of selected text

Font link

Figure 8-4: Paragraph format modified in the Reveal Formatting task pane

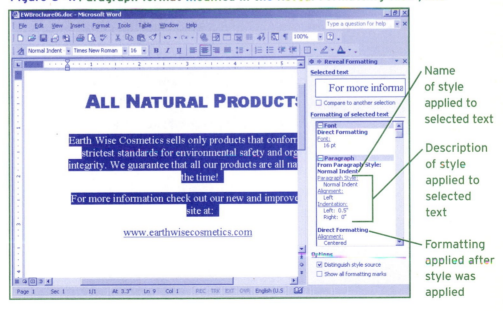

Name of style applied to selected text

Description of style applied to selected text

Formatting applied after style was applied

Skill Set 8
Formatting Documents

Create and Format Document Sections
Clear Formatting

Once you have applied formats to paragraphs and characters in a document, you can clear them quickly with the Clear Formatting command in the Reveal Formatting or the Styles and Formatting task panes. This can be faster than changing the formatting of one element at a time.

tip

To format a document automatically, click Format on the menu bar, click AutoFormat, select a document type, then click OK. Open the Reveal Formatting task pane to see exactly what formats were applied.

Activity Steps

 open EWBrochure07.doc

1. Click **View** on the menu bar, click **Task Pane**, click the **Other Task Panes list arrow** in the task pane title bar, then click **Reveal Formatting**, if necessary, to open the Reveal Formatting task pane

2. Select the first line of text in the document

3. Point to the box under **Selected text** at the top of the Reveal Formatting task pane, click the **list arrow** that appears, then click **Clear Formatting** as shown in Figure 8-5

4. Click the **Other Task Panes list arrow** in the task pane title bar, then click **Styles and Formatting**

5. Click **Edit** on the menu bar, then click **Select All** to select all of the text in the document

6. Click **Clear Formatting** in the Pick formatting to apply list in the task pane
   See Figure 8-6.

7. Click the **Close button** in the task pane title bar, then click anywhere in the document to deselect the text

 close EWBrochure07.doc

Figure 8-5: Using the Clear Formatting command in the Reveal Formatting task pane

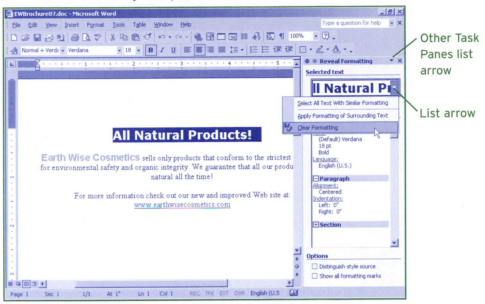

Other Task Panes list arrow

List arrow

Figure 8-6: Clear Formatting command in the Styles and Formatting task pane

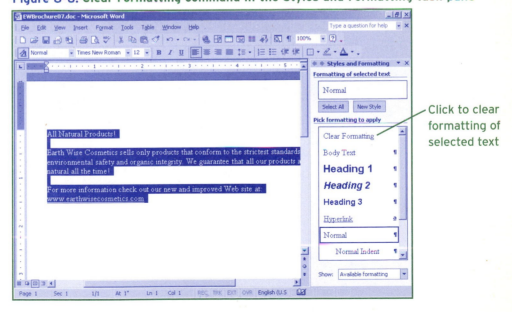

Click to clear formatting of selected text

Skill Set 8
Formatting Documents

Create and Apply Character and Paragraph Styles
Create and Apply Character Styles

You will quickly see the real advantage to using styles when you work with longer documents or with the same type of text over and over again. You can create a new style based on your needs, then apply that style wherever you want. The easiest way to create a new style is to format text the way you want, select it, then define a new style based on the selected text.

Activity Steps

 open EWBrochure08.doc

1. Select the text **Earth Wise Cosmetics** in the first paragraph in the document

2. Click the **Font list arrow** `Times New Roman`, click **Arial**, click the **Bold button** `B`, click the **Font Color list arrow** `A`, then click the **Lavender box**

3. Click the **Styles and Formatting button** `A` to open the Styles and Formatting task pane, then click **New Style** in the task pane to open the New Style dialog box

4. Type **Company Name** in the Name box, click the **Style type list arrow**, then click **Character**
   See Figure 8-7.

5. Click **OK** to complete the styles definition, then click **Company Name** in the Pick formatting to apply list in the task pane to apply the new style to the selected text

6. Select **Earth Wise Cosmetics** in the second paragraph in the document, click **Company Name** in the Pick formatting to apply list in the task pane, then click anywhere in the document to deselect the text

7. Point to **Company Name** in the Styles and Formatting task pane, click the **list arrow**, click **Modify**, click the **Bold button** `B` to turn off bold formatting, click the **Italic button** `I`, then click **OK** to change the style definition and update the document
   See Figure 8-8.

8. Click the **Close button** `X` in the Styles and Formatting task pane

 close EWBrochure08.doc

Click the Add to template check box in the New Style or Modify Style dialog box to make your new style available to all documents based on the template you are using (including the Normal template).

Figure 8-7: New Style dialog box

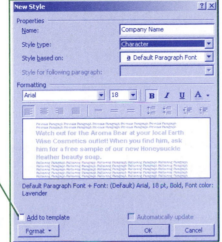

Click to make available to other documents that are based on this template

Figure 8-8: Format changed after modifying style

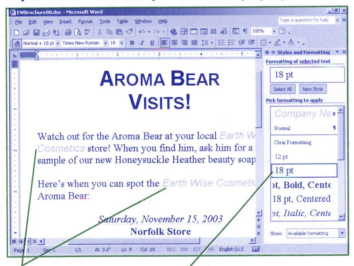

Format changed automatically to reflect modifications to style definition

Selected style on your screen will differ depending on where you clicked to deselect the text

extra!

Updating style definitions

If you click the Automatically update check box in the New Style or Modify Style dialog box, any change you make to text with that style will cause the definition of the style to change to reflect your modification. If the style is not defined to update automatically, you can still change the definition to reflect changes you make. Simply apply the style, make the changes you want, point to the style name in the Styles and Formatting task pane, click the list arrow, then click Update to Match Selection.

Skill Set 8
Formatting Documents

Create and Apply Character and Paragraph Styles

Create and Apply Paragraph Styles

Paragraph styles are applied to entire paragraphs. As with character styles, one way to create a paragraph style is to format a paragraph the way you want, then define a new paragraph style based on this format. Another easy way to define a style is to modify the definition of a style that already exists.

Activity Steps

 open EWPriceList03.doc

1. Click the **Styles and Formatting button** to open the Styles and Formatting task pane, then click **New Style** to open the New Style dialog box

2. Type **My Heading Style** in the Name box, then make sure that **Paragraph** is selected in the Style type box

3. Click the **Style based on list arrow**, scroll up the list, then click **Heading 1** to base your new style on the existing Heading 1 style

4. Click the **Style for following paragraph list arrow**, then click **Main Text** to automatically apply the Main Text style to a new paragraph created by pressing [Enter] after a My Heading Style paragraph

5. Click the **Font Size list arrow** 18, click **14**, then click the **Italic button**

6. Click **Format**, click **Paragraph**, click the **Indents and Spacing tab**, click the **Alignment list arrow**, click **Left**, click the **After up arrow** to change the spacing after the paragraph to **6 pt**, then click **OK**
   See Figure 8-9.

7. Click **OK**, select the heading **Papaya Cleansing Milk**, click **My Heading Style** in the Pick formatting to apply list in the task pane, then apply the **My Heading Style style** to the heading **Lavender Soap Gel**

8. Click the **Close button** in the task pane title bar, scroll down and select the heading **Pineapple Wash**, click the **Style list arrow** Normal + 12 pt, click **My Heading Style**, position the insertion point immediately after the word **Wash**, press [Enter], then type **Recommended for oily skin.**
   See Figure 8-10.

 close EWPriceList03.doc

To change the list of styles displayed in the Styles and Formatting task pane or on the Style list on the toolbar, click the Show list arrow in the Styles and Formatting task pane, click Custom to open the Format Settings dialog box, then select the check boxes of the styles you want to display.

Figure 8-9: New Style dialog box after creating paragraph style definition

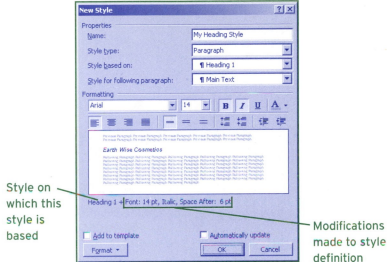

Style on which this style is based

Modifications made to style definition

Figure 8-10: Document with new paragraph style applied

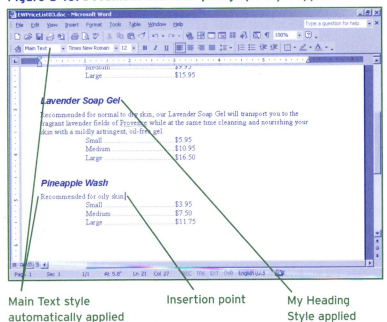

Main Text style automatically applied

Insertion point

My Heading Style applied

Skill Set 8
Formatting Documents

Create and Update Document Indexes and Tables of Contents, Figures, and Authorities
Create an Index

To create an index, you first mark words in the document as **index entries**. Word inserts an **index field** for each entry. The index field is inserted between braces and is labeled *XE*. You can see index fields only if paragraph marks are turned on. After you mark all the index entries, you compile them into an index. Word automatically sorts the entries alphabetically, adds the page references, and removes any duplicate entries.

Activity Steps

 open EWReport01.doc

1. Click the **Show/Hide ¶ button** to display paragraph marks, if necessary, scroll down to page 2 and select the words **Naturally Yours** in the paragraph below the heading **Marilyn Arnold, Mobile Store**, then press **[Alt][Shift][X]** to mark the selected text as an index entry and open the Mark Index Entry dialog box

2. Make sure **Naturally Yours** appears in the Main entry box and that the **Current page option button** is selected, then click **Mark**

3. With the Mark Index Entry dialog box still open, select the words **massage therapist** in the paragraph below the heading **Sandra Grant, Atlanta Store**, click in the Main Index Entry dialog box to make it active, then click **Mark**

4. Scroll down and select **Mobile** in the heading below **Franchise Locations**, click in the Mark Index Entry dialog box, select all of the text in the Main entry box, type **Franchise Locations**, press **[Tab]**, type **Mobile, Alabama** in the Subentry box, then click **Mark All** to mark all instances of **Mobile** in the text as an index entry

5. Scroll down and select the word **Atlanta** in the next heading, click in the Mark Index Entry dialog box, replace the text in the Main entry box with **Franchise Locations**, press **[Tab]**, type **Atlanta, Georgia** in the Subentry box, click **Mark All**, then click **Close**
   See Figure 8-11.

6. Press **[Ctrl][End]**, click the **Show/Hide ¶ button** to hide paragraph marks and the field entries so the document will be paginated correctly, click **Insert** on the menu bar, point to **Reference**, click **Index and Tables**, make sure the **Index tab** is on top, click the **Formats list arrow**, then click **Classic**
   See Figure 8-12.

7. Click **OK** to create the index
   See Figure 8-13.

 close EWReport01.doc

To insert a cross-reference instead of the page number for an index entry, click the Cross-reference option button in the Mark Index Entry dialog box, and type the cross-reference after the word "See" in the Cross-reference box.

Figure 8-11: Index entries marked in document

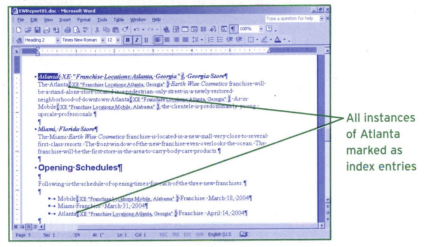

All instances of Atlanta marked as index entries

Figure 8-12: Index tab in Index and Tables dialog box

Index will appear in two columns

Click to change index format

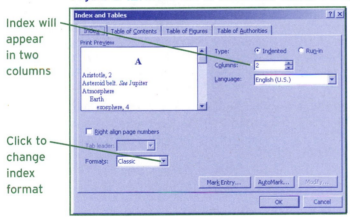

extra!

Customizing the index format

To customize the format of your index, click From template on the Formats list in the Index and Tables dialog box, then click Modify to open the Style dialog box. Select an index style, click Modify to open the Modify Style dialog box, then make whatever changes you want. If you want to format entries with the page number in bold or italics, click the Bold or Italic check boxes in the Mark Index Entry dialog box when you mark the index entry.

Figure 8-13: Index in document

Skill Set 8

Formatting Documents

Create and Update Document Indexes and Tables of Contents, Figures, and Authorities

Update an Index

The index that Word creates is actually a field, and you can update it if you make changes to the document. You modify the index by marking new entries in the document, deleting an index field, or changing the format of the index.

Activity Steps

 open EWReport02.doc

1. Press **[Ctrl][End]** to see the current index
   See Figure 8-14.

2. Click the **Show/Hide ¶ button** ¶ to display paragraph marks, if necessary, scroll up to the last paragraph on page 3, select the words **opening day events**, press **[Alt][Shift][X]**, then click **Mark** in the Mark Index Entry dialog box to mark a new entry for the index

3. With the Mark Index Entry dialog box still open, scroll up to the paragraph above the heading **Opening Schedules**, select **Miami** in the heading, click in the Mark Index Entry dialog box to make it active, replace the text in the Main entry box with **Franchise Locations**, press **[Tab]**, type **Miami, Florida**, click **Mark All** to mark new entries for the index, then click **Close**

4. Scroll up to the middle of page 2, click immediately before the index field for **marketing** below the **Marilyn Arnold, Mobile Store** heading, press and hold **[Shift]**, then press **[➡]** to select the entire field
   See Figure 8-15.

5. Press **[Delete]** to delete the field from the index

6. Press **[Ctrl][End]** to jump to the end of the document

7. Click the **Show/Hide ¶ button** ¶ to hide paragraph marks and the field entries so the document will be paginated correctly, right-click anywhere on the index, then click **Update Field** on the shortcut menu to update the index

8. Click anywhere in the index, click **Insert** on the menu bar, point to **Reference**, click **Index and Tables**, click the **Formats list arrow**, click **Modern**, click **OK**, then click **OK** in the dialog box that appears asking if you want to replace the selected index to reformat the index
   See Figure 8-16.

 close EWReport02.doc

Step 7
You can also click anywhere in a field and press [F9] to update it.

Figure 8-14: Original index in document

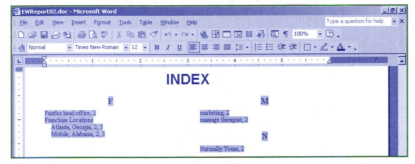

Figure 8-15: Entire index field selected

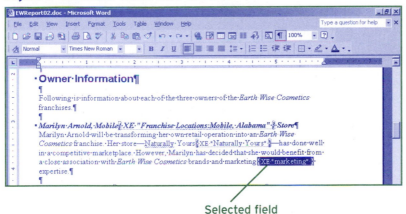

Selected field

Figure 8-16: Modified index in document

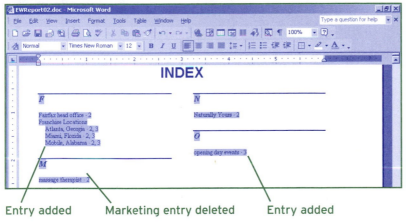

Entry added   Marketing entry deleted   Entry added

Skill Set 8

Formatting Documents

Create and Update Document Indexes and Tables of Contents, Figures, and Authorities

Insert and Update a Table of Contents

The easiest way to create a table of contents is to use the built-in heading styles for the headings in a document, then tell Word how many levels of headings you want to include in the table of contents. (If you did not use the built-in heading styles in your document, you need to assign the styles you used to a heading level, as explained in the extra! box on the following page.) When you create the table of contents, you can choose a number of formatting options, including whether to show page numbers, whether to right-align the page numbers, and whether to format the entries as hyperlinks.

Activity Steps

 open EWReport03.doc

1. Scroll down to page 2, then position the insertion point in the empty paragraph below the heading **Table of Contents**

2. Click **Insert** on the menu bar, point to **Reference**, click **Index and Tables**, then click the **Table of Contents tab**

3. Click the **Formats list arrow**, then click **Distinctive**

4 Click the **Tab leader list arrow**, then click the **dotted line** below **(none)** in the list

5. Click the **Show levels down arrow** to change the number of levels shown to **2**
   See Figure 8-17.

6. Make sure the **Use hyperlinks instead of page numbers check box** is selected, then click **OK** to insert the table of contents

7. Press **[Ctrl][End]**, scroll up a little and select the heading **Wrap-up**, type **Conclusion**, scroll up, select the heading **January Information Meeting**, click the **Style list arrow** Heading 3, then click **Heading 2**

8. Scroll back up to the table of contents and right-click anywhere on it, then click **Update Field** on the shortcut menu to update the table of contents
   See Figure 8-18.

 close EWReport03.doc

Step 6
If you format the entries as hyperlinks, you can position the insertion point over an entry, press and hold [Ctrl], and then click the mouse button to jump to that heading in the document.

Figure 8-17: Table of Contents tab in the Index and Tables dialog box

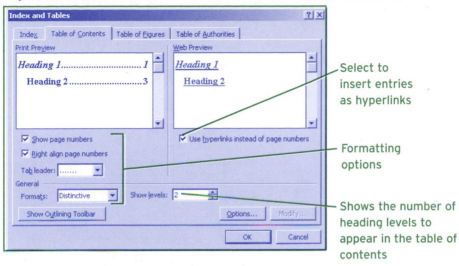

Select to insert entries as hyperlinks

Formatting options

Shows the number of heading levels to appear in the table of contents

Figure 8-18: Updated table of contents

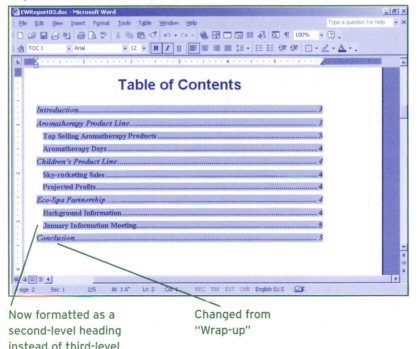

Now formatted as a second-level heading instead of third-level

Changed from "Wrap-up"

extra!

Creating a table of contents using custom heading styles
You can create a table of contents even if you did not use the built-in heading styles. Open the Table of Contents tab in the Index and Tables dialog box, then click Options to open the Table of Contents Options dialog box. The styles you used in your document will be listed on the left, and you can assign each of your styles a level in your table of contents.

Skill Set 8
Formatting Documents

Create and Update Document Indexes and Tables of Contents, Figures, and Authorities
Insert and Update a Table of Figures

A **table of figures** is a list of all the illustrations in a document. You can have Word create one as an updateable field. First, you select each figure, then you use the Caption command to add a numbered caption. After you create the figure captions, you position the insertion point at the place in the document where you want the table of figures to appear, and then have Word create the table. As with a table of contents or an index, you can make changes to the figure captions or add or delete captions, and then update the table field.

To add a new label to the available labels in the Label list, click New Label in the Caption dialog box. To customize the caption numbering, click Numbering in the Caption dialog box.

Activity Steps

 open EWReport04.doc

1. Scroll down and click the **pie chart** on page 4, click **Insert** on the menu bar, point to **Reference**, then click **Caption**

2. Make sure that **Figure** is listed in the Label list box and **Below selected item** is listed in the Position list box

3. Type **:** (a colon) in the Caption box after **Figure 1**, press **[Spacebar]**, then type **Top-selling Essential Oils**
   See Figure 8-19.

4. Click **OK**

5. Scroll up to page 3 and position the insertion point below the heading **Table of Figures**

6. Click **Insert** on the menu bar, point to **Reference**, click **Index and Tables**, click the **Table of Figures tab**, make sure that **Figure** is listed in the Caption label list box, then click **OK**

7. Scroll down to page 5 and click the **worksheet chart** below the heading **Projected Profits** to select it, click **Insert** on the menu bar, point to **Reference**, click **Caption**, type **:** (a colon), click in the Caption box after **Figure 2**, press **[Spacebar]**, type **Children's Line Projected Sales**, then click **OK**

8. Scroll back up to page 3, right-click anywhere on the table of figures, click **Update Field** on the shortcut menu, click the **Update entire table option button** in the Update Table of Figures dialog box, then click **OK**
   See Figure 8-20.

 close EWReport04.doc

Figure 8-19: Caption dialog box

Figure 8-20: Updated table of figures

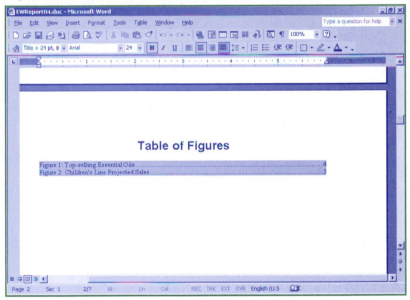

extra!

Creating a table of figures using custom styles

You can create a table of figures even if you added captions to your figures first. Make sure you assign a style to the captions, then open the Table of Figures tab in the Index and Tables dialog box. Click Options to open the Table of Figures Options dialog box. Click the Style check box, click the Style list arrow, then select the style you applied to the captions.

Skill Set 8

Formatting Documents

Create Cross-references

A **cross-reference** is a reference to a figure, table, or other element that appears somewhere else in the document. You can add a cross-reference as a field that changes to reflect an item's new position in the document whenever the document changes. Cross-references are inserted as hyperlinks.

Activity Steps

 open EWReport05.doc

1. Scroll to page 3, click to position the insertion point immediately before the **)** (close parenthesis) in the line below the heading **Top Selling Aromatherapy Products**

2. Click **Insert** on the menu bar, point to **Reference**, then click **Cross-reference** to open the Cross-reference dialog box

3. Click the **Reference type list arrow**, then click **Figure**

If you don't want a cross-reference to be inserted as a hyperlink, click the Insert as hyperlink check box to deselect it in the Cross-reference dialog box.

4. Click the **Insert reference to list arrow**, click **Only label and number**, then make sure the first caption in the list is selected
   See Figure 8-21.

5. Click **Insert**

6. With the Cross-reference dialog box still open, click immediately before the last **)** (close parenthesis) in the paragraph, after the word **page**

7. Click the **Reference type list arrow** in the Cross-reference dialog box, click **Heading**, click the **Insert reference to list arrow**, click **Page number**, click **Eco-Spa Partnership** in the For which heading list, click **Insert**, then click **Close**
   See Figure 8-22.

8. Press and hold **[Ctrl]**, position the pointer over the page number **4** in the cross-reference, then click to jump to the cross-referenced **Eco-Spa Partnership** heading

 close EWReport05.doc

Figure 8-21: Cross-reference dialog box

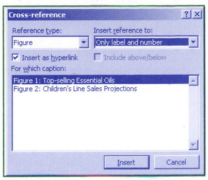

Figure 8-22: Cross-references in document

Cross-references

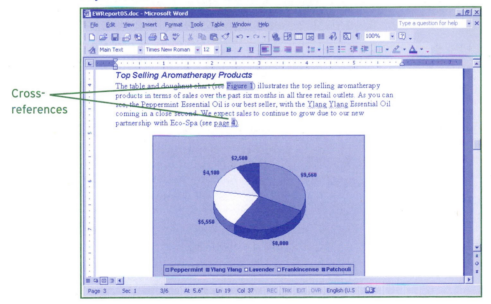

Skill Set 8

Formatting Documents

Add and Revise Endnotes and Footnotes

Footnotes are notes at the bottom, or foot, of a page. **Endnotes** are footnotes that are listed at the end of a document instead of at the bottom of each page. When you insert a footnote, a number or symbol appears at the insertion point, then you type your note. You can insert custom marks to denote a footnote, or you can have the footnotes numbered automatically.

Activity Steps

 open EWSummary01.doc

1. Scroll to the bottom of the page, then double-click the number **1** in the footnote that appears in the footer area to jump to the place in the document where the note reference mark is located, after **Williamsburg**

2. Position the insertion point immediately after the , (comma) after the word **Norfolk** in the first paragraph, click **Insert** on the menu bar, point to **Reference**, then click **Footnote** to open the Footnote and Endnote dialog box

3. Make sure that the **Footnotes option button** is selected and that **Bottom of page** appears in the Footnotes list box

4. Click **Insert** to insert a note reference mark next to the text and move the insertion point down to the number **1** in the footer area at the bottom of the page
See Figure 8-23.

5. Type **The Norfolk outlet is located at 1602 Federal St.**, then scroll back up so you can see that the note reference mark was added in the document and that the note reference mark next to Williamsburg automatically changed to **2**

6. Position the pointer directly over the note reference mark **1** so that the note text appears in a ScreenTip

7. With the insertion point anywhere in the current section, click **Insert** on the menu bar, point to **Reference**, click **Footnote**, click the **Number format list arrow**, click **A, B, C, ...,** then click **Apply**
See Figure 8-24.

8. Double-click directly on the note reference mark **A** to jump down to the note text at the bottom of the page, double-click **1602** in the footnote numbered **A**, then type **3502**

 close EWSummary01.doc

tip

To insert a character such as an asterisk instead of a number for a note reference mark, click in the Custom mark box in the Footnote and Endnote dialog box, then type the character you want to use, or click Symbol and select the character you want to use.

Figure 8-23: Entering note text in a footnote

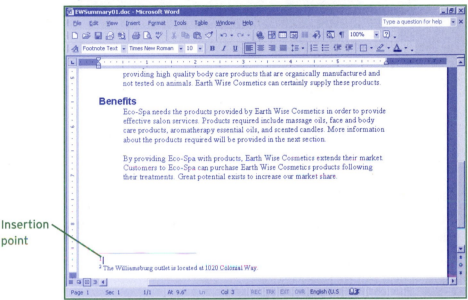

Insertion point

Figure 8-24: Note reference marks reformatted

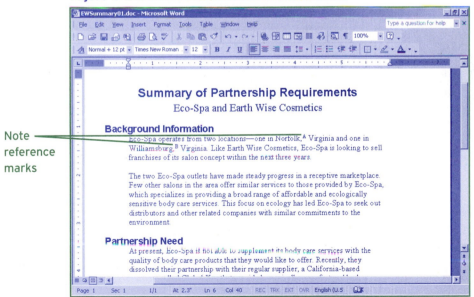

Note reference marks

Skill Set 8
Formatting Documents

Create and Manage Master Documents and Subdocuments
Create and Open Master Documents and Subdocuments

You can convert a document into a main document—the **master document**—that contains shorter documents—**subdocuments**. You can either designate a document as a master or sub document as you create it, or you can convert an existing document into a master or sub document. To work with master and sub documents, you must be in Outline view.

Activity Steps

 open EWProposal02.doc

1. Click the **Outline View button** to see the heading styles displayed as outline levels and to open the Outlining toolbar

2. Click the **Show Level list arrow** [Show All Levels ▾] on the Outlining toolbar, then click **Show Level 1**

3. Select all of the text in the outline, then click the **Create Subdocument button** on the Outlining toolbar to create a subdocument from every level 1 heading as shown in Figure 8-25
   A separate file was created for each subdocument.

4. Click **File** on the menu bar, click **Save As**, type **My Master Document** in the File name box, navigate to the drive and folder where you are storing your project files, then click **Save**

5. Click the **Collapse Subdocuments button** on the Outlining toolbar to collapse the subdocuments into hyperlinks, then scroll down so you can see the links to the subdocuments
   See Figure 8-26.

6. Press and hold **[Ctrl]**, position the pointer over the **Introduction subdocument link** so that the pointer changes to 👆, then click to open that subdocument and open the Web toolbar

7. Click the **Back button** on the Web toolbar to jump back to the master document

8. Click the **Expand Subdocuments button** on the Outlining toolbar to display the content of the documents as part of the master document, click the **Print Layout View button**, right-click any toolbar, then click **Web** to close the Web toolbar

 close My Master Document.doc
Introduction.doc

Step 7
When you click the Back button to jump back to the Master document, the subdocument remains open.

Figure 8-25: Subdocuments listed in the master document

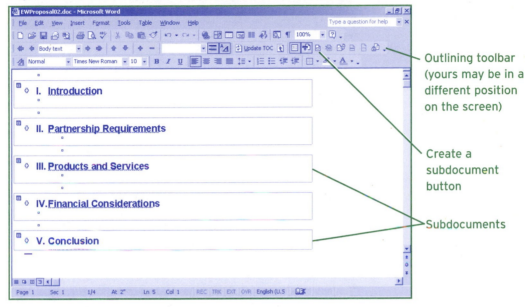

Outlining toolbar (yours may be in a different position on the screen)

Create a subdocument button

Subdocuments

Figure 8-26: Subdocuments collapsed to links

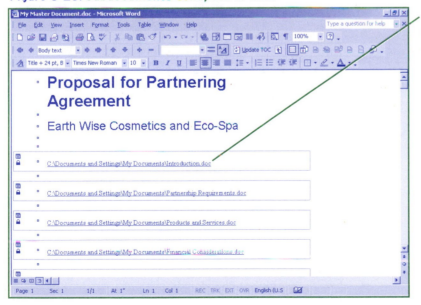

Introduction subdocument link (path to file may differ on your screen)

extra!

Printing master and sub documents

You can print subdocuments from the master document. Expand the subdocuments in the master document, click the Show Level list arrow `Show All Levels` on the Outlining toolbar, then click Show All Levels. Switch to Print Layout view, then print the document as you normally would.

Skill Set 8
Formatting Documents

Create and Manage Master Documents and Subdocuments
Manage Master Documents and Subdocuments

You can add, delete, and rename subdocuments, combine several subdocuments into one subdocument, or remove a subdocument so that it becomes part of the master document again. Subdocuments must remain stored in the same folder in which they were created, so that the links in the master document will remain connected.

Activity Steps

 open EWProposal03.doc

1. Click the **Show Level list arrow** `Show All Levels ▾` on the Outlining toolbar, click **Show Level 1**, select all of the text in the outline, then click the **Create Subdocument button** 📄 on the Outlining toolbar

2. Click **File** on the menu bar, click **Save As**, navigate to the location where your project files are stored, double-click the folder **EWProposal03 Folder**, select all of the text in the File name box, type **EWProposal03 Master Document**, then click **Save**

3. Click the **Introduction subdocument icon** 📄, press and hold **[Shift]**, then click the **Partnership Requirements subdocument icon** 📄

4. Click the **Merge Subdocument button** 📄 on the Outlining toolbar to combine these two subdocuments into one

5. Click the **plus sign** ➕ next to **Partnership Requirements**, then click the **Split Subdocument button** 📄 on the Outlining toolbar to split that outlining level into its own subdocument again
   A new subdocument named PartnershipRequirement1 is created. The Partnership Requirements subdocument created in step 1 still exists.

6. Drag the **Financial Considerations subdocument icon** 📄 up until the vertical line indicator is below the **Partnership Requirements** heading, as shown in Figure 8-27, to make Financial Considerations a subdocument within the Partnership Requirements subdocument

7. With the **Financial Considerations subdocument** still selected, click the **Remove Subdocument button** 📄 on the Outlining toolbar to remove that subdocument and combine the text into its master document (the Partnership Requirements subdocument)
   See Figure 8-28.

8. Click above the **Conclusion subdocument box** to the right of the small squares to position the insertion point there, click the **Insert Subdocument button** 📄 on the Outlining toolbar to open the Insert Subdocument dialog box, make sure that **EWProposal03 Folder** is listed in the Look in box, click **January Meeting**, then click **Open** to insert a new subdocument

 close EWProposal03 Master Document.doc

tip

To rename a subdocument or to change its location, collapse the subdocuments in the master document, press and hold [Ctrl] and then click the subdocument link, then use the Save As command in the subdocument window that opens.

Figure 8-27: Repositioning a subdocument

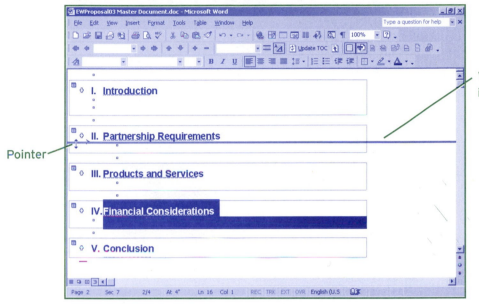

Vertical line indicator

Pointer

Figure 8-28: Subdocument removed as a subdocument and combined with its master document

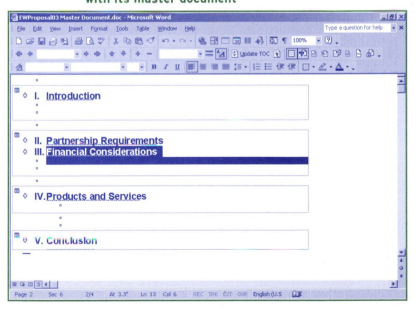

extra!

Locking subdocuments
Subdocuments are automatically locked for editing when they are collapsed in the master document or when a subdocument is already open. You can manually lock a subdocument so that no one can modify it. Expand the subdocuments in the master document, click anywhere in the subdocument you want to lock, then click the Lock Document button on the Outlining toolbar.

Skill Set 8
Formatting Documents

Move within Documents
Use Bookmarks

When you are navigating in a longer document, it can be time-consuming to scroll through it looking for a specific section. You can insert a **bookmark**, a named location in a document, and use it to jump to a frequently accessed part of the document. You must use a letter as the first character in a bookmark name, and the bookmark name cannot contain any spaces.

Activity Steps

 open EWMemo09.doc

1. Scroll down and position the insertion point immediately before the heading **Aromatherapy Day**

2. Click **Insert** on the menu bar, then click **Bookmark** to open the Bookmark dialog box

3. Type **AromatherapyDay** in the Bookmark name box, then click **Add**

4. Click **Insert** on the menu bar, click **Bookmark**, click **OnlineOrderingInfo** in the list of bookmarks, then click **Go To** to scroll the document to the location of the OnlineOrderingInfo bookmark
   See Figure 8-29.

5. With **OnlineOrderingInfo** still selected in the bookmark list, click **Delete** to delete that bookmark, then click **Close**

6. Click **Edit** on the menu bar, then click **Go To** to open the Go To tab in the Find and Replace dialog box

7. Click **Bookmark** in the Go to what list, click the **Enter bookmark name list arrow**, click **StockLevels**, then click **Go To**
   See Figure 8-30.

8. Click **Close**

 close EWMemo09.doc

To see bookmarks in your document, click Options on the Tools menu, click the View tab, then click the Bookmarks check box to select it.

Figure 8-29: Using the Bookmark dialog box to jump to a location in a document

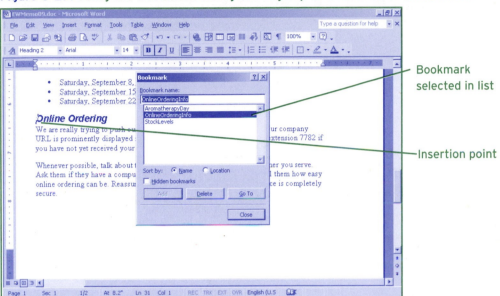

Bookmark selected in list

Insertion point

Figure 8-30: Go To tab in the Find and Replace dialog box

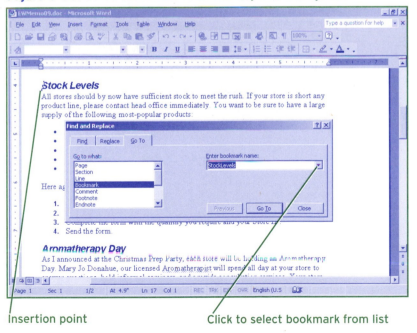

Insertion point

Click to select bookmark from list

Skill Set 8
Formatting Documents

Move within Documents
Use the Document Map

The **Document Map** is a pane that lists the headings in your document in outline form. Word recognizes the headings in your document if they are formatted with the built-in heading styles. If you use other styles, Word attempts to find headings and applies an outline level to the headings it finds. If you don't use the built-in heading styles, Word may not represent your outline accurately in the Document Map. You can click headings in the Document Map to jump to that section of the document.

Activity Steps

 open EWReport06.doc

1. Click the **Document Map button** to open the Document Map
   See Figure 8-31.

2. Click **Sky-rocketing Sales** in the Document Map to jump to that location in the document

3. Right-click in the Document Map, then click **Show Heading 1** in the shortcut menu

4. Click the **plus sign** next to **Eco-Spa Partnership** in the Document Map to display the headings under this heading
   See Figure 8-32.

5. Click the **minus sign** next to **Eco-Spa Partnership** in the Document Map to collapse the subheadings under this heading

6. Click the **Document Map button** to close the Document Map

 close EWReport06.doc

To change the width of the Document Map, drag the right edge of the Document Map pane.

Figure 8-31: Document Map open

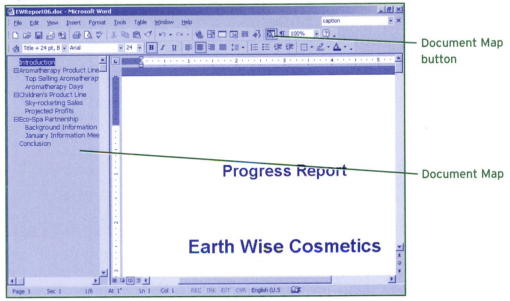

— Document Map button

— Document Map

Figure 8-32: Using the Document Map to see the document structure

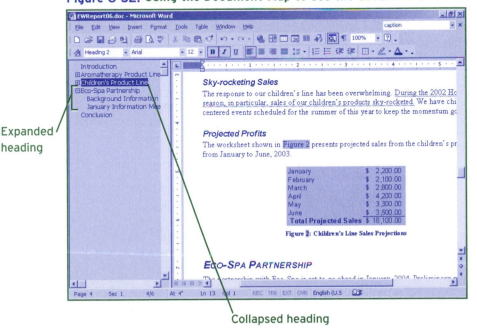

Expanded heading

Collapsed heading

extra!

Returning to a previous edit

It can be helpful to return to the location of an edit you made earlier. Word remembers the location of the last three edits made, even after you save or close and reopen the document. Press [Shift][F5] to jump to the location of the last edit made. Press it again to jump to the location of the second-to-last edit you made, and again to the location of the edit made before that.

Skill Set 8

Formatting Documents

Create and Modify Forms Using Various Form Controls

Create Forms

Forms are used to collect information in a structured format. To create a form, you add **form controls** that display or request information. An easy way to design a form is to start with a table. You save a form as a template, so that each user who opens the form can save their filled-in form as a document.

Activity Steps

 open EWForm01.doc

1. Right-click any toolbar, then click **Forms**

2. Click in the third column in the top row in the table, then click the **Text Form Field button** `ab|` on the Forms toolbar to enter a text field form control

3. Click the **Form Field Options button** on the Forms toolbar

4. Click the **Type list arrow**, click **Current date**, click the **Date format list arrow**, then click **M/d/yy** (the fourth style in the list) *See Figure 8-33*.

5. Click **OK**, press [↓], click the **Text Form Field button** `ab|`, click the **Form Field Options button** to verify that a regular text field was inserted, then click **OK**

6. Press [↓], click the **Drop-Down Form Field button** on the Forms toolbar to enter a drop-down list field form control, right-click the field you just inserted, then click **Properties** on the shortcut menu

7. Type **Choose from list** in the Drop-down item box, press **[Spacebar]**, click **Add**, type **Gift Baskets**, click **Add**, type **Aromatherapy Products**, click **Add**, type **Children's Products**, click **Add**, then click **OK**

8. Click after **Yes** in the last cell in the table, press **[Ctrl][Tab]**, click the **Check Box Form Field button** on the Forms toolbar, press [↓], press **[Ctrl][Tab]**, then click the **Check Box Form Field button** *See Figure 8-34*.

9. Click **File** on the menu bar, click **Save As**, click the **Save as type list arrow**, click **Document Template (*.dot)**, navigate to the location where you are storing your project files, select all of the text in the File name box, type **My Form Template**, click **Save**, then click the **Close button** on the Forms toolbar

 close My Form Template.dot

If you want to print a form, click the Print Preview button to see how it will look when printed. Note that only the first item in a drop-down list will print.

Figure 8-33: Adding a current date field

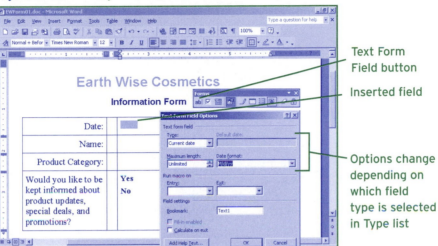

Text Form
Field button

Inserted field

Options change
depending on
which field
type is selected
in Type list

Figure 8-34: Completed form

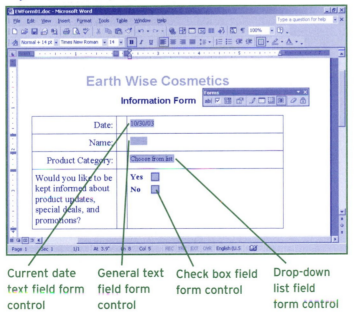

Current date
text field form
control

General text
field form
control

Check box field
form control

Drop-down
list field
form control

extra!

**Making form
templates available
as a new document**
If you save your form
template to the default
Templates folder that
opens when you
change the Save as file
type to Document
Template, your tem-
plate will be listed on
the General tab in the
Templates dialog box.
That means that you
can access your tem-
plate by clicking the
General Templates link
on the New Document
task pane to open the
General tab in the
Templates dialog box.

Skill Set 8
Formatting Documents

Create and Modify Forms Using Various Form Controls

Modify Forms

As with other types of Word documents, you can modify a form once you have created it. You can add or delete field form controls, or you can modify the properties of existing controls. You can also change the static text in the form. You must open the form template as a template, not as a new document to make and save changes to it.

You can change the format of the form field results by selecting the entire field and using font formatting commands.

Activity Steps

1. Click the **Open button** 📂 to open the Open dialog box, navigate to the folder where your project files are stored, click **EWForm02.dot**, then click **Open** to open the template as a template instead of as a new document

2. Right-click any toolbar, click **Forms** to open the Forms toolbar

3. Click anywhere in the row in the table containing **Name**, click **Table** on the menu bar, point to **Insert**, then click **Rows Below**

4. Click in the first cell in the newly inserted row, type **E-mail Address:**, then press **[Tab]** twice

5. Click the **Text Form Field button** abl on the Forms toolbar to insert a regular text form field

6. Right-click the **check box field** after Yes, click **Properties** on the shortcut menu, click the **Checked option button** under Default value
   See Figure 8-35.

7. Click **OK**, click anywhere in the document window to deselect the field, then click the **Form Field Shading button** 🗇 to turn shading off in the form fields
   See Figure 8-36.

8. Right-click any toolbar, then click **Forms** to close the Forms toolbar

    close EWForm02.dot

Figure 8-35: Check Box Form Field Options dialog box

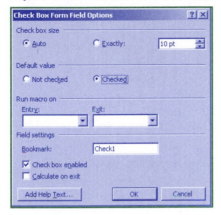

Figure 8-36: Modified form

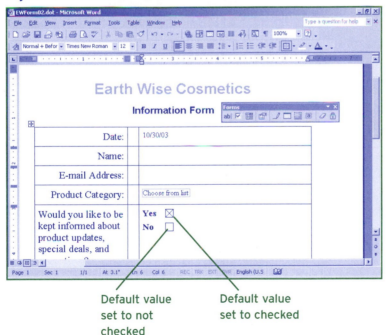

Default value
set to not
checked

Default value
set to checked

extra!

Preparing a form to be used on the Web

You prepare a form to be used on the Web in essentially the same manner as you do for use in Word, but instead of creating controls by using commands on the Forms toolbar, you use commands on the Web Tools toolbar. The controls you insert appear between Top and Bottom of Form boundaries. To change the properties of a control, you click the Properties button on the Web Tools toolbar to open the Properties dialog box. You can change the values of each property individually by selecting or typing a new value in the box next to the property you want to change. The Web Tools toolbar includes a Submit button and a Submit with Image button . You should always include one of these buttons so that the person who fills out your form on the Web has a means for sending the completed form back to you.

Skill Set 8
Formatting Documents

Create Forms and Prepare Forms for Distribution
Protect Forms and Prepare for Distribution

You cannot enter any information into form fields until you protect the form. Conversely, you cannot change the field properties or the form itself when a form is protected. You can protect the form with a password before you distribute it, so that users cannot turn protection off and change the form structure. Note that passwords are case sensitive, so that *PASSWORD* is not the same as *password* or *Password*. Once you have protected a form, it is ready to be distributed.

Activity Steps

1. Open a new, blank document, click the **Open button** , navigate to the folder where your project files are stored, click **EWForm03.dot**, click **Open**, right-click any toolbar, click **Forms** to open the Forms toolbar, then click the **Protect Form button** on the Forms toolbar
   See Figure 8-37.

2. Type **Graham Long** in the Name form field, press **[Tab]** to move to the next unprotected field, then type **glong@earthwisecosmetics.com** in the E-mail Address form field

3. Press **[Tab]**, click the **Choose from list list arrow**, then click **Children's Products** as shown in Figure 8-38

4. Click the **No check box** to select it, then click the **Yes check box** to deselect it

5. Click in the **Name: cell** to see the insertion point jump to the Name form field because the form is protected

6. Click the **Protect Form button** to unprotect the form so you can set a password

7. Click **Tools** on the menu bar, click **Protect Document** to open the Protect Document dialog box, click the **Forms option button** if necessary, type **password** (all lowercase) in the Password (optional) box, click **OK**, type **password** in the Reenter password to open box, then click **OK**

8. Click the **Protect Form button** on the Forms toolbar to see that protection cannot be turned off without entering the password, click **Cancel** in the Unprotect Document dialog box, then click the **Close button** on the Forms toolbar

 close EWForm03.dot

tip

Step 7
If the form is in a separate section in the document, click Sections in the Protect Document dialog box, then click the form's section number.

Figure 8-37: Protected form

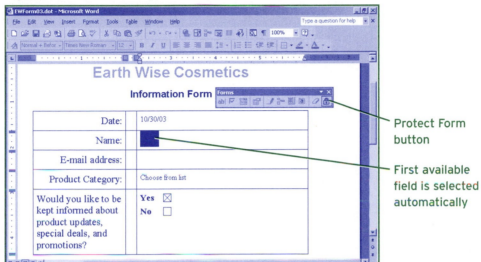

Protect Form button

First available field is selected automatically

Figure 8-38: Filling out a form

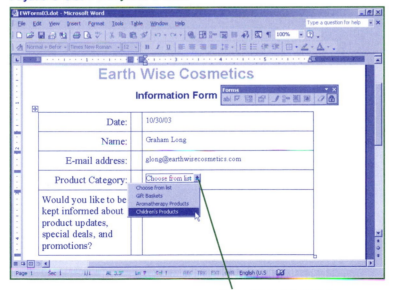

Drop-down list arrow becomes available when field is selected in protected form

Target Your Skills

 EWMemo11.doc

1 Create the document shown in Figure 8-39 by formatting the Aromatherapy Day flyer as a separate section that starts on a new page. Apply a new character style named Headline to the Aromatherapy Day title, then apply a new paragraph style named Flyer Body to the body text in the flyer. Verify the formats used when you are finished.

Figure 8-39

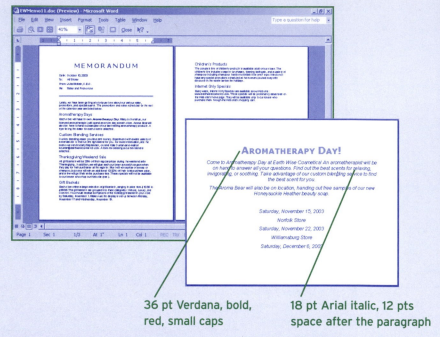

36 pt Verdana, bold, red, small caps

18 pt Arial italic, 12 pts space after the paragraph

2 Create the form shown in Figure 8-40. Insert the same drop-down list in each of the Scent fields. Insert Date type text fields for the Pickup date and Pickup time fields. Format the Pickup date field as **MMMM d, yyyy,** and format the Pickup time field as **HH:mm.** Save the form as a template named **Custom Blend Form.dot.** (*Hint:* Don't forget to lock the form.)

Figure 8-40

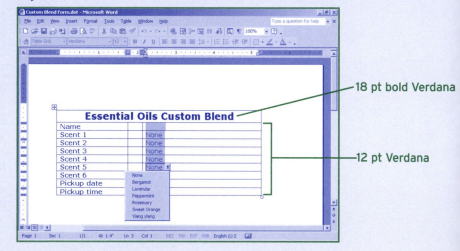

18 pt bold Verdana

12 pt Verdana

Skill List

1. Use Excel data in tables
2. Perform calculations in Word tables

Tables are an easy way to organize data in rows and columns in a document. If you want to include data that already exists in an Excel workbook, you can copy and paste the data from an Excel worksheet directly into a Word table. You can link the data so that if the Excel worksheet changes, the table will update automatically. If you want to be able to modify the worksheet directly from within the Word document, you can embed the worksheet, and Excel will open when you double-click the embedded worksheet object. You can also use simple formulas to perform calculations within a table.

If the structure of a table needs to be modified, you can merge or split cells. For example, you can merge two or more cells to create one cell that spans the columns if a table has a heading that spans several columns. If you need to create two or more cells from one existing cell, you can split the cell. Tables are a versatile way to display and manipulate data in columns and rows.

Skill Set 9
Customizing Tables

Use Excel Data in Tables
Linking Excel Data Using the Paste Command

You can copy data from an Excel worksheet (the **source file**), and then paste it into a Word document (the **destination file**). When you paste the data, the Paste Options button appears so that you can choose whether the data will be pasted or linked and the format of the data. When you **link** data, the data is represented in the destination file as fields. The fields are updated automatically when the data in the source file changes.

Activity Steps

 open GCMemo08.doc

1. Click the **Start button** on the taskbar, point to **Programs**, click **Microsoft Excel**, click the **More workbooks link** in the New Workbook task pane, navigate to the location where your project files are stored, click **GCProjections01.xls**, then click **Open**

2. Click the **Word program button** on the taskbar, right-click an empty part of the taskbar, then click **Tile Windows Vertically** Note that all open windows tile when you execute this command, so close all windows except the two used in this activity.

3. Click in the **GCProjections01.xls window**, drag to select **cells A4:C11**, then click the **Copy button** in the Excel window

4. Click in the **GCMemo08.doc window**, press **[Ctrl][End]**, then click the **Paste button** on the Word Standard toolbar to insert the data with the source formatting (the default option)

If the linked data in the destination file does not update when you make a change in the source file, right-click the linked data, then click Update Link on the shortcut menu.

5. Click the **Paste Options button** below the pasted data, then click **Match Destination Table Style and Link to Excel** to link the Excel data to the document in the default Word table style *See Figure 9-1.*

6. Right-click anywhere in the table, point to **Linked Worksheet Object** on the shortcut menu, then click **Edit Link** to jump to the linked data in the source file

7. Click the **Maximize button** in the GCProjections01.xls window if necessary, click **cell B9**, type **45**, then press **[Enter]** to accept that entry and update the link in the Word window *See Figure 9-2.*

8. Click the **Save** button on the Excel toolbar to save the changed data, then click the Close button in the Excel program window

 close GCMemo08.doc

Figure 9-1: Excel data linked to a new Word table

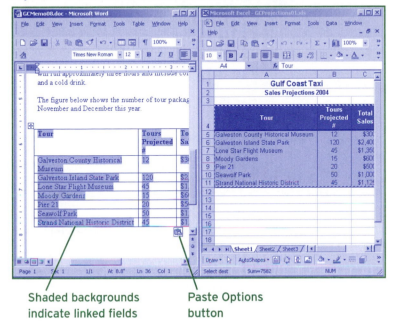

Shaded backgrounds indicate linked fields

Paste Options button

Figure 9-2: Linked data automatically updated in document

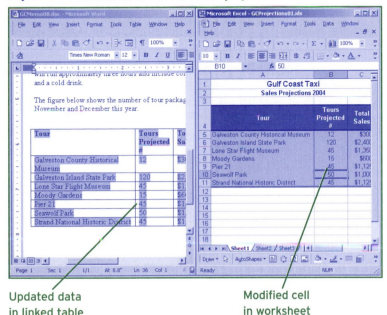

Updated data in linked table

Modified cell in worksheet

extra!

Using the Links dialog box

To open the Links dialog box, right-click the linked data, point to Linked Worksheet Object, then click Links; or click anywhere in the document, click Edit on the menu bar, then click Links. The default is for links to be updated automatically, but you can change this if you want. First, make sure the link is selected in the Source file list, then click the Manual update option button. If you move the source file to a new location, you can click Change Source, then navigate to the new location of the source file and click the source filename. You can also click the Locked check box to lock a link and prevent it from updating when the source data changes.

Skill Set 9

Customizing Tables

Use Excel Data in Tables

Embedding Excel Data in a Word Document

When you **embed** data, a copy of the source data becomes part of the destination file, and it contains a link to the source program. To edit embedded data, double-click the embedded object. The source program and the embedded file open in a new window. The original source file does not change when you edit embedded data.

Activity Steps

 open GCMemo09.doc

1. Position the insertion point between the two body paragraphs, click **Insert** on the menu bar, click **Object** to open the Object dialog box, then click the **Create from File tab**

2. Click **Browse**, navigate to the location where your project files are stored, click **GCSales01.xls**, then click **Insert**
   See Figure 9-3.

3. Click **OK** to embed a copy of the GCSales01 workbook

4. Double-click the **embedded worksheet object** to open the workbook in an Excel window in the document, click the **Next Sheet button** ▶ to the left of the worksheet tabs, click the **Oct & Nov Sales sheet tab**, click **cell C6**, type **150**, then press **[Enter]**
   See Figure 9-4.

5. Drag the **bottom middle sizing handle** up to just below row 9, then click anywhere in the document window outside the object

6. Click the **Start button** on the taskbar, point to **Programs**, click **Microsoft Excel**, click the **More workbooks link** in the task pane, navigate to the location where your project files are stored, click **GCSales01.xls**, click **Open** to open the original GCSales01 workbook file, then click the **Oct & Nov Sales sheet tab** and notice that the value in cell C6 has not changed

7. Click the **Dec & Jan Projections sheet tab**, select **cells A1:C12**, click the **Copy button** 📋, click the **Word program button** on the taskbar, position the insertion point below the last paragraph, click **Edit** on the menu bar, then click **Paste Special**

8. Click **Microsoft Excel Worksheet Object** in the list, make sure the **Paste option button** is selected, then click **OK**

9. Click the **Excel program button** on the taskbar, then click the **Close button** ☒ in the Excel program title bar

 close GCMemo09.doc

Step 1
To embed a new Excel worksheet in a document, click the Insert Microsoft Excel Worksheet button, or click the Create New tab in the Object dialog box, then click Microsoft Excel Object in the Object type list.

Figure 9-3: Object dialog box ready to embed existing data

Click to insert a new file

Path name on your screen may differ

Click to link file instead of embed it

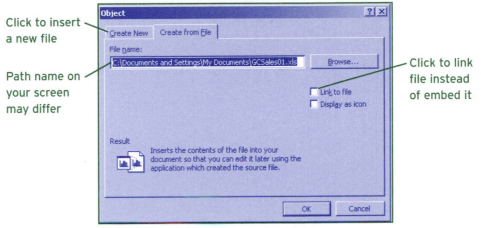

Figure 9-4: Embedded data's source program opened in window

Next Sheet button

Selected sheet tab

Edited value

Sizing handle

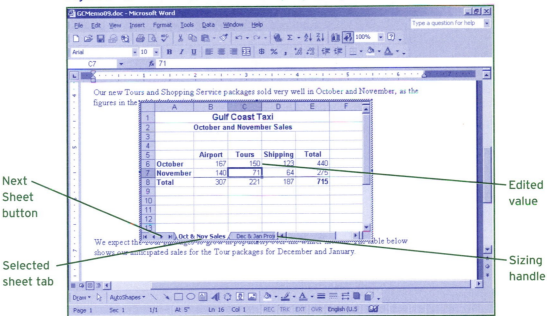

Skill Set 9
Customizing Tables

Perform Calculations in Word Tables
Use Formulas in Tables

You can use formulas in a Word table to perform simple calculations. When you click the AutoSum button on the Tables and Borders toolbar, it automatically checks for data in the cells above; if the cells above do not contain any data, it checks in the cells to the left. It then adds the data and displays the total. Every cell must contain data, so if a cell is empty, you must enter a zero in it. You can insert other formulas by using the Formula dialog box. Formulas always begin with an equal sign. When you insert a formula, you refer to the table cells in the same manner as in a Microsoft Graph data sheet or an Excel worksheet: the columns are labeled A, B, C, D, etc., and the rows are labeled 1, 2, 3, 4, etc., so the first cell—the cell in the upper-left corner—is cell A1, the cell just below it is cell A2, and the cell just to the right of the first cell is cell B1. When a formula is calculated, the result is displayed as a field.

Activity Steps

 open GCMemo10.doc

1. Right-click any toolbar, then click **Tables and Borders** if necessary to display the Tables and Borders toolbar

2. Scroll down so you can see the first table, click in the cell to the right of **Average Cost** (cell B9), then click the **AutoSum button** [Σ] on the Tables and Borders toolbar to insert a formula that adds the values in the cells above the current cell
   See Figure 9-5.

3. With the insertion point still in cell B9 (the cell to the right of the **Average Cost** cell), click **Table** on the menu bar, then click **Formula** to open the Formula dialog box

4. Select the contents of the Formula box, then press **[Delete]**

5. Type = (equal sign), click the **Paste function list arrow**, then click **AVERAGE** to insert the Average function in the Formula box

6. Type **b2:b8** between the parentheses in the Formula box to calculate the average of the values in cells B2 through B8, inclusive (in other words, the cells directly above the current cell)
   See Figure 9-6.

7. Click **OK** to insert the new formula into the cell and calculate the average cost

8. Click **View** on the menu bar, point to **Toolbars**, then click **Tables and Borders** to close the Tables and Borders toolbar

 close GCMemo10.doc

tip

It is not necessary to click the AutoSum button if you know you want to insert a different formula.

Figure 9-5: Adding numbers using the AutoSum button

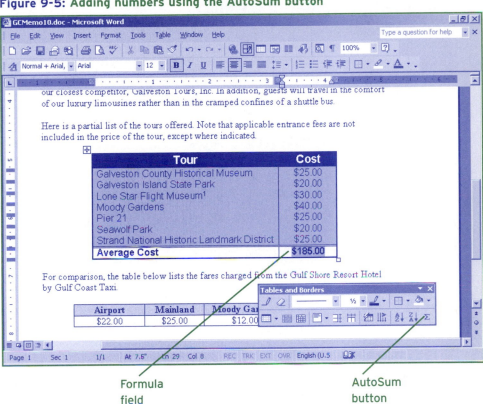

Formula
field

AutoSum
button

Figure 9-6: Formula dialog box

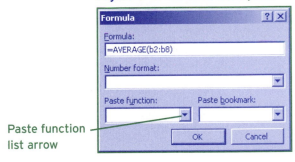

Paste function
list arrow

Skill Set 9
Customizing Tables

Perform Calculations in Word Tables
Merge and Split Table Cells

Some tables are more complex than others. You might, for example, need to combine cells to create a table with secondary headings. To do this, you can use the Merge Cells command. Conversely, you may need to split a cell into two or more cells. This is easy to do with the Split Cells command. When you split cells, you may need to reformat the table—or at least the cells you just split—to adjust the widths of the new cells.

Activity Steps

 open GCAnnouncement05.doc

1. Right-click any toolbar, click **Tables and Borders** if necessary to display the Tables and Borders toolbar, scroll down so that you can see the table, then select the three cells in the **Malls row**

2. Click the **Merge Cells button** on the Tables and Borders toolbar to merge the three cells into one cell, then click anywhere in the document to deselect the cells
See Figure 9-7.

3. Merge the cells in the **Factory Outlets** and **Outdoor Markets rows**

4. Click in the top row in the table, then click the **Split Cells button** on the Tables and Borders toolbar to open the Split Cells dialog box

5. Click the **Number of columns up arrow** so that it changes to **3**, then click **OK**

6. Press **[Delete]**, type **Destination**, press **[Tab]**, type **Average Time**, press **[Tab]**, then type **Average Fare**

7. Position the pointer over the border between **Destination** and **Average Time** so that it changes to +‖+, then drag the border to the right, so that the border aligns with the border between the first and second columns in the table as shown in Figure 9-8

8. Drag the border between **Average Time** and **Average Fare** to the right so that it aligns with the border between the second and third columns in the table, right-click any toolbar, then click **Tables and Borders** to close the Tables and Borders toolbar

 close GCAnnouncement05.doc

Step 7
If you can't get the borders to align, press and hold [Alt] while you are dragging.

Figure 9-7: Cells merged in table

Merged cells

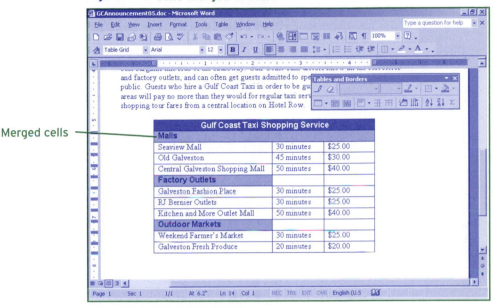

Figure 9-8: Table with merged and split cells

Cell split into three cells

Merged cells

Pointer

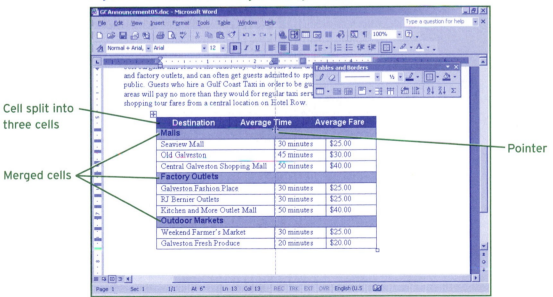

Skill Set 9

Customizing Tables

Target Your Skills

 GCMemo11.doc

Figure 9-9

1 Create the finished document shown in Figure 9-9. First paste the data from the Excel worksheet **GCChart01.xls** as a link formatted to match the destination file. Then change both the **Driver Courtesy** and **Cost** numbers to **2** in the Excel workbook. Save the revised workbook, then close it. In the document, modify the table as shown in Figure 9-9.

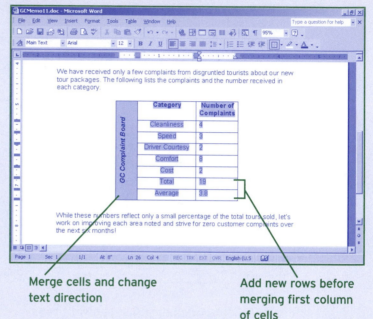

Merge cells and change text direction

Add new rows before merging first column of cells

 GCBrochure07.doc

Figure 9-10

2 Use Figure 9-10 as a guide for creating the table shown. Use the merge and Split Cells commands.

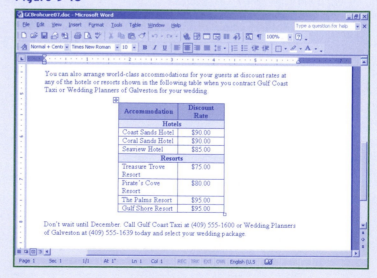

Skill List

1. Create, modify, and position graphics
2. Create and modify charts using data from other applications
3. Align text and graphics

In this skill set, you will learn how to create and add graphics to your documents. You will use a variety of tools on the Drawing toolbar to draw and color graphics. To avoid re-creating existing data, you will also learn how to import data from other programs to a Microsoft Graph chart. Finally, you will learn advanced methods for positioning graphics in a document.

Skill Set 10

Creating and Modifying Graphics

Create, Modify, and Position Graphics

Create and Insert Graphics in a Document

You use the tools on the Drawing toolbar to create and insert graphics into a document. When you click a button on the Drawing toolbar, the drawing canvas appears. The **drawing canvas** is the name for the area on which you draw shapes. When you click a drawing tool on the Drawing toolbar, the pointer changes to ╋ and you can drag it to draw the shape you selected. After you draw a shape, **sizing handles**, small white circles, appear around the edge of the drawn object. You can drag a sizing handle to resize the object. You can also drag entire objects to reposition them.

Activity Steps

To draw a freeform shape, click the AutoShapes button, point to Lines, then click Curve to draw curved line segments, click Freeform to draw curved or straight line segments, or click Scribble to use the pointer like a pencil.

1. Create a new, blank document, then click the **Drawing button** 🖉 to open the Drawing toolbar, if necessary

2. Click the **Rectangle button** ▢ on the Drawing toolbar
   Note that the drawing canvas appears.

3. Position the ╋ pointer on the drawing canvas at approximately the intersection of the ½" marks on the rulers, then drag to create a rectangle about 4" wide and ⅛" high (refer to Figure 10-1)

4. Click the **AutoShapes button** AutoShapes ▾ on the Drawing toolbar, point to **Flowchart** on the menu, then click the **Flowchart: Manual Input button** ◻ (third row, third column)

5. Drag below the rectangle shape to create a shape approximately 1" wide and ¼" long
   See Figure 10-1.

6. With the second drawn shape still selected, click the **Fill Color list arrow** 🎨 ▾ on the Drawing toolbar, then click the **Sea Green box** (third row, fourth column)

7. Press and hold [Alt] so that you can position the graphic exactly, then drag the **second shape** on top of the right end of the rectangle shape, as shown in Figure 10-2, to create an oar shape

8. Click in a blank area of the document outside of the drawing canvas to deselect the object and hide the drawing canvas

 close file

Figure 10-1: Rectangle shape drawn on the drawing canvas

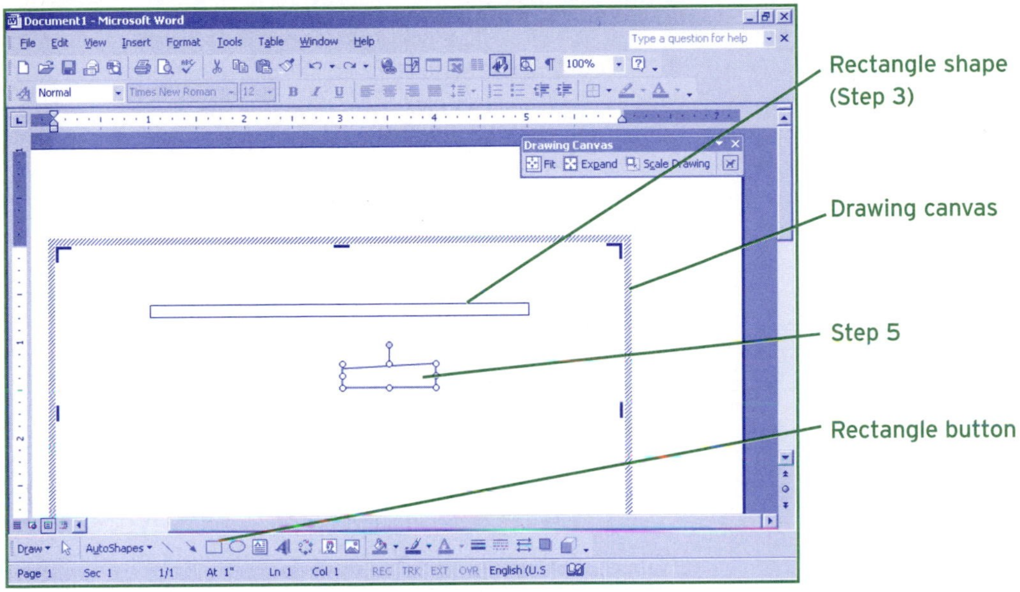

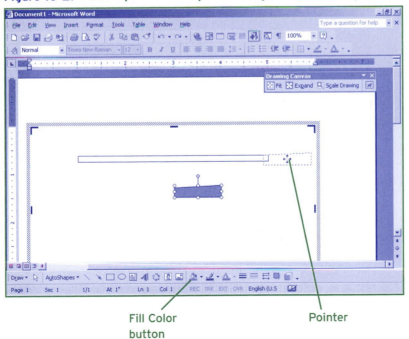

Rectangle shape
(Step 3)

Drawing canvas

Step 5

Rectangle button

Figure 10-2: Oar shape created by combining two drawn shapes

Fill Color
button

Pointer

extra!

Understanding the drawing grid

When you position an object in a document, it snaps to an invisible grid. This is useful when you need to align objects, but it can be troublesome if you try to position an object and it keeps snapping to the grid. To override the grid, press and hold [Alt] while you drag the object you want to position.

Skill Set 10
Creating and Modifying Graphics

Create, Modify, and Position Graphics
Modify Graphics in a Document

You can modify the graphics that you create in a document. You can draw one object on top of another, and then rearrange the order of the objects so that an object that appeared to be behind another object can be brought forward and appear to be in front. You can group objects together so they are treated as a unit, you can rotate them, and you can copy and paste or reposition them. When you place shapes on the drawing canvas, you can move and resize the shapes as a single unit by dragging the white circle sizing handles on the drawing canvas. You can also resize the drawing canvas around an object.

Activity Steps

 open CCLogo01.doc

1. Click the **handle section** of the oar shape, drag it approximately ½" to the left, then click the **Undo button** 🔙

2. With the handle section still selected, click the **Draw button** `Draw ▾` on the Drawing toolbar, point to **Order**, then click **Send to Back** to send the handle drawn object behind the blade object

3. Press and hold **[Shift]**, click the **blade section** of the oar shape to select both drawn objects, click the **Draw button** `Draw ▾` on the Drawing toolbar, then click **Group** to combine the two shapes into a single object

4. Position the pointer over the **rotate handle** so that it changes to 🔄, then drag the handle to the left so that the dotted outline of the grouped object rotates approximately 45 degrees *See Figure 10-3*.

5. With the object still selected, click the **Copy button** 📋, then click the **Paste button** 📋

6. Click the **Draw button** `Draw ▾` on the Drawing toolbar, point to **Rotate or Flip**, click **Flip Horizontal**, then press [⬆]twice to cross the oars approximately at their centers

7. Click the **Fit Drawing to Contents button** 🔲 on the Drawing Canvas toolbar to shrink the drawing canvas so it fits exactly around the object

8. Click the **Scale Drawing button** 🔳 on the Drawing Canvas toolbar, position the pointer over the **lower-right sizing handle** of the drawing canvas so that the pointer changes to ↖, then drag up and to the left so that the object is approximately 2" wide, as shown in Figure 10-4

 close CCLogo01.doc

Step 7
If the Drawing Canvas toolbar is not visible, right-click on the edge of the drawing canvas, then click Show Drawing Canvas Toolbar on the shortcut menu.

Figure 10-3: Object rotated 45 degrees

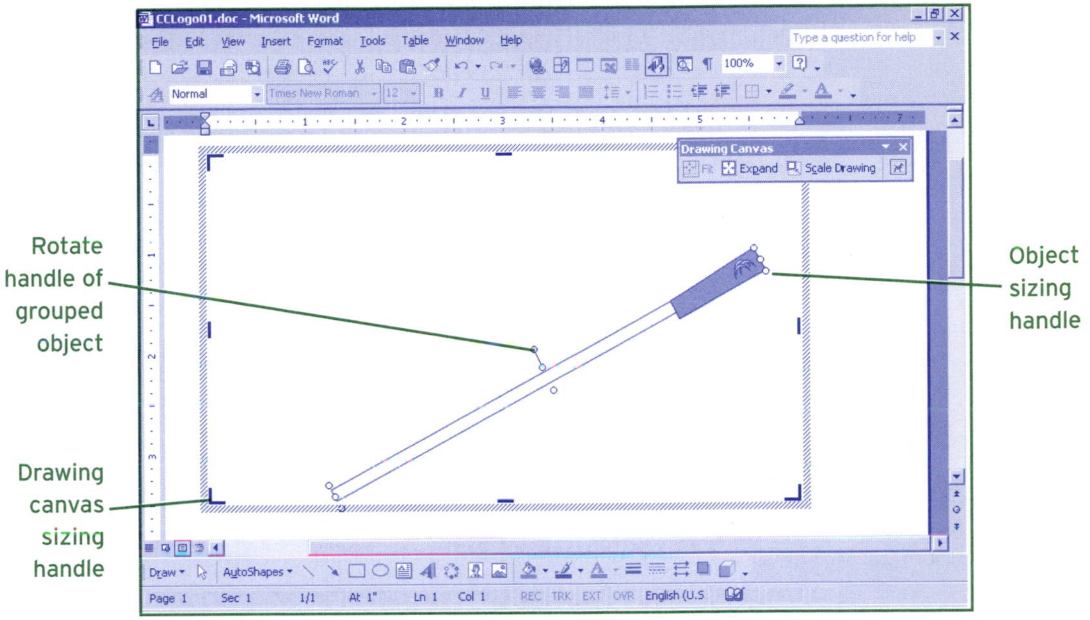

Rotate
handle of
grouped
object

Object
sizing
handle

Drawing
canvas
sizing
handle

Figure 10-4: Drawing canvas tight around the object

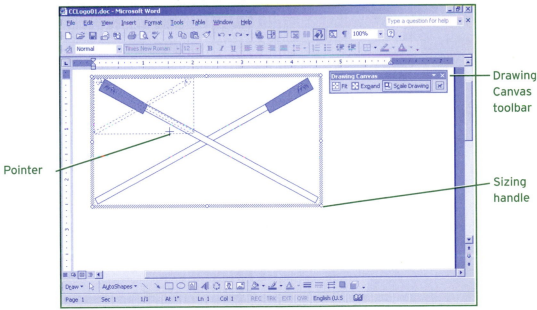

Drawing
Canvas
toolbar

Pointer

Sizing
handle

Skill Set 10
Creating and Modifying Graphics

Create, Modify, and Position Graphics
Add Text to Graphics in a Document

You can add text to graphics or other objects. To do this, you use the Text Box button on the Drawing toolbar to create a text object. When you add a text box, the border of the text box is composed of slanted lines, which indicates that the text box is ready to accept any text you type. If you want to format the entire text box, you select the entire object by clicking the slanted line border so that it changes to a border composed of dots. When the border is the dotted line border, all formatting commands apply to the entire object.

Activity Steps

 open CCDrawing01.doc

1. Click the **Text Box button** on the Drawing toolbar

2. Scroll down below the new drawing canvas so you can see the T-shirt graphic

3. Position the pointer inside the T-shirt just under the left sleeve, then drag down and to the right to create a text box approximately ½" high and 1 ½" wide
See Figure 10-5.

4. Type **Property of CCC Crew**

5. Click the **slanted line border** of the text box so that it changes to a dotted line border, click the **Font list arrow** `Times New Roman ▾`, click **Arial**, click the **Font Size list arrow** `12 ▾`, click **9**, then click the **Bold button** `B`

6. With the entire text object still selected, click the **Line Color list arrow** on the Drawing toolbar, then click **No Line** on the pop-up menu

7. Click in a blank area of the document to deselect the text object and hide the drawing canvas
See Figure 10-6.

 close CCDrawing01.doc

To add text to an AutoShape object quickly, right-click the object, then click Add Text on the shortcut menu.

Figure 10-5: Creating a text box in a drawn object

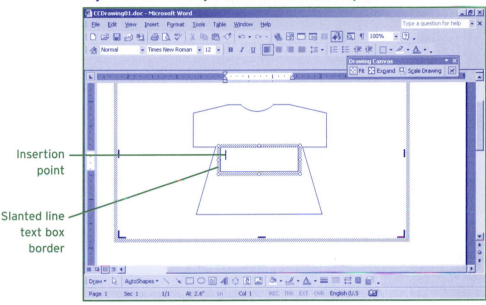

Insertion point

Slanted line text box border

Figure 10-6: Formatted text box

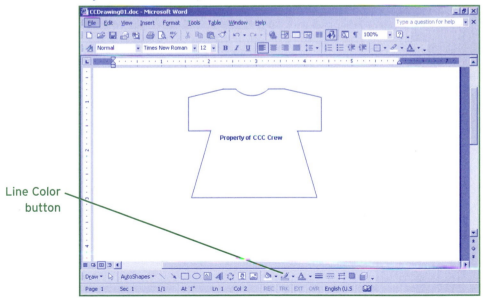

Line Color button

Skill Set 10
Creating and Modifying Graphics

Create, Modify, and Position Graphics
Position Graphics in a Document

The default position for graphics in a document is **inline** with the text; that is, objects are positioned at the insertion point and moved with the text around them. They are part of the paragraph in which they are positioned. This is usually the easiest way to work with graphics. To reposition an inline graphic, you drag it by its border or by the border of the drawing canvas. A vertical line follows the pointer to indicate where the inline graphic will be positioned when you release the mouse button.

To add color behind a drawn object, select the drawing canvas, click the Fill Color list arrow on the Drawing toolbar, then select a color.

Activity Steps

 open CCLetterhead01.doc

1. Click the **Show/Hide ¶ button** ![¶] to display paragraph marks, if necessary

2. Click the graphic to select it, then drag it by the drawing canvas border to position it immediately in front of the word **Culver** in the first line in the document, as shown in Figure 10-7

3. Click anywhere in the document to deselect the graphic, then click between the inline graphic and the word **Culver** to position the insertion point

4. Press **[Enter]** twice

5. Drag to select the graphic, the blank paragraph below the graphic, and all four lines of the address

6. Click the **Center button** ![center] to center the graphic and the text on the page
   See Figure 10-8.

7. Click in a blank area of the document to deselect the text and the object, then click the **Show/Hide ¶ button** ![¶] to hide paragraph marks

 close CCLetterhead01.doc

Figure 10-7: Inline graphic and text selected

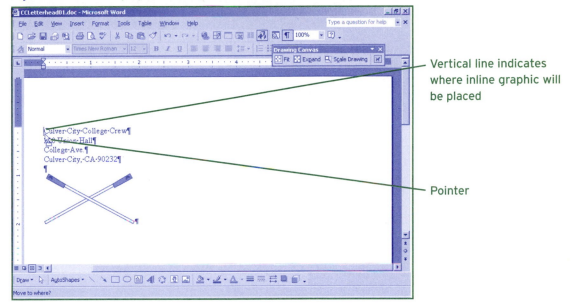

Vertical line indicates where inline graphic will be placed

Pointer

Figure 10-8: Inline graphic and text centered on page

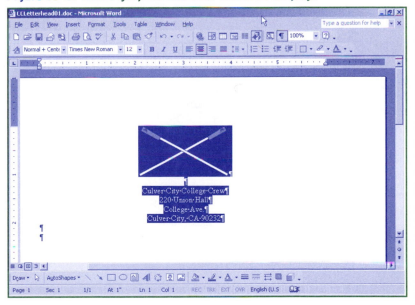

extra!

Editing wrap points
You can change the way text wraps around the shape of an object by editing its wrap points. **Wrap points** are the vertexes of the object, the point where two line segments meet or the highest point in a curved line. Select the drawing canvas, click the Text Wrapping button on the Drawing Canvas toolbar, then click Edit Wrap Points to display the vertexes. Drag any wrap point to change the invisible border around which the text wraps.

Skill Set 10
Creating and Modifying Graphics

Create and Modify Charts Using Data from Other Applications

If you want to include a chart in a document, and the data already exists in an Excel worksheet or in an Access table, you can import the data and then use Graph to display the chart. You can then change the data or the chart to suit your needs.

Activity Steps

 open CCMemo02.doc

1. Press [Ctrl][End], click **Insert** on the menu bar, click **Object** to open the Object dialog box, scroll down and click **Microsoft Graph Chart** in the Object type list, then click **OK**

2. Click the **top-left gray box** in the datasheet to select all of the cells in the datasheet as shown in Figure 10-9, then click the **Import File button** to open the Import File dialog box

3. Navigate to the location where your project files are stored, click **CCBudget01.xls**, then click **Open**

4. In the Import Data Options dialog box that opens, make sure **Budget** is selected in the list of worksheets, make sure the **Overwrite existing cells check box** is selected, then click **OK**

5. Click the **By Column button** to switch the data plotted on the chart so that it represents the data in the data sheet's columns, not its rows, click the **Close button** in the datasheet, then drag the lower-right sizing handle of the chart object down and over to the right margin of the document

6. Right-click one of the labels on the x-axis, click **Format Axis** on the shortcut menu to open the Format Axis dialog box, click the **Font tab**, click **Regular** in the Font style list, click **8** in the Size list if necessary, then click **OK** to resize the x-axis labels so that all six are visible

7. Click **Chart** on the menu bar, click **Chart Options**, click the **Titles tab**, click in the **Chart title box**, type **Crew Budget**, then click **OK**

8. Click in a blank area of the document to exit Graph
   See Figure 10-10.

 close CCMemo02.doc

Step 2
It is not always necessary to select all the existing cells before importing data, because the default is for the data you import to start at the upper-left corner of the datasheet.

Skill 2

Create and Modify Charts Using Data from Other Applications

Figure 10-9: All the cells in the datasheet selected

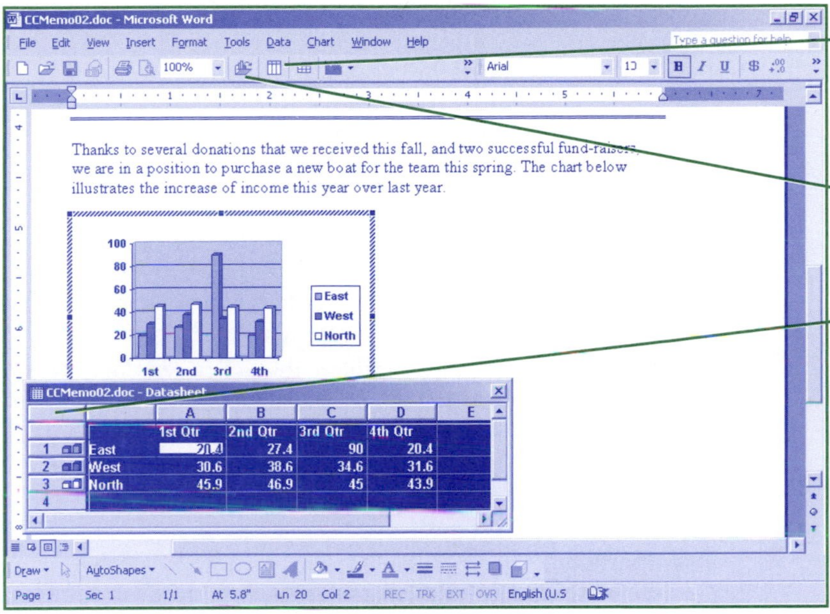

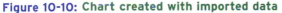

By Column button

Import File button

Click this box to select all cells in the datasheet

Figure 10-10: Chart created with imported data

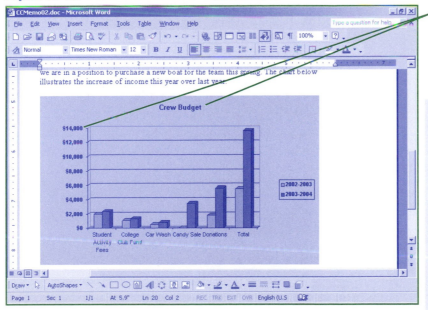

Font sizes may vary depending on how you resized the chart

extra!

Using Access data in a chart

You can also use data from an Access table in a chart. Open the table in Access, copy the table to the clipboard, then paste the data into the Graph datasheet. The chart will update as soon as you paste the new data.

Skill Set 10
Creating and Modifying Graphics

Align Text and Graphics

You can choose to have a drawn object or a graphic **float** in the document so that you can position it on the page by dragging it. If you choose to make an object a floating object, you need to select the way you want the text to wrap around the object. See Table 10-1 for a list of wrapping styles available.

Activity Steps

 open CCNewsletter01.doc

1. Click the **inline graphic** to select it, then drag it by the edge of the drawing canvas to just before the word **News** in the heading **Alumni News**, using the vertical line that follows the pointer to identify exactly where the graphic will be positioned

2. With the drawing canvas still visible, click the **Text Wrapping button** on the Drawing Canvas toolbar, then click **Square**

3. Drag the **floating graphic** by the drawing canvas border to the middle of the page, using the dotted outline of the graphic to help position it as shown in Figure 10-11
   Note that the text wraps around the square edge of the drawing canvas.

4. With the graphic still selected, click the **Text Wrapping button** on the Drawing Canvas toolbar, click **Tight** to wrap the text around the object's shape, then click in a blank area of the document
   See Figure 10-12.

5. Click the **graphic** to select it and display the drawing canvas, click the edge of the drawing canvas to select it, click **Format** on the menu bar, click **Drawing Canvas**, then click the **Layout tab**

6. Click **Advanced** on the Layout tab, then click the **Text Wrapping tab**

7. Click the **Right only option button**, click **OK**, then click **OK** again

 close CCNewsletter01.doc

tip

Step 1
When you drag the graphic, make sure you drag the edge of the drawing canvas, not the graphic itself.

Table 10-1: Wrapping styles for floating objects

wrapping style	description
Square	text wraps around the object in a square
Tight	text wraps around the object in the shape of the object, but does not fill in any white space within the object itself
Behind Text	text does not wrap around the object at all; instead the object is placed behind the text
In Front of Text	text does not wrap around the object at all; instead the object is placed on top of the text
Top and Bottom	text wraps around the top and bottom of the object, but does not wrap on the sides
Through	text wraps around the object in the shape of the object, but also fills in any white space in the object itself

Figure 10-11: Floating graphic with text wrapped square around it

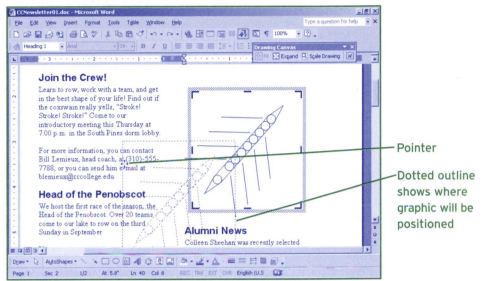

Pointer

Dotted outline shows where graphic will be positioned

Figure 10-12: Floating graphic with text wrapped tight only on the right

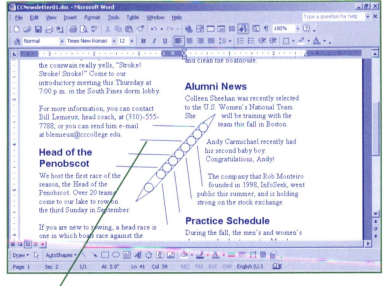

Text wraps around shape of graphic

extra!

Additional layout options

On the Text Wrapping tab in the Advanced Layout dialog box, you can customize the distance that is maintained between the graphic and the text that wraps around it. A distance of 0" means that no text will appear on that side of the graphic. You can also precisely adjust the position of the graphic by specifying exactly where it will go on the page. Click the Picture Position tab in the Advanced Layout dialog box, then specify the horizontal and vertical positions.

Skill Set 10
Creating and Modifying Graphics

Target Your Skills

 CCAnnouncement03.doc

Figure 10-13

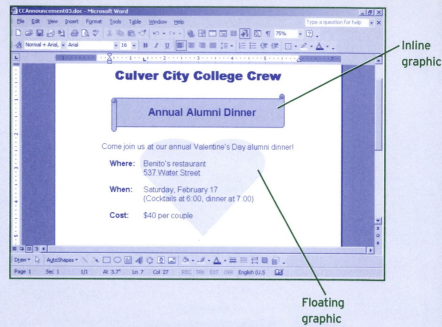

Inline graphic

Floating graphic

1 Use Figure 10-13 as a guide for creating and positioning the graphic shown. Use buttons on the AutoShapes menus to create the two graphics. (*Hint*: To change the color of the heart AutoShape, click the Fill Color list arrow, click More Colors, then select a very light gray.)

 CCMemo03.doc

2 Create the document shown in Figure 10-14. To create the chart, import the Expenses worksheet of the Excel file **CCExpenses01.xls**. Change the chart type to a pie chart, then plot the data series by columns. To add the values as data labels, right-click a pie slide, click Format Data Series, click the Data Labels tab, then click the Value check box. To change the font size of the data labels, right click one, click Format Data Labels, then click the Font tab.

Figure 10-14

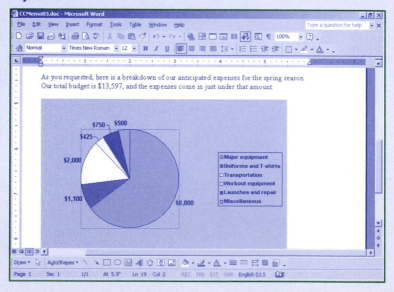

Skill List

1. Create, edit, and run macros
2. Customize menus and toolbars

You can customize Word in several ways to make it fit your work style. You can record a **macro**, a single command that you execute to perform a series of commands, to handle an often-repeated task. If you want to change a recorded macro, you can re-record it or edit it using Microsoft Visual Basic Editor.

You can add new custom menus to the current menu bar or to any toolbar. You can also add and remove buttons from toolbars to make it easier to perform tasks that you perform on a regular basis. Spending a few minutes customizing Word to suit your work habits will make you more efficient.

Create, Edit, and Run Macros
Create Macros

A macro is a single command that you execute to perform a series of commands. Macros are useful because you can perform all of the steps necessary to execute a task by pressing a keyboard shortcut or clicking one command. To create a macro, you name the macro and start recording, execute the tasks, then stop recording. You must use a letter as the first character in a macro name, and the macro name cannot contain any spaces. You can store a macro in the Normal template (this is the default), any other open template, or in an open document. If you store a macro in a document, it is available only when that document is open. You can assign a keyboard shortcut to run the macro, or you can assign the macro to a toolbar or menu command.

Activity Steps

1. Open a new, blank document, click **Tools** on the menu bar, point to **Macro**, then click **Record New Macro** to open the Record Macro dialog box

2. Type **SignatureLine** in the Macro name box

3. Click the **Store macro in list arrow**, then click the **document name** of the new document (for example, **Document1 (document)**) to store the macro in the current document instead of in the Normal template
   See Figure 11-1.

Step 4
Click the Toolbars button to open the Customize dialog box and assign the macro to a toolbar button or menu command.

4. Click the **Keyboard button** to open the Customize Keyboard dialog box

5. Press **[Ctrl][Shift][Y]** to insert a shortcut key combination in the Press new shortcut key box, click the **Save changes in list arrow**, click the **document name** of the new document (for example, **Document1**) to store the shortcut key in the current document instead of in the Normal template, click **Assign**, then click **Close** to close the dialog box and open the Stop Recording toolbar

6. Type **Sincerely,** (including the comma), press **[Enter]** four times, type **Terry Farris**, press **[Enter]**, then type **Sales Manager**
   See Figure 11-2.

7. Click the **Stop Recording button** on the Stop Recording toolbar

8. Click **Tools** on the menu bar, point to **Macro**, click **Macros** to open the Macros dialog box, notice that the **SignatureLine** macro is listed, then click **Cancel** to close the dialog box

 close file

Figure 11-1: Record Macro dialog box

Your document may have a different number

Information here will differ on your screen

Figure 11-2: Recording a macro

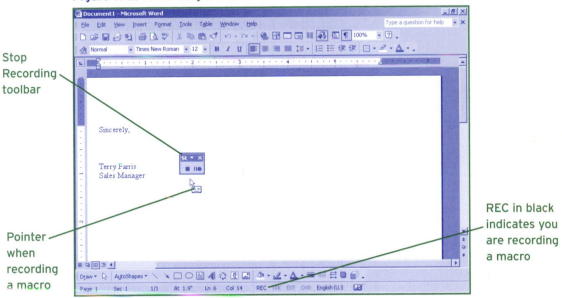

Stop Recording toolbar

Pointer when recording a macro

REC in black indicates you are recording a macro

Create, Edit, and Run Macros
Run Macros

Once you have created a macro, you need to run it to test it. You can run macros stored in the current document or template. If macro security is set to High, Word automatically disables macros in the documents that you open. If you know that a document is from a trusted source, you can change the macro security setting to Medium and then choose to enable macros in documents or templates that you open, or to Low to enable macros automatically.

To copy a macro from one template or document to another, click Organizer in the Macros dialog box to open the Macro Project Items tab in the Organizer dialog box, select the macro you want to copy, then click Copy.

Activity Steps

1. Create a new, blank document, click **Tools** on the menu bar, click **Options** to open the Options dialog box, click the **Security tab**, click **Macro Security** to open the Security dialog box, make sure the **Security Level tab** is selected, note which option button is selected, then click the **Medium option button**, if necessary

2. Click **OK** to close the Security dialog box, click **OK** to close the Options dialog box, click the **Close button** ☒ in the title bar of the document window, click the **Open button** 🖼, navigate to the location where your project files are stored, click **EWLetter10.doc**, click **Open**, then, in the dialog box that opens asking if you want to enable macros, click **Enable Macros**

3. Open the project file **EWLetter11**, enabling macros when asked, then press **[Ctrl][End]** to position the insertion point at the end of the document

4. Click **Tools** on the menu bar, point to **Macro**, then click **Macros** to open the Macros dialog box
   See Figure 11-3.

5. Make sure **TerrySignatureLine** is selected in the macro list, then click **Run** to insert a signature line

6. Click **Window** on the menu bar, click **EWLetter10.doc** to switch to that document, then press **[Ctrl][End]**

7. Press **[Ctrl][Shift][Y]** to run the SignatureLine macro by using the shortcut key assigned to it
   See Figure 11-4.

8. Click **Tools** on the menu bar, click **Options**, click **Macro Security** on the **Security tab**; *if* High was selected before you began this activity, click the **High option button**; *if* Low was selected before you began this activity, click the **Low option button**; then click **OK** twice

 close EWLetter10.doc
    EWLetter11.doc

Figure 11-3: Macros dialog box

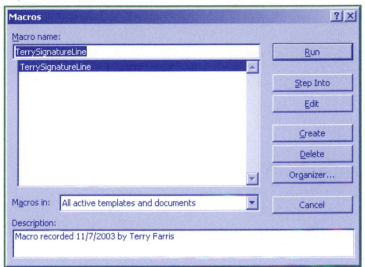

Figure 11-4: Signature line inserted in document

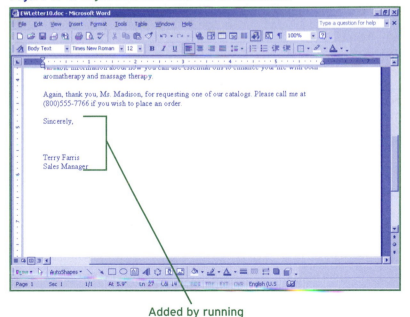

Added by running
TerrySignatureLine
macro

extra!

Understanding more about macros

If the name you assign to a macro is the same as the name assigned to a built-in command, your new macro will override the existing commands. To make sure that you don't create a macro with the same name as a built-in command, click the Macros in list arrow in the Macros dialog box, then click Word commands. Another thing to keep in mind when you are recording a macro is that, while the macro recorder will record mouse clicks on a menu command or toolbar button, it will not record the mouse actions in the document window, for example, dragging to select text or clicking to position the insertion point. Finally, not all formatting changes made using the buttons on the Formatting toolbar are recorded when you record a macro, so it's a good idea to open the appropriate formatting dialog box to change any character or paragraph formats.

Skill Set 11
Customizing Word

Create, Edit, and Run Macros
Edit Macros

If you make a mistake when you record a macro, or if you change your mind about any of the actions you included in the macro, you can re-record or edit the macro. For simple changes, it can be easier to edit the existing macro. Macros are recorded in Visual Basic for Applications, a programming language. If you know the steps you took to record a macro, it is fairly easy to figure out which line of code executes which step.

Note: This activity continues on page 248. Make sure you turn the page and complete all nine steps.

To re-record a macro, first delete it by opening the Macros dialog box, selecting the macro, then clicking Delete, then close the Macros dialog box and start the recording process again.

Activity Steps

1. Open a new, blank document, click **Tools** on the menu bar, click **Options**, click the **Security tab**, click **Macro Security**, note which option button is selected on the **Security Level tab**, click the **Medium option button** if necessary, click **OK** twice, close the blank document, open the project file **EWMemo10**, then click **Enable Macros**

2. Press **[Ctrl][End]**, click **Tools** on the menu bar, point to **Macro**, click **Macros**, make sure **MemoHeader** is selected, then click **Run**
   This macro created memo header lines, but made the name **Julia McNair** in the **From** line bold, added an extra **Re** line, and added a red border line.

3. Click **Tools** on the menu bar, point to **Macro**, click **Macros**, make sure **MemoHeader** is selected, then click **Edit** to open the Microsoft Visual Basic Editor window
   See Figure 11-5.

4. Click immediately after the quotation mark after **From:** in the eighth line of code after the comments, press **[Enter]**, press **[Delete]**, type **Selection.T**, click the down scroll arrow in the list that appeared when you typed the period, double-click **TypeText**, press the **[Spacebar]**, type **Text**, type : (a colon), type = (an equal sign), then press **[Delete]**

5. Click ✍ to the left of the next line (**Selection.Font.Bold = wdToggle**) to select it, click the **Cut button** ✂, press **[↑]**, then click the **Paste button** 📋 to move the Bold toggle command so it comes before the line that inserts Julia's name
   See Figure 11-6.

Do not close the file. Continue with Step 6 on page 248.

Figure 11-5: Microsoft Visual Basic Editor window

Insertion point

Project window (may not be visible on your screen)

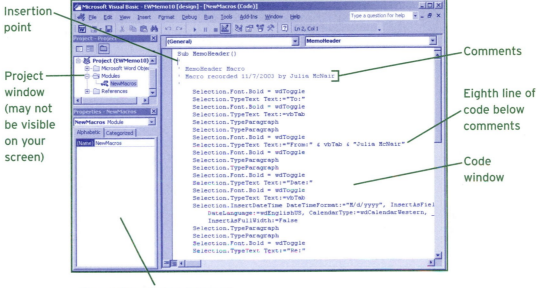

Properties window (may not be visible on your screen)

Comments

Eighth line of code below comments

Code window

Figure 11-6: Edited macro program code in the Code window

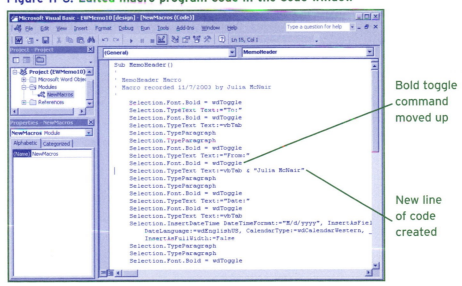

Bold toggle command moved up

New line of code created

Create, Edit, and Run Macros
Edit Macros (continued)

In Steps 4 and 5 on page 246, you moved code so that the toggle command to turn off bold formatting now appears before Julia McNair's name. In the steps on this page, you will delete the extra Re line and change the color of the border line to dark blue.

Activity Steps

6. Click below the scroll box in the vertical scroll bar to scroll down a screen, position ✎ to the left of the *second* line that inserts **Re: (Selection.TypeText Text:="Re:"**, about eight lines down), drag to select it and the next four lines (through the second **Selection.TypeParagraph** line as shown in Figure 11-7, then press **[Delete]** to delete the lines of code that inserted the *second* **Re** line in the memo header

7. Press **[↓]** six times, press **[End]** to position the insertion point at the end of the line (after **ColorRed**), press **[Backspace]** 12 times to delete **wdColorRed** and the equal sign, type **=** (equal sign), click the **down scroll arrow** in the list that appeared when you typed the equal sign, then double-click **wdColorDarkBlue**

8. Click **File** on the menu bar, click **Close and Return to Microsoft Word**, select everything in the document from the **To** line to the end, press **[Delete]**, click **Tools** on the menu bar, point to **Macro**, click **Macros**, make sure **MemoHeader** is selected in the list, then click **Run** to run the edited macro

9. Click **Tools** on the menu bar, click **Options**, click **Macro Security** on the **Security tab**, *if* **High** was selected before you began this activity, click the **High option button**, *if* **Low** was selected before you began this activity, click the **Low option button**, then click **OK** twice

 close EWMemo10.doc

Figure 11-7: Selecting lines that insert the second Re: line

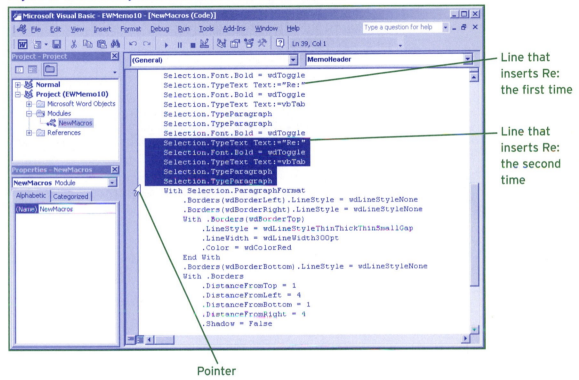

Line that inserts Re: the first time

Line that inserts Re: the second time

Pointer

extra!

Understanding the Visual Basic Editor

The Code window on the right side of the Visual Basic Editor window contains the macro program code. The lines of code are called programming **statements**. Statements that provide explanatory text but do not execute are called **comments**; comments are preceded by a quotation mark. A macro is a **subroutine**, a series of statements that executes a specific task. It begins with the keyword **Sub**, the macro name, and an empty set of parentheses and ends with the keywords **End Sub**. **Keywords** are words that have a specific meaning in Visual Basic. A macro can be composed of program statements and subroutines that contain their own programming statements. The other windows in the Visual Basic Editor window are the Project Explorer window at the top left, which contains a list of the current macro projects, and the Properties window at the bottom left, which lists the properties by macro name and category. If these windows are closed, you can open them by clicking the appropriate name on the View menu.

Skill Set 11

Customizing Word

Customize Menus and Toolbars

Create Menus

You can create a custom menu that contains commands that you use often. Custom menus can be added to a toolbar or to the menu bar. To create a new, custom menu, you open the Customize dialog box and click New Menu on the Toolbars tab. You can store a custom menu in the current document or template.

Activity Steps

1. Open a new, blank document, click **Tools** on the menu bar, click **Customize** to open the Customize dialog box, click the **Commands tab**, click the **Save in list arrow**, then click the **document name** of the new document (for example, **Document1**) so that your customizations are saved only in the current document

2. Scroll down to the bottom of the Categories list, click **New Menu**, then drag the **New Menu command** from the Commands list to the menu bar and position it to the right of the Help menu on the menu bar, as shown by the dark I-beam indicator

3. Scroll back to the top of the Categories list, click **Edit**, then scroll down the Commands list until you can see the **Go To command**

4. Drag the **Go To command** on top of New Menu on the menu bar so that a small box appears below New Menu, then release the mouse button when the dark I-beam indicator is in the box, as shown in Figure 11-8

5. Scroll down the Commands list so that you can see the next four **Go To commands**, drag the **Go To Next Page command** on top of New Menu on the menu bar, then drag down until the dark horizontal line indicates that the command will be positioned below the **Go To command**

6. Drag the **Go To Previous Page command** so that it is inserted below the Go To Next Page command on the New Menu

7. Click **New Menu** on the menu bar, click **Modify Selection** in the Customize dialog box, select all of the text in the Name box on the pop-up menu, then type **Go To Menu**
   See Figure 11-9.

8. Click anywhere in the Customize dialog box to close the pop-up menu and rename the new menu you added, click **Close**, click **Go To Menu** on the menu bar, click **Go To** to open the Go To tab in the Find and Replace dialog box, then click **Close**

 close file

To delete a custom menu, open the Customize dialog box, then drag the menu name off of the menu bar or toolbar where it is located.

Figure 11-8: Adding a command to a custom menu

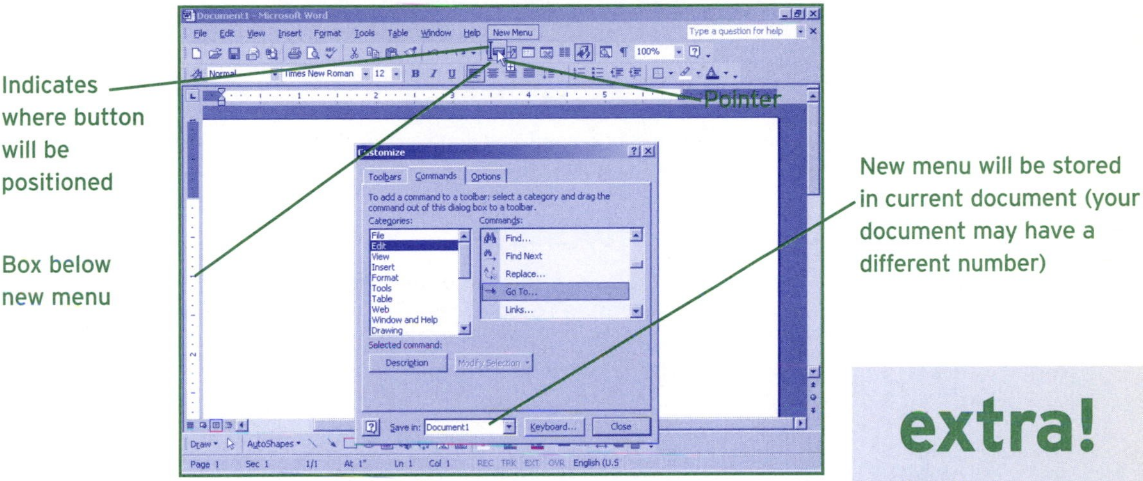

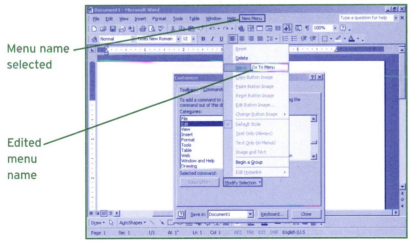

Indicates where button will be positioned

New menu will be stored in current document (your document may have a different number)

Box below new menu

Figure 11-9: Menu name changed in the Modify Selection pop-up menu

Menu name selected

Edited menu name

extra!

Creating a new toolbar

You can also add menus and toolbar buttons to new, customized toolbars that you create. To do this, open the Customize dialog box, click the Toolbars tab, click New to open the New Toolbar dialog box, type a name for your new toolbar, then click OK. Drag the buttons that you want to add to the new toolbar. If you want the toolbar to be available only to the current document, click the Make toolbar available to list arrow in the New Toolbar dialog box, then click the current document name. To delete a custom toolbar, scroll down the list on the Toolbars tab in the Customize dialog box, select the new toolbar, then click Delete.

Customize Menus and Toolbars

Add Buttons to and Remove Buttons from Toolbars

You can add buttons to and remove buttons from toolbars so that you can have one-click access to the commands that you frequently use. To add or remove toolbar buttons, you must open the Customize dialog box. You can store the customizations in the current document or template.

tip

To assign a keyboard shortcut to a command, open the Customize dialog box, click Keyboard, select the command, click in the Press new shortcut key box, then press the shortcut key(s) you want to use.

Activity Steps

1. Open a new, blank document, right-click any toolbar, click **Customize** to open the Customize dialog box, click the **Commands tab**, click the **Save in list arrow**, then click the **document name** of the new document (for example, **Document1**)

2. Click **Edit** in the Categories list, then scroll down the Commands list until you can see the **Find, Find Next**, and **Replace commands**

3. Drag the **Find command** to the right end of the Standard toolbar, then release the mouse button when the dark I-beam indicator is positioned on the toolbar, as shown in Figure 11-10

4. Drag the **Find Next command** to the right of the Find button on the Standard toolbar

5. Drag the **Replace command** to the Standard toolbar so that it is between the Find and Find Next buttons you just added
   See Figure 11-11.

6. Drag the **Replace button** off the Standard toolbar, releasing the mouse button when the button is no longer on any toolbar

7. Click **Close** in the Customize dialog box

   file close file

Figure 11-10: Customize dialog box open

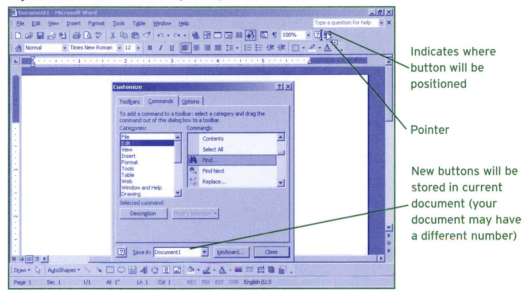

Indicates where button will be positioned

Pointer

New buttons will be stored in current document (your document may have a different number)

Figure 11-11: Command dragged to custom toolbar

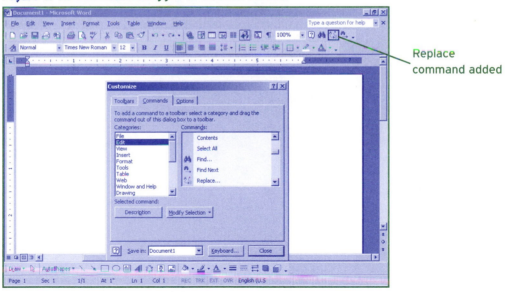

Replace command added

Skill Set 11

Customizing Word

Target Your Skills

1 Open a new, blank document and record a macro named **EarthWiseCoName** that inserts the text and blank paragraphs shown in Figure 11-12. Save the macro in the current document and not in the Normal template. Run the macro, then edit it so that the text is formatted as Lavender instead of Green, and is italicized as well as bold. (*Hint*: Set the value of italic to True.) Re-run the macro in the document below the second company heading.

Figure 11-12

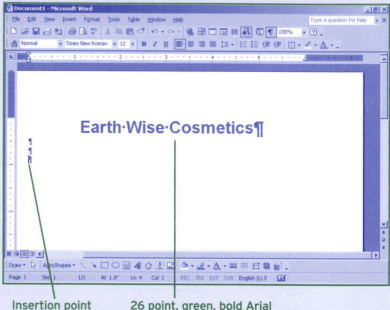

Insertion point   26 point, green, bold Arial

2 Open a new, blank document. Create the custom menu shown in Figure 11-13. Add the Insert Date and Insert Time custom toolbar buttons as shown. All of the menu commands and the two toolbar buttons are in the Insert category. Save your customizations in the current document and not in the Normal template.

Figure 11-13

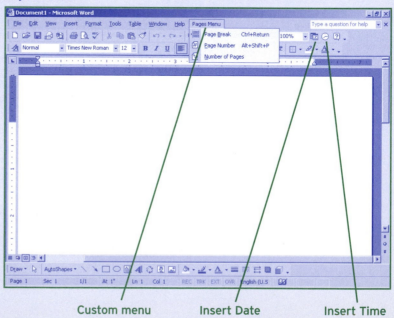

Custom menu   Insert Date   Insert Time

Skill List

1. Track, accept, and reject changes to documents
2. Merge input from several reviewers
3. Insert and modify hyperlinks to other documents and Web pages
4. Create and edit Web documents in Word
5. Create document versions
6. Protect documents
7. Define and modify default file locations for workgroup templates
8. Attach digital signatures to documents

Being able to collaborate with others easily to finalize documents is one of the strengths of Word. Word offers several ways to share documents with others. You can edit documents and see the edits on screen. You can send a document to others to review and have their changes automatically marked so that you can decide whether to incorporate the changes. If you would rather not see the edits on screen, but you still want a record of them, you can save various versions of a document.

If you are sharing a document with others, you can protect it so that changes aren't made to it accidentally. You can also add a digital signature to a document so that anyone you send it to will know that it came from you and that it hasn't changed since you created it. You can also change the default location for document templates that are shared by a group.

To make it easy to move around in a document or from one document to another, you can add hyperlinks to your document that allow you to jump to another location. You can also add hyperlinks to jump to a Web page on the World Wide Web.

Word makes it easy to create a Web page using the Web Page Wizard. Once you have created a Web page, you can edit it as easily as any Word document.

Track, Accept, and Reject Changes to Documents
Track Changes

You can see edits you make to a document on the screen when you use the Track Changes command. When Tracking Changes is turned on, text you add is in another color and underlined; text you cut or delete appears in a balloon to the right of the text in the same color as the insertions in Print layout view (the default), or with a line through it in Normal view. If you share a document with others, each person's changes are tracked in a different color.

Activity Steps

 open GCBrochure08.doc

1. Click **Tools** on the menu bar, click **Track Changes** to turn on tracking and open the Reviewing toolbar, then click the **Show/Hide ¶ button** ¶ to display paragraph marks, if necessary

2. Select the text **We at Gulf Coast Taxi recognize that the** in the first paragraph, type **Because**, then press the **[Spacebar]** if necessary to insert a space between **Because** and **seniors**
   See Figure 12-1.

3. Click immediately after the word **needs** at the end of the first sentence, press **[Delete]** to delete the period, type **,** (a comma), press **[→]**, press **[Delete]**, then type **w**

4. Scroll down and select the entire **Details line**, then press **[Delete]**

5. Press **[←]** to position the insertion point immediately before the paragraph mark at the end of the first paragraph, press **[Delete]**, click immediately before **We** at the beginning of the last sentence in the combined first paragraph, then press **[Enter]**

6. Select the **three bulleted list items**, then click the **Bold button** B

7. Position the insertion point over the bottom edit balloon to see the registered user's name and the current date appear in a ScreenTip, along with a brief description of the change
   See Figure 12-2.

8. Click the **Track Changes button** on the Reviewing toolbar to turn tracking off, right-click any toolbar, click **Reviewing** to close the Reviewing toolbar, then click the **Show/Hide ¶ button** ¶ to hide paragraph marks

 close GCBrochure08.doc

tip

Click the Reviewing Pane button on the Reviewing toolbar to see the changes in a pane at the bottom of the screen in addition to in the document and in the edit balloons.

Figure 12-1: Tracked change

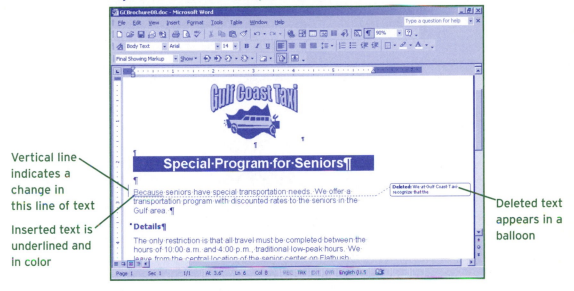

Vertical line indicates a change in this line of text

Inserted text is underlined and in color

Deleted text appears in a balloon

Figure 12-2: ScreenTip identifying tracked change

Selected Track Changes button indicates Track Changes feature is active

Registered user's name and the current date will appear on your screen

Bold TRK indicates Track Changes is turned on

Skill Set 12

Workgroup Collaboration

Track, Accept, and Reject Changes to Documents
Review Changes

When you work with a document that contains edits made with Track Changes turned on, you can see all of the changes that were made to the document. If you position the pointer over a change, a ScreenTip appears identifying the reviewer who made the change, the date and time the change was made, and the type of change that was made (for example, a formatting change, an insertion, or a deletion). You can choose to display changes by only selected reviewers, only insertions and deletions, or only comments.

Activity Steps

 open GCBrochure09.doc

1. Click **View** on the menu bar, point to **Toolbars**, then click **Reviewing** to display the Reviewing toolbar, if necessary

2. Click the **Next button** on the Reviewing toolbar to jump to the first change made in the document, then position the pointer over the highlighted text to see the reviewer's name, the date the change was made, and a description of the change

3. Click the **Show button** on the Reviewing toolbar, point to **Reviewers**, notice that the registered user's name is listed as a reviewer, then click **Jean Hanson** to hide all of the changes made by that reviewer

4. Click the **Next button** to jump to the next displayed change in the document, then position the pointer over the balloon to see that Billy Bob Grantham made the change
   See Figure 12-3.

5. Click the **Show button** on the Reviewing toolbar, point to **Reviewers**, then click **All Reviewers** to display changes by all the reviewers again

6. Click the **Show button** on the Reviewing toolbar, then click **Formatting** to hide all formatting changes

7. Scroll down so you can see the comment, click the **Show button** on the Reviewing toolbar, then click **Comments** to hide all comments, leaving only insertions and deletions displayed
   See Figure 12-4.

8. Right-click any toolbar, then click **Reviewing** to close the Reviewing toolbar

 close GCBrochure09.doc

tip

To see the original document with all the changes (including insertions) noted in edit balloons, click the Display for Review list arrow on the Reviewing toolbar, then click Original Showing Markup.

Figure 12-3: One reviewer's changes hidden

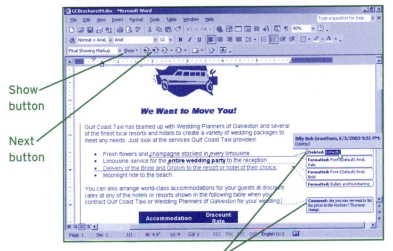

Show button

Next button

Only changes and comments made by Billy Bob Grantham are displayed

Figure 12-4: All changes hidden except insertions and deletions

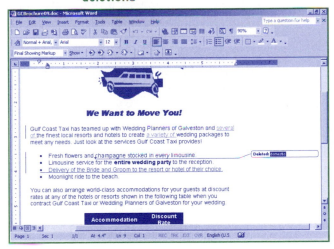

extra!

Changing options for the Track Changes command

To modify how changes are displayed on screen, click the Show button on the Reviewing toolbar, then click Options to open the Track Changes dialog box. You can click the Color list arrow to assign a color to mark changes in the document, rather than having Word assign a different color to each reviewer. Click the Insertions and the Formatting list arrows to change the way that insertions and formatting changes are displayed. You can choose whether to use balloons, how large the balloons should be, whether to print in landscape with the balloons to the side, or whether to keep portrait orientation if the document is in portrait. You can customize the appearance of the balloons by selecting options in the Balloons section in the dialog box. Finally, you can decide whether to mark all changes by adding a line to the left or right margin and what color that line will be.

Skill Set 12
Workgroup Collaboration

Track, Accept, and Reject Changes to Documents
Respond to Changes

After you review a tracked change, you can decide whether to accept it and incorporate it into the document, reject it and delete the suggested insertion, or re-insert the suggested deletion. You can also accept or reject all of the changes in a document at once. Finally, if the document contains any comments, usually you want to delete them before you finalize the document.

Activity Steps

 open GCBrochure10.doc

1. Right-click any toolbar, then click **Reviewing** to open the Reviewing toolbar, if necessary

2. Click the **Next button** on the Reviewing toolbar to highlight the first change in the document, the insertion of the text **several of**

3. Click the **Reject Change/Delete Comment button** on the Reviewing toolbar to reject this change, then click the **Next button**

4. Click the **Accept Change button** on the Reviewing toolbar to accept the insertion of **a variety of**, then click the **Next button** to highlight the next change
See Figure 12-5.

5. Click the **Accept Change button** to accept the deletion of the word **domestic**, click the **Next button**, then click the **Accept Change button** to accept the formatting change

6. Click the **Next button**, click the **Show/Hide ¶ button** to display paragraph marks if necessary, then press [**←**]
See Figure 12-6.

7. Click the **Accept Change button** to accept the insertion of a new paragraph, click the **Next button**, then click the **Reject Change/Delete Comment button** to delete the comment

8. Scroll to the bottom of the page, click the **Accept Change list arrow**, click **Accept All Changes in Document** to accept the rest of the suggested changes, click the **Show/Hide ¶ button** to hide paragraph marks, right-click any toolbar, then click **Reviewing** to close the Reviewing toolbar

 close GCBrochure10.doc

If you track changes and add comments to a document and then save it as a Web page without accepting or rejecting the changes or deleting the comments, the tracked changes and comments will appear on the Web page.

Figure 12-5: Suggested deletion highlighted in balloon

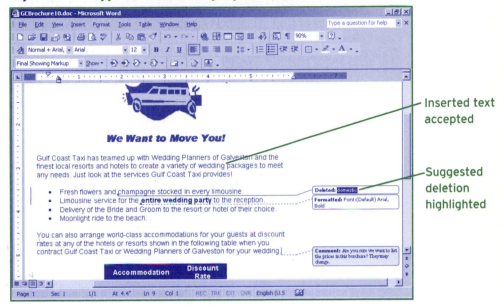

Inserted text accepted

Suggested deletion highlighted

Figure 12-6: Suggested insertion of new paragraph

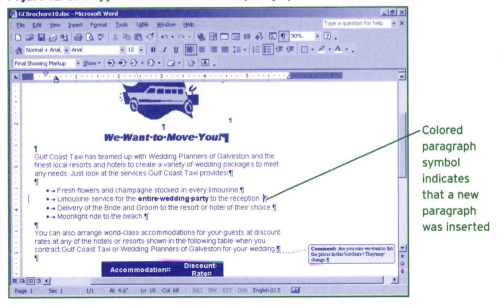

Colored paragraph symbol indicates that a new paragraph was inserted

Skill Set 12

Workgroup Collaboration

Merge Input from Several Reviewers
Distribute Documents for Review via E-mail

To send a document for review, you use the Send To Mail Recipient (for Review) command. When the reviewer receives the message and opens the document, tracking changes is turned on, and the Reply with Changes button appears on the Reviewing toolbar. The reviewer clicks the Reply with Changes button to send the reviewed document back to you.

Note: We assume you are using Microsoft Outlook as your e-mail program.

Activity Steps

 open GCReport03.doc

1. Make sure you are connected to the Internet, click **File** on the menu bar, point to **Send To**, then click **Mail Recipient (for Review)** *See Figure 12-7*.

2. Type your e-mail address in the **To box**, then click the **Send button** 🖂 to send the message

3. Click the **Start button** 🏁 Start on the taskbar, point to **Programs**, then click **Microsoft Outlook**

4. If the message is in the Outbox, click the **Send/Receive button** 📧 Send/Receive to send the message; then, if the message you sent is not yet in your Inbox, click the **Send/Receive button** 📧 Send/Receive again to check for and retrieve the messages

5. Click **Outlook Today** in the Outlook Shortcuts bar, click the **Inbox link** under Messages on the right, then double-click the message **Please review 'GCReport03'**

6. Double-click **GCReport03.doc** in the Attachments line, if a dialog box opens asking if you want to open the document or save it, click the **Open it option button**, click **OK**, then click **No** in the dialog box asking if you want to merge changes *See Figure 12-8*.

7. Right-click the **Outlook program button** on the taskbar, click **Close**, then click **No** if asked if you want to save changes

8. Click **Window** on the menu bar, click **GCReport03.doc**, right-click any toolbar, click **Reviewing** to display the Reviewing toolbar if necessary, click the **End Review button** End Review... on the Reviewing toolbar, click **Yes** in the dialog box to end the reviewing cycle, then close the Reviewing toolbar, if necessary

 close GCReport03.doc
GCReport031.doc

Step 1
If the document is stored in a location on a network, such as on a company intranet, the e-mail message will contain a link to the file rather than including it as an attachment.

Figure 12-7: E-mail message in Outlook with document attached

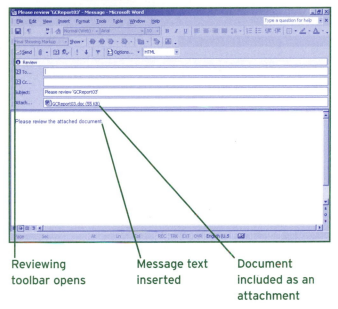

Reviewing toolbar opens

Message text inserted

Document included as an attachment

Figure 12-8: Reviewed document opened on sender's computer

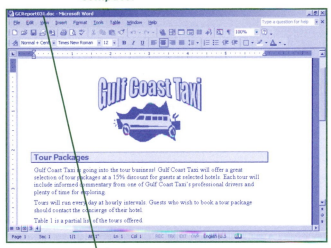

Number added to the end of the filename to indicate that it is a temporary file (may be a different number on your screen)

extra!

Using the other Send To commands

If you click Mail Recipient on the Send To sub menu (which is the same as clicking the E-mail button), the e-mail message header opens at the top of the document, and the entire document is sent as the body of the e-mail rather than as an attachment. Clicking Mail Recipient (as Attachment) sends the document as an attach-ment, but the Track Changes command is not turned on. If you click Routing Recipient, the Routing Slip dialog box opens with the One after another option button selected by default. You can then select several e-mail addresses to send the document to. When you click Route, the docu-ment is sent as an attachment to the first person on the list with the Track Changes com-mand turned on. When the reviewer is finished making changes, he or she clicks File on the menu bar, points to Send To, then clicks Next Routing Recipient and so on until the last recipient returns the document to you.

Skill Set 12
Workgroup Collaboration

Merge Input from Several Reviewers
Merge Revisions

If you sent a document for review and you receive the document back from several reviewers, you can merge all of the changes and comments into one document. To do this, you open the edited document, click the Compare and Merge Documents command, then select the original document. You can click the Merge list arrow in the Compare and Merge Documents dialog box to choose from three merge options: Merge; Merge into current document; and Merge into new document. If you click Merge, the changes are merged into the original document. Changes will be made whether or not the reviewer turned on Track Changes.

If reviewer changes conflict with one another, you may see a confusing markup on screen. Try clicking the Display for Review list arrow, then click Original Showing Markup; or click the Show button, point to Reviewers, and click each reviewer name to hide all reviewer comments except for the one whose change you want to see.

Activity Steps

 open GCReport04BG.doc

1. Scroll down to see the changes made in the document, then position the pointer over any change to see that Billy Bob Grantham made these changes

2. Click **Tools** on the menu bar, then click **Compare and Merge Documents** to open the Compare and Merge Documents dialog box

3. Navigate to the location where your project files are stored, click **GCReport04.doc** (the original document), then click **Merge** to merge the changes made in GCReport04BG into GCReport04
   See Figure 12-9.

4. Click the **Open button** 🖝, navigate to the location where your project files are stored, click **GCReport04JH.doc**, click **Open**, then scroll down and position the pointer over the inserted sentence under Table 1 to see that Jean Hanson made the change in this file

5. Click **Tools** on the menu bar, click **Compare and Merge Documents**, click **GCReport04.doc** (the original document), then click **Merge** to merge the changes into GCReport04

6. Scroll down and position the pointer to see that Jean Hanson's change was inserted

7. Open the project file **GCReport04SW**, position the pointer over the balloon to see that Scott West made the changes in this document, then merge the changes into the original document **GCReport04**
   See Figure 12-10.

8. Right-click any toolbar, then click **Reviewing** to close the Reviewing toolbar

 close GCReport04.doc   GCReport04JH.doc
          GCReport04SW.doc   GCReport04BG.doc

Figure 12-9: Tracked changes merged into original document

Current document is original document

Reviewing toolbar opened automatically

Edited document is still open

Figure 12-10: Tracked changes from three documents merged into original document

One of the changes made in Billy Bob Grantham's file

Change made in Jean Hanson's file

All three edited files still open

Changes made in Scott West's file

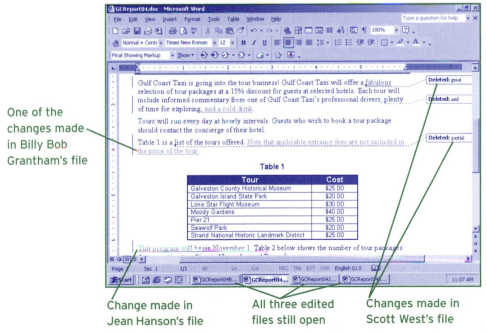

Skill Set 12
Workgroup Collaboration

Insert and Modify Hyperlinks to Other Documents and Web Pages
Insert Hyperlinks to Another Place in the Document or to Another Document

You can insert hyperlinks into your documents. A **hyperlink**, or **link**, is specially formatted text that, when clicked, moves you to another location in the document or opens another document or a Web page. To insert a link to another place in the current document or to another document, you select the text that you want to format as a link, then click the Insert Hyperlink button . Hyperlinks are formatted as blue underlined text. After you click a hyperlink, it changes to a **followed hyperlink**, and its color changes to purple.

Activity Steps

 open GCMemo11.doc

1. Scroll down and select the third bulleted item in the list, then click the **Insert Hyperlink button** to open the Insert Hyperlink dialog box

2. Click **Place in This Document** under Link to on the left, then click **Young Driver Training Classes** in the Select a place in this document list
See Figure 12-11.

3. Click **OK**, position the pointer over the newly inserted hyperlink, press and hold [Ctrl], then click to jump to the Young Driver Training Classes heading

4. Select the text **Young Driver Training Class Announcement** in the last paragraph, then click the **Insert Hyperlink button**

5. Click **Existing File or Web Page** under Link to on the left, click the Look in list arrow and navigate to the location where your project files are stored, click **GCAnnouncement06.doc** in the list, then click **OK**

6. Position the pointer over the newly inserted hyperlink, press and hold [Ctrl], then click to open and jump to the file **GCAnnouncement06** and open the Web toolbar
See Figure 12-12.

7. Click the **Back button** on the Web toolbar to return to the location of the hyperlink

8. Click **Window** on the menu bar, click **GCAnnouncement06.doc**, click the **Close button** in the title bar, if necessary click **No** in the dialog box that opens asking if you want to save changes, right-click any toolbar, then click **Web** to close the Web toolbar

 close GCMemo11.doc

To change the ScreenTip associated with a hyperlink, click ScreenTip in the Insert Hyperlink or in the Edit Hyperlink dialog box, then type the text you want to add as a ScreenTip.

Figure 12-11: Insert Hyperlink dialog box

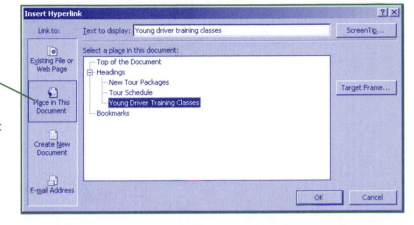

Click to list headings and bookmarks in this document

Figure 12-12: Document and Web toolbar open after hyperlink is clicked

Back button

Web toolbar (address shown on your screen may differ)

Young Driver Training Classes

The Young Drivers of Texas organization will be holding a special, three-day, introductory course for the young drivers of Galveston Island. The children, nieces, and nephews of taxi drivers may attend the course for free!

Here's the course schedule:

Date	Time
October 11	7:00 p.m.
October 15	9:00 a.m.
October 22	9:00 a.m.

Original document still open

Skill Set 12

Workgroup Collaboration

Insert and Modify Hyperlinks to Other Documents and Web Pages

Insert Hyperlinks to Web Pages

You can insert hyperlinks to any location on an intranet or the Internet. In addition, Word recognizes URLs and e-mail addresses when you type them, so that when you press the [Spacebar] or [Enter], Word formats the text automatically as a hyperlink.

Note: In this activity, you are directed to go to two specific locations on the World Wide Web. These locations were active Web sites at the time of publication. If they are no longer active, link to any currently active Web site.

Step 1
To turn off automatic formatting of hyperlinks, click AutoCorrect Options on the Tools menu, click the AutoFormat As You Type tab, then click the Internet and network paths with hyperlinks check box to deselect it.

Activity Steps

 open GCAnnouncement07.doc

1. Click immediately before the word **if** in the last sentence in the paragraph below the table, type **www.mapquest.com**, then press the **[Spacebar]** to convert the text to a hyperlink

2. Make sure you are connected to the Internet, press and hold **[Ctrl]**, then click the newly inserted hyperlink to open your browser and jump to the MapQuest Web page

3. Click the **Back button** ⬅ Back to jump back to the Word document and close the browser window

4. Select the text **Drive Home Safe Web site** in the last sentence in the document, then click the **Insert Hyperlink button** 🔗 to open the Insert Hyperlink dialog box

5. Click **Existing File or Web Page** under Link to on the left, then click the **Browse the Web button** 🔍 to open your Web browser

6. Click in the Address or Location box, type **drivehomesafe.com**, press **[Enter]** to jump to that Web site, then click **Word program button** on the taskbar to switch back to your document and automatically insert the address of the current Web page in the Address box in the Insert Hyperlink dialog box
See Figure 12-13.

7. Click **OK**

8. Press and hold **[Ctrl]**, click the newly inserted hyperlink to open a new browser window displaying the Web page, click the **Back button** ⬅ Back to jump back to the Word document, click the **browser window program button** on the taskbar, click the **Close button** ❎ in the title bar to switch back to the Word document, right-click any toolbar, then click **Web** to close the Web toolbar
See Figure 12-14.

 close GCAnnouncement07.doc

Figure 12-13: Inserting a hyperlink to a Web page

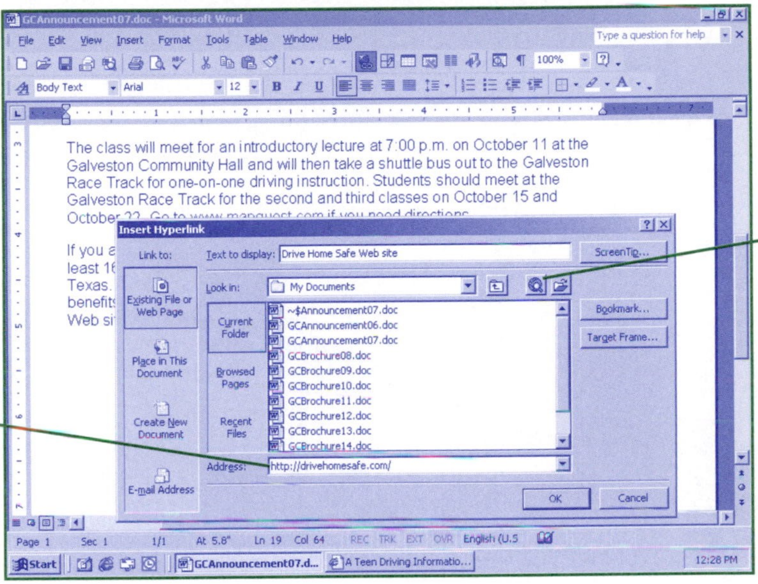

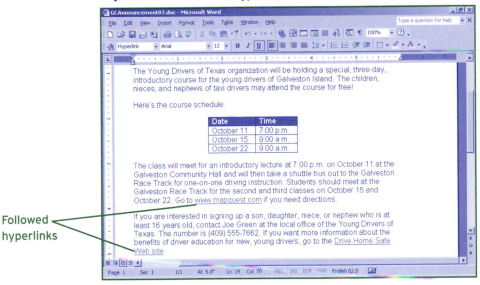

Browse the Web button

Address of hyperlink destination

Figure 12-14: Followed hyperlinks in a document

Followed hyperlinks

Insert and Modify Hyperlinks to Other Documents and Web Pages
Modify hyperlinks

Once you've inserted a hyperlink, you can modify it. You can change the location of the link, the text displayed, or the ScreenTip displayed when you point to the link, or you can remove the link formatting altogether.

Activity Steps

 open GCMemo12.doc

1. Right-click any toolbar, click **Web** to open the Web toolbar, scroll down so you can see the bulleted list, press and hold **[Ctrl]**, then click the **Young driver training classes hyperlink** in the third bullet

2. Click the **Back button** ⬅ on the Web toolbar to return to the location of the hyperlink, right-click the **Young driver training classes hyperlink** in the third bullet, then click **Edit Hyperlink** on the shortcut menu to open the Edit Hyperlink dialog box and notice that the address of the hyperlink is to the file GCAnnouncement06.doc
See Figure 12-15.

3. Click **Create New Document** under Link to on the left, click **Change** to open the Create New Document dialog box, type **New Linked Document** in the File name box, click the **Save as type list arrow**, click **Documents (*.doc)**, navigate to the location where you are saving your project files, then click **OK**

4. Click the **Edit the new document later option button**, then click **OK**

5. Press and hold **[Ctrl]**, click the **Young driver training classes hyperlink** in the third bullet to open and jump to the new document file **New Linked Document**
See Figure 12-16.

6. Click the **Back button** ⬅ on the Web toolbar to return to the location of the hyperlink

7. Right-click the **Tour schedules hyperlink** in the second bullet, then click **Remove Hyperlink** on the shortcut menu to remove the hyperlink

8. Click **View** on the menu bar, point to **Toolbars**, then click **Web** to close the Web toolbar

 close GCMemo12.doc
New Linked Document.doc
GCAnnouncement06.doc

tip

Step 3
If you don't need to change the folder in which you are storing the new document you are creating, simply type the filename—with a filename extension—of the new document in the Name of new document box in the Insert Hyperlink or in the Edit Hyperlink dialog box.

Figure 12-15: Edit Hyperlink dialog box

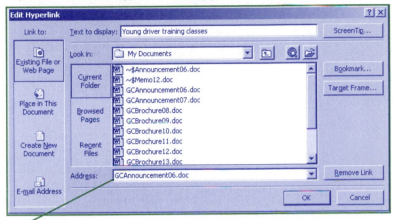

Hyperlink address
links to another file

Figure 12-16: New linked document open

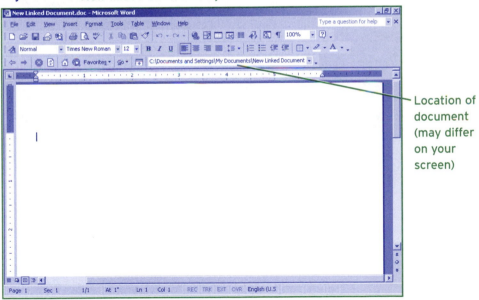

Location of
document
(may differ
on your
screen)

Skill Set 12
Workgroup Collaboration

Create and Edit Web Documents in Word
Create a Web Site in Word

When you create a Web site using a Web page template, you create a Web site with one page, no **theme** (a background design and set of colors for headings and other text) and no **frames** (a section of a Web page that acts as if it were a different window or pane on the screen). When you use the Web Page Wizard, the default is to create a Web site with a home page and two blank pages, along with a theme and a frame that contains links to jump to each page in the Web site.

Activity Steps

1. Click **File** on the menu bar, click **New** to open the New Document task pane, click the **General Templates link** in the task pane to open the Templates dialog box, click the **Web Pages tab**, click the **Web Page Wizard icon**, then click **OK**

2. Click **Next** to move to the Title and Location screen in the Web Page Wizard, type **Gulf Coast Taxi** in the Web site title box, click **Browse**, navigate to the location where you are saving your project files, click the **Create New Folder button** in the toolbar at the top of the Copy dialog box, type **Gulf Coast Taxi Web site**, click **OK**, then click **Open**
   See Figure 12-17.

3. Click **Next** to go to the Navigation screen, then make sure the **Vertical frame option button** is selected

4. Click **Next** to move to the Add Pages screen, click **Add Existing File**, navigate to the location where your project files are stored, click **GCBrochure11.htm**, then click **Open**

5. Click **Next** to move to the Organize Pages screen, make sure **GCBrochure11** is selected in the list, then click **Move Up** twice

6. Click **Next** to go to the Visual Theme screen, click **Browse Themes**, scroll down and click **Sumi Painting** in the Choose a Theme list, click **OK**, click **Next**, then click **Finish** to open a document in Web Layout view with the filename **default** and to open the Frames toolbar

7. Click **File** on the menu bar, click **Save As**, type **Gulf Coast Taxi Web site** in the File name box, note that **Web Page** is listed in the Save as type box, then click **Save**
   See Figure 12-18.

8. Click the **Close button** on the Frames toolbar to close it

 **close Gulf Coast Taxi Web site.htm**

Step 7
The file default.htm still exists in the folder where your Web page is stored.

Figure 12-17: Title and Location screen in the Web Page Wizard

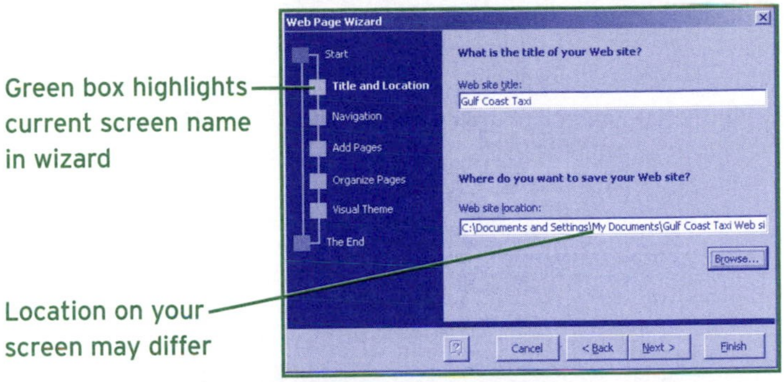

Green box highlights current screen name in wizard

Location on your screen may differ

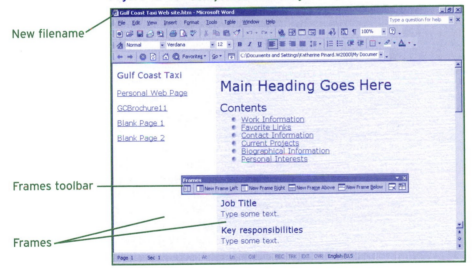

Figure 12-18: Completed Web Page

New filename

Frames toolbar

Frames

extra!

Understanding the files created by the Web Page Wizard

Each page in a Web site that you created using the Web Page Wizard is a separate HTML file. In this activity, you created the files default.htm, the original file for the entire Web site; Gulf Coast Taxi Web Site.htm, the renamed file for the entire Web site; Personal Web Page.htm, the default filename for the home page (the first page) of the Web site; Blank Page 1.htm, Blank Page 2.htm, and GCBrochure11.htm, the additional pages in the Web site that you added in the Add Pages screen in the Wizard; and TOCFrame.htm, the filename for the vertical frame that contains links to all the pages in the site. Each HTML file for an individual Web page has an associated folder with the same name as the file; for example, there is a folder named GCBrochure11_files. If you delete the HTML file, the associated folder is deleted automatically. If you copy the HTML file to a new location, you must also copy the associated folder.

Create and Edit Web Documents in Word
Open and Edit Web Documents in Word

You can open a Web site in Word and edit it. Be aware of unexpected changes when you edit a Web site. Depending on how the Web site was created, a new document window may open when you click a link to a page, or edits may result in hyperlink formatting being removed so that the link no longer works.

Activity Steps

1. Click the **Open button** to open the Open dialog box, navigate to the location where your project files are stored, make sure the Files of type box lists **All Word Documents**, double-click the **GCWebSite01 folder**, click **GCWebSite01.htm**, then click **Open**

2. Select the text **Main Heading Goes Here**, type **Gulf Coast Taxi**, press **[Enter]**, click the **Italic button** *I*, then type **We Want to Move You!**

3. Click anywhere in the yellow frame on the left to make it the active frame, right-click the **Personal Web Page link**, click **Select Hyperlink** on the shortcut menu, then type **Home**

4. Press and hold **[Ctrl]**, click the **Wedding link**, which opens the wedding package brochure Web page in a new document
   See Figure 12-19.

5. Click anywhere in the yellow frame on the left to make it the active frame, right-click the **Wedding link**, click **Select Hyperlink** on the shortcut menu, type **WeddingPackageInformation** (without any spaces), press **[←]** as many times as necessary to position the insertion point between the **e** in **Package** and the **I** in **Information**, press the **[Spacebar]**, then insert a space between the **g** in **Wedding** and the **P** in **Package**

6. Click **Format** on the menu bar, point to **Frames**, click **Frame Properties** to open the Frame Properties dialog box, click the **Borders tab**, click the **Show all frame borders option button**, click the **Show scrollbars in browser list arrow**, click **Always**, then click **OK**
   See Figure 12-20.

7. Press and hold **[Ctrl]**, click the **Home link**, click the **Close button** ⊠ in the title bar to close the second document window (with **:2** after the filename in the title bar), click **No** when asked if you want to save changes, right-click any toolbar, then click **Web** to close the Web toolbar
   To save your changes, you need to click the Save button, or to rename the file, you need to click Save As Web Page on the File menu.

 close GCWebSite01.htm

tip

Step 5
If you make a typing mistake or press the [Spacebar] accidentally and the underline that indicates that this text is a hyperlink disappears, click the Undo button, then type the new link name again.

Figure 12-19: New document window opened after clicking link

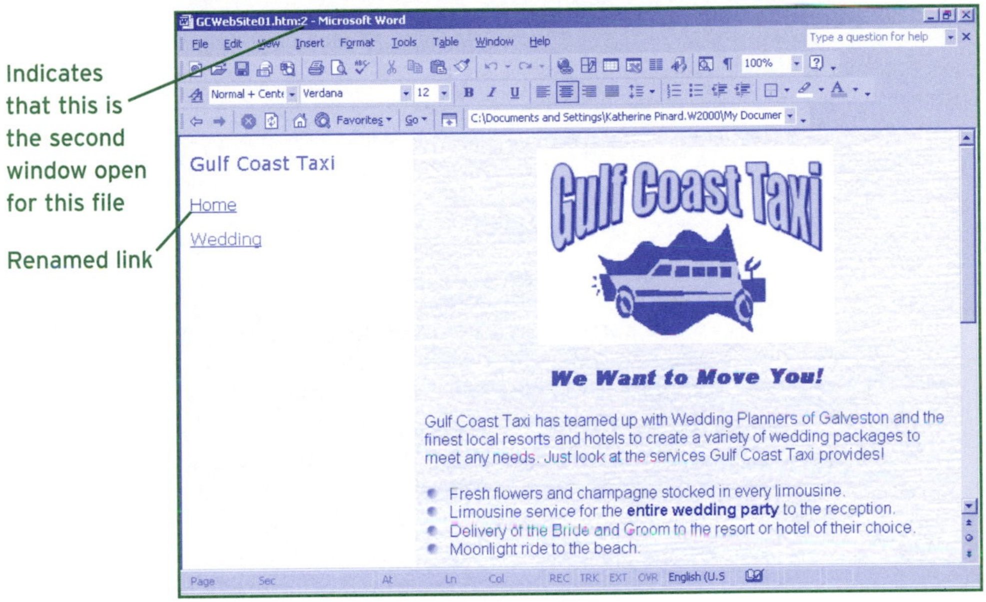

Indicates that this is the second window open for this file

Renamed link

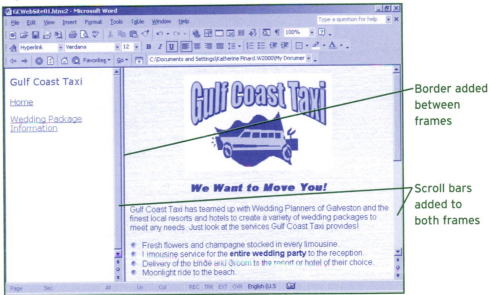

Figure 12-20: Web page with frame borders and scroll bars displayed

Border added between frames

Scroll bars added to both frames

Skill Set 12
Workgroup Collaboration

Create and Edit Web Documents in Word
Save Word Documents to the Web

To post your Web site on the World Wide Web, you need permission from the server's owner to copy your files to a Web server and the exact address of a folder on that server. Then copy the files that are connected to the Web page by hyperlinks, and edit the hyperlinks so that they link to the new locations.

Note: We assume you are using Internet Explorer as your Web browser.

Activity Steps

 open GCWebSite02.htm

1. Make sure that you are connected to the Internet, click **File** on the menu bar, click **Save as Web Page** to open the Save As dialog box, then click **My Network Places** under Save in on the left *See Figure 12-21*.

2. If a Web server is listed in the dialog box, and if you have permission to post files to it, double-click it, then skip to Step 5

3. If you have permission to post to a Web server but it is not listed in the dialog box, double-click **Add Network Place** to start the Add Network Place Wizard, make sure the **Create a shortcut to an existing Network Place option button** is selected, click **Next**, type the **URL** of the server in the Location box, press **[Tab]**, type a shortcut name for the server, click **Finish**, then skip to Step 5 *The folder should now be listed in the Save in box.*

4. If you do not have permission to save files to a Web server, navigate to the location where you are saving your files

5. Select all of the text in the File name box, type **My Saved Web Site**, then click **Save**

6. Click the **Start button** on the taskbar, point to **Programs**, then click **Internet Explorer**

7. Click **File** on the menu bar, click **Open**, click **Browse**, navigate to the location on the Web server where you saved your Web site or to the location where you are saving your files, click **My Saved Web Site.htm**, click **Open**, then click **OK** *See Figure 12-22*. The Wedding Package Information hyperlink is linked to the Wedding.htm file in the folder where the file GCWebSite02.htm is stored. To copy the linked file, right-click the hyperlink, click Edit Hyperlink, then navigate to the file's new location.

8. Click the **Close button** ☒ in the Internet Explorer program window

 close My Saved Web Site.htm

If you use the Web Page Wizard to create a Web site, when you click Browse in the Title and Location screen, you can click My Network Places in the Copy dialog box and select a location on a Web server.

Figure 12-21: Save As dialog box after clicking My Network Places

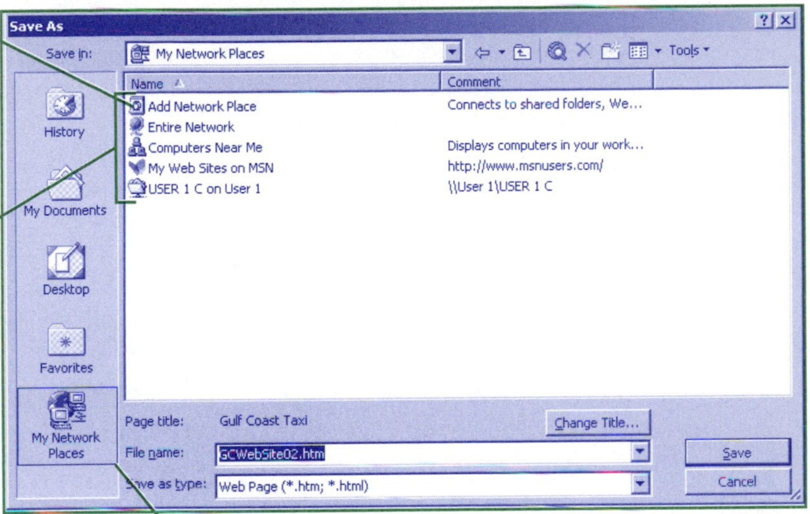

Click to add the address for a Web server to the Save in list

List of folders and drives available on the network (your list will differ)

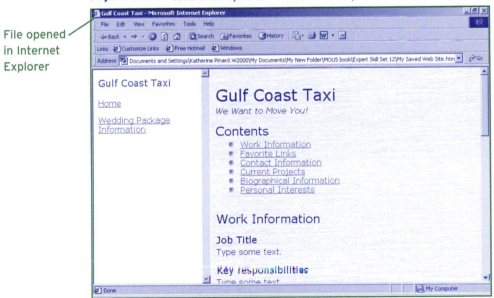

Click to display the list of folders and drives available on your network

Figure 12-22: Web site opened in Internet Explorer

File opened in Internet Explorer

Create Document Versions

If you don't want to use the Track Changes command but you still want to save a record of the changes you make to a document, you can save versions of your document. A **version** is the document saved at some point during its creation. When you are editing and you reach a point at which you would like to save the document, you use the Versions command on the File menu. Versions of a document are saved in the same file as the document file.

Activity Steps

 open GCBrochure12.doc

1. Click **File** on the menu bar, then click **Versions** to open the Versions in GCBrochure12.doc dialog box

2. Click **Save Now** to open the Save Version dialog box

3. Type **Original draft** in the Comments on version box
   See Figure 12-23.

You cannot save changes that you make to a document version unless you save that version as a separate document.

4. Click **OK**, select the entire **Details heading line**, press **[Delete]**, click **File** on the menu bar, then click **Versions**
   See Figure 12-24.

5. Click **Save Now**, type **Details heading deleted**, then click **OK**

6. Double-click **Special** in the title line, type **Transportation**, click **File** on the menu bar, click **Versions**, click **Save Now**, type **Title changed**, then click **OK**

7. Click **File** on the menu bar, click **Versions**, then click the last version in the list (with **Original draft** in the Comments column)

8. Click **Open** to open the Original draft version of the document in a new window arranged under the window containing the open document, click **File** on the menu bar of the Original draft version document window, click **Save As**, type **Original Transportation Brochure** in the File name box, navigate to the location where you are saving your project files, then click **Save**
   See Figure 12-25.

 close Original Transportation Brochure.doc
    GCBrochure12.doc

Figure 12-23: Save Version dialog box

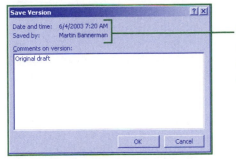

Current date and time and
registered user's name
appears here (information
on your screen will differ)

Figure 12-24: Versions in GCBrochure12.doc dialog box

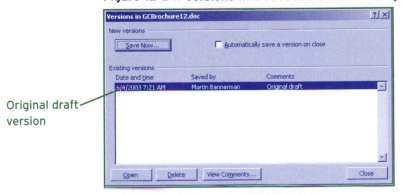

Original draft
version

Figure 12-25: Original draft version open

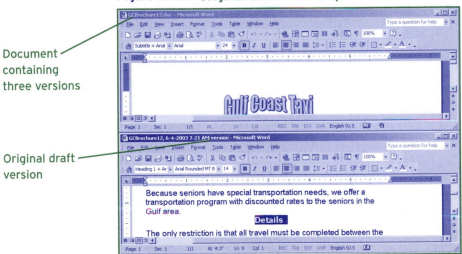

Document
containing
three versions

Original draft
version

Skill Set 12

Workgroup Collaboration

Protect Documents

If you do not want others to make changes to a document, or if you want to be able to see those changes as tracked changes, you can protect the document. For extra security, you can protect it with a password. When you protect a document, you can choose to protect it so that users are allowed to make changes that are tracked with the Track Changes feature; or you can choose to prevent users from making any changes except to insert comments.

Activity Steps

 open GCBrochure13.doc

1. Click **Tools** on the menu bar, then click **Protect Document**

2. Make sure the **Tracked changes option button** is selected, then type **password** in the Password (optional) box
   See Figure 12-26.

3. Click **OK**, type **password** in the Confirm Password dialog box, then click **OK**

4. Select **every day** in the first line in the second paragraph, type **daily**, click **Insert** on the menu bar, click **Comment**, then type **Change this**

5. Click **Tools** on the menu bar, click **Unprotect Document**, type **password** in the Unprotect Document dialog box, then click **OK**

6. Click **Tools** on the menu bar, then click **Protect Document**, type **password** in the Password (optional) box, click the **Comments option button**, click **OK**, type **password**, then click **OK**

7. Select the number **3** in the first paragraph, type **three**, and note that the change is not recorded

8. Click the **New Comment button** on the Reviewing toolbar, type **Change to three**, right-click any toolbar, then click **Reviewing** to close the Reviewing toolbar
   See Figure 12-27.

tip

Another way to protect your document from changes is to click Options on the Tools menu, click the Security tab, then click the Read-only recommended check box to select it.

 close GCBrochure13.doc

Figure 12-26: Protect Document dialog box

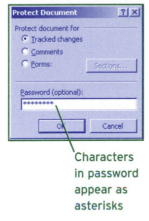

Characters
in password
appear as
asterisks

Figure 12-27: **Protected document with tracked changes and comments**

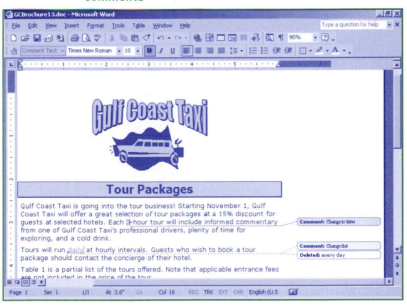

extra!

Using advanced protection options

In addition to the protection options discussed in this activity, you can also make it necessary to use a password to even open a document or to make any changes at all. To do this, click Options on the Tools menu, then click the Security tab. Type a password in the Password to open box to require users to type a password before they can open the document. Type a password in the Password to modify box to require users to enter a password to open the document normally rather than as read-only. When a document is opened as **read-only**, users cannot make changes or insert comments.

Skill Set 12

Workgroup Collaboration

Define and Modify Default File Locations for Workgroup Templates

Define and Modify Default File Locations for Workgroup Templates

If you work on a network and want custom templates to be available to everyone on that network, you can change the default file location for workgroup templates. Basically, when you do this, you add tabs to the Templates dialog box that correspond to folders within the folder or on the drive that you specify.

The default setting is for the location or workgroup templates to be undefined so that only the standard tabs appear in the Templates dialog box. Once you have defined a location for workgroup templates, you cannot change it back to an undefined location; in other words, the change is permanent. You can modify the location, but you cannot reset it to its default undefined location.

WARNING: Do not attempt this on your computer unless you are sure you want to define the default location of workgroup templates permanently. If you are working on a network, do not attempt to do this at all. Ask your network support person for assistance.

To change the default location for workgroup templates and permanently add additional tabs to the Templates dialog box, click Tools on the menu bar, click Options to open the Options dialog box, then click the File Locations tab in the Options dialog box. Next, click Workgroup templates in the File types list. The default is that no location is specified in the Location column on the right; but if you are working on a network, your network administrator may have specified a location. See Figure 12-28.

Click Modify to open the Modify Location dialog box. The folder or drive listed in the Look in box at the top of the dialog box will become the location listed for workgroup templates on the File Locations tab. All folders in this folder or drive will appear as tabs in the Templates dialog box, and any files stored in those folders will appear on each tab. Click Cancel to leave the location of workgroup templates unchanged. For example, if you modify the location to be a folder named Group Templates, and that folder contains folders for the Development Group, the Production Group, and General Office Templates, those three folders will appear as tabs in the Templates dialog box. See Figure 12-29.

Note that if a folder in the new workgroup template location does not contain any documents or templates, it will not appear as a tab in the Templates dialog box.

Figure 12-28: File Locations tab in the Options dialog box

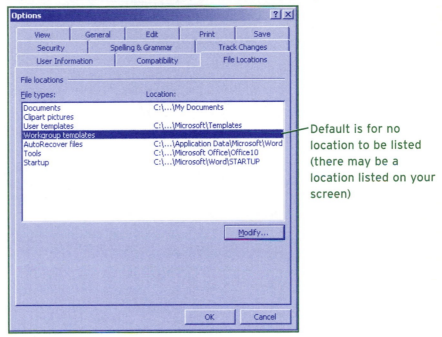

Default is for no location to be listed (there may be a location listed on your screen)

Figure 12-29: Templates dialog box with new tabs

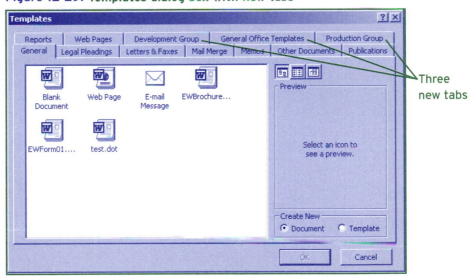

Three new tabs

Skill Set 12
Workgroup Collaboration

Define and Modify Default File Locations for Workgroup Templates
Modify and Re-post HTML Documents

You can open an HTML document in Internet Explorer, and then switch to Word to edit it. Then, you can repost a file or Web site to the Web.

Note: We assume you are using Internet Explorer as your Web browser.

Activity Steps

1. Click the **Start button** on the taskbar, point to **Programs**, then click **Internet Explorer**

2. Click **File** on the menu bar, click **Open**, click **Browse**, navigate to the location where your project files are stored, double-click the **GCWebSite03 folder**, click **GCWebSite03.htm**, then click **Open** *See Figure 12-30.*

3. Click **OK**, click **File** on the menu bar, then click **Edit with Microsoft Word** to open the HTML file in Word

4. Double-click **Work** below the list of links, then type **Company**

5. Make sure that you are connected to the Internet, click **File** on the menu bar, click **Save as Web Page** to open the Save As dialog box, then click **My Network Places** under Save in on the left *See Figure 12-31.*

6. If a Web server is listed in the dialog box, and if you have permission to post files to it, double-click it, then skip to Step 9

7. If you have permission to post to a Web server but it is not listed in the dialog box, double-click **Add Network Place** to start the Add Network Place Wizard, make sure the **Create a shortcut to an existing Network Place option button** is selected, click **Next**, type the **URL** of the server in the Location box, press **[Tab]**, type a shortcut name for the server, click **Finish**, then skip to Step 9

8. If you do not have permission to save files to a Web server, navigate to the location where you are saving your files

9. Select all of the text in the File name box, type **Reposted Web Page**, click **Save**, right-click the **Internet Explorer program button** on the taskbar, then click **Close** on the shortcut menu

 close Reposted Web Page.htm

tip

Step 9
If you have already copied the file Wedding.htm to the location where you saved the Reposted Web Page file, right-click the Wedding Package Information hyperlink, click Edit Hyperlink, then click the Wedding.htm file in the location to which you saved your file.

Figure 12-30: Open dialog box in Internet Explorer

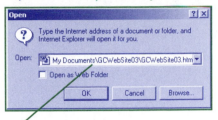

Your path may differ

Figure 12-31: Save As dialog box after clicking My Network Places

Click to add the address for a Web server to the Save in list

List of folders and drives available on the network (your list will differ)

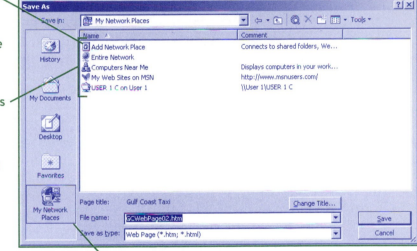

Click to display the list of folders and drives available on your network

Skill Set 12
Workgroup Collaboration

Attach Digital Signatures to Documents
Attach Digital Signatures

You can attach a **digital signature** to a document to verify that you created the document and prove that the file has not been modified since you attached the signature. A **digital certificate** is electronic verification that you actually created the digital signature by ensuring that the digital signature matches a special code in the software that created it. You can purchase a digital certificate from a company that sells them. If you don't have a digital certificate, you can still attach a digital signature to a document, but it will not be authenticated by any outside source, and when you view the certificate, you will see a warning that tells you this. When a document has a digital signature attached to it, **(Signed)** appears in the title bar, and a small red and yellow symbol appears in the status bar.

To remove a digital signature, open the Digital Signature dialog box, click the digital signature in the list, then click Remove.

Activity Steps

 open GCBrochure14.doc

1. Click **File** on the menu bar, click **Save As**, type **Signed Brochure** in the File name box, navigate to the location where you are saving your project files, then click **Save**

2. Click **Tools** on the menu bar, click **Options** to open the Options dialog box, then click the **Security tab**

3. Click **Digital Signatures** to open the Digital Signature dialog box

4. Click **Add** to open the Select Certificate dialog box, then if necessary click **Yes** in the dialog box to continue

5. Make sure the registered user's name is listed and selected, then click **View Certificate**
   See Figure 12-32.

6. Click **OK** to close the Certificate dialog box, then click **OK** to close the Select Certificate dialog box

7. Click **OK** to close the Digital Signature dialog box, click **OK** to close the Options dialog box, then click the **Save button** 🖫 to save the document with the digital signature you just created
   See Figure 12-33.

 close Signed Brochure.doc

Figure 12-32: Certificate dialog box

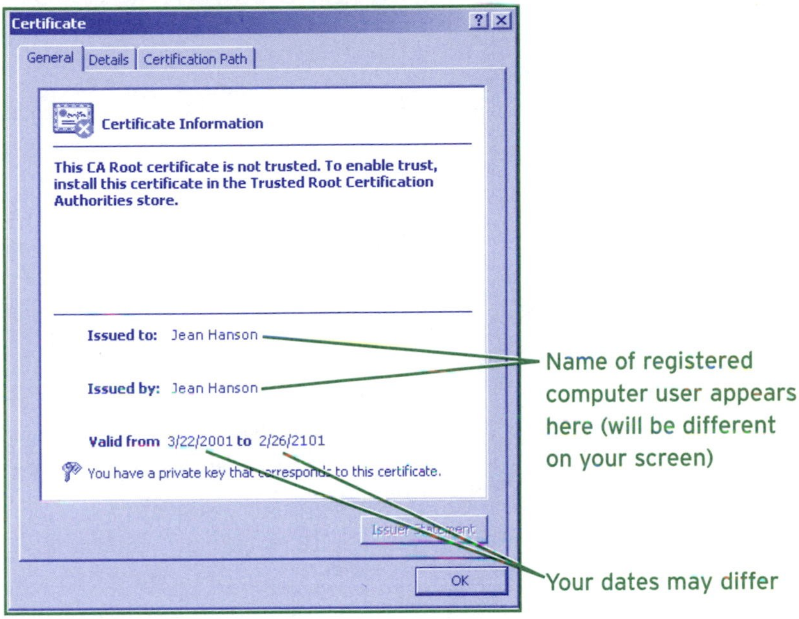

Name of registered computer user appears here (will be different on your screen)

Your dates may differ

Figure 12-33: Digitally signed document

Indicates document has a digital signature

Indicates document has a digital signature

Skill Set 12
Workgroup Collaboration

Attach Digital Signatures to Documents
Use Digital Signatures to Authenticate Documents

If a digital signature is attached to a document, you can open and view the document to verify that it is from someone you trust. You can also view the digital certificate that accompanies it.

Activity Steps

 open GCBrochure15.doc

1. Note in the title and status bars that the project file GCBrochure15 is digitally signed, click **Tools** on the menu bar, click **Options**, click the **Security tab**, then click **Digital Signatures**

2. Make sure the certificate from **Course Technology** is selected, then click **View Certificate**

3. Note the names next to **Issued to** and **Issued by**, then make sure the certificate is still valid
See Figure 12-34.

4. Click **OK** three times to exit out of all the open dialog boxes

5. Double-click **November** in the first line in the first paragraph, type **December**, then click the **Save button** 💾
See Figure 12-35.

6. Click **No** in the dialog box that opens asking if you want to remove all digital signatures in the document

7. Click **File** on the menu bar, click **Save As**, type **Unsigned Brochure** in the File name box, make sure the current folder is the folder where you are saving your project files, click **Save**, then click **OK** in the dialog box that opens warning you that a copy of this document will not contain any digital signatures

 close Unsigned Brochure.doc

Step 6
If you click Yes in the dialog box that asks if you want to remove all digital signatures, the change you made will be saved and the digital signatures will be removed from the current document.

Figure 12-34: Certificate dialog box

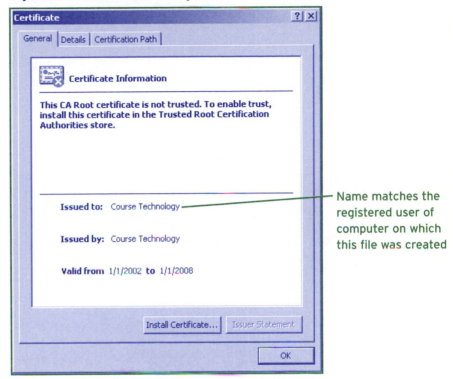

Name matches the registered user of computer on which this file was created

Figure 12-35: Dialog box opens when trying to save changes to a digitally signed document

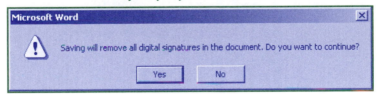

Skill Set 12

Workgroup Collaboration

Target Your Skills

GCAnnouncement08.doc
GCAnnouncement08JH.doc
GCAnnouncement08SW.doc

1 Create the document shown in Figure 12-36. Start by merging the changes and comments from **GCAnnouncement08JH** and **GCAnnouncement08SW** into the original document, **GCAnnouncement08**, then turn on tracked changes and add the changes as noted in the figure. Accept all of the changes and delete all of the comments, save the final file as **Signed Announcement**, then add a digital signature and save your changes.

Figure 12-36

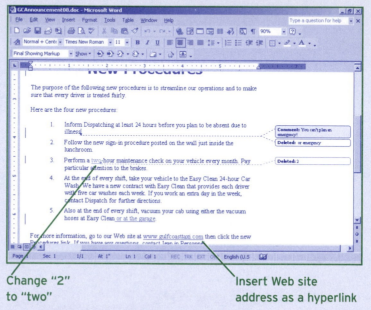

Change "2" to "two"

Insert Web site address as a hyperlink

GCBrochure16.doc

2 Create the document shown in Figure 12-37. First insert the hyperlink on the word **resorts** and link it to the heading **Hotels**. Save a version of the document at this point. Next, insert the hyperlink on the words **activity tours** and link it to the heading **Activity Tours**. Save another version of the document. Finally, protect the document so that only comments can be made. Use the password **GulfCoast**.

Figure 12-37

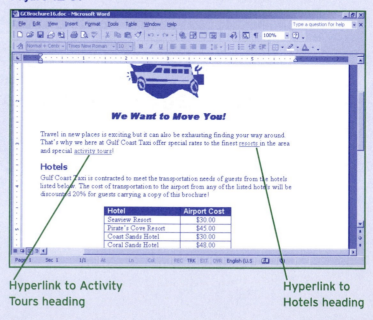

Hyperlink to Activity Tours heading

Hyperlink to Hotels heading

Skill List

1. Merge letters with a Word, Excel, or Access data source
2. Merge labels with a Word, Excel, or Access data source
3. Use Outlook data as a mail merge data source

When you need to send the same letter to many people, you can use the Mail Merge Wizard to merge names and addresses from a list with your form letter. The wizard takes you through a series of steps. First, you choose to use the current document as your form letter or to create the form letter as part of the process when you run the Mail Merge Wizard. You then choose the file that contains the list of names with which you want to merge the form letter. Finally, you merge the letter with a list of people in Word, Excel, Access, or Outlook. The Mail Merge Wizard can save you quite a bit of time.

Skill Set 13

Using Mail Merge

Merge Letters with a Word, Excel, or Access Data Source

The **Mail Merge Wizard** is a series of six steps that leads you through the process of merging a letter or other document (the **main document**) with a list of names and addresses from another document (the **data source**), such as a Word document, an Excel worksheet, or an Access database. Using the wizard, you first define or create the main document. Next, you select the data source, then you insert the merge fields into the main document. The **merge fields** are the placeholders for the data that you will use from the data source, for example, the inside address and the greeting line.

Note: This activity continues on page 294. Make sure you turn the page and complete all nine steps.

Activity Steps

 open CCLetter03.doc
CCMailList01.doc

1. Make sure **CCMailList01** is the active document, notice that the data is arranged in a table, click **Window** on the menu bar, click **CCLetter03.doc**, click **Tools** on the menu bar, point to **Letters and Mailings**, click **Mail Merge Wizard**, then position the insertion point in the main document below the date so that there is one blank line between it and the date
See Figure 13-1.

Step 3
You can use source data from a Word document, Excel worksheet, or Access table.

2. Make sure the **Letters option button** is selected in the Mail Merge task pane, click the **Next: Starting document link** at the bottom of the task pane, make sure the **Use the current document option button** is selected, then click the **Next: Select recipients link**

3. Make sure the **Use an existing list option button** is selected, click the **Browse link** to open the Select Data Source dialog box, navigate to the drive and folder where your project files are stored, click **CCMailList01.doc**, then click **Open** to open the Mail Merge Recipients dialog box
See Figure 13-2.

4. Click **OK**, click the **Next: Write your letter link** in the task pane, then click the **Address block link** to open the Insert Address Block dialog box

5. Make sure **Mr. Joshua Randall Jr.** is selected in the list at the top of the dialog box, click the **Only include the country/region if different than option button**, click in the text box below that option button, then type **US**

Do not close the files. Continue with step 6 on page 294.

Figure 13-1: Starting the Mail Merge Wizard

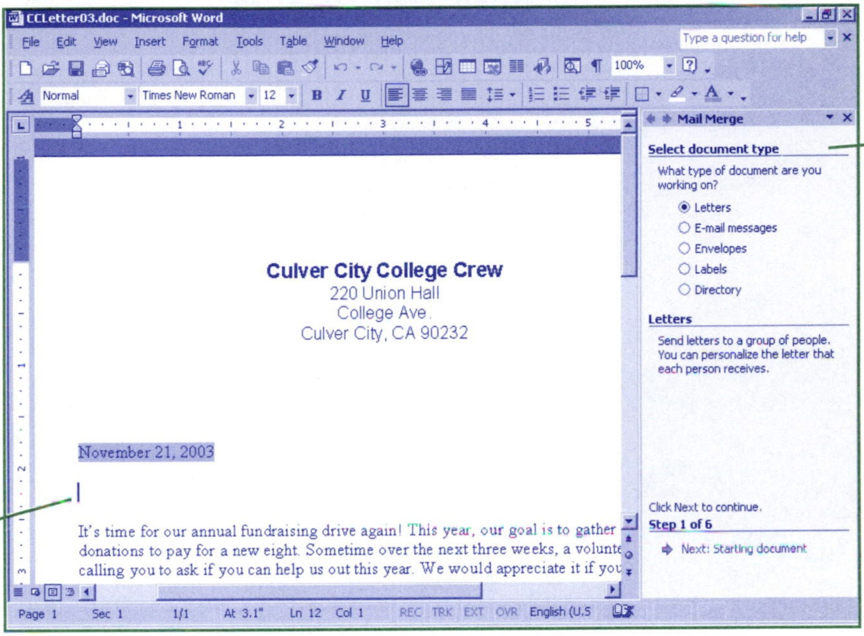

Insertion point

Mail Merge Wizard taskpane

---

extra!

Editing the recipient list

In Steps 3 and 5 of the Mail Merge Wizard, you can click the Edit recipient list link to open the Mail Merge Recipients dialog box and edit the list from the data source (see Figure 13-2). To exclude recipients from the merge, click the check box in the first column to deselect the person you want to exclude. To include only people that meet certain criteria, click the list arrow that appears next to each field name to filter the list.

Figure 13-2: Mail Merge Recipients dialog box

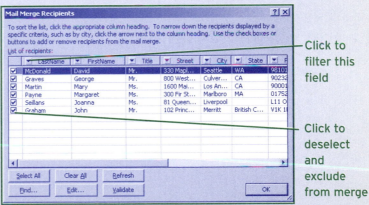

Click to filter this field

Click to deselect and exclude from merge

Skill Set 13

Using Mail Merge

Merge Letters with a Word, Excel, or Access Data Source (continued)

The Mail Merge Wizard will try to match the field names in your data source with its preset fields. You may need to specify any that the Wizard cannot assign. Finally, after reviewing your merged documents, you can save them as one document or send them directly to a printer.

Activity Steps

6. Click **Match Fields** to open the Match Fields dialog box, click the **Address 1 list arrow**, click **Street**, click the **Postal Code list arrow**, then click **Postal_Code**
   See Figure 13-3.

7. Click **OK** to close the Match Fields dialog box, then click **OK** again to close the Insert Address Block dialog box and insert the Address Block merge field into the main document

8. Press **[Enter]** twice, click the **Greeting line link** in the task pane to open the Greeting Line dialog box, click the list arrow next to **Mr. Randall**, scroll down and click **Joshua**, click **OK** to close the dialog box and insert the Greeting Line merge field into the main document, click the **Next: Preview your letters link**, then click the >> in the task pane five times to scroll through the merged letters
   See Figure 13-4.

9. Click the **Next: Complete the merge link**, click the **Edit individual letters link**, make sure the **All option button** is selected in the Merge to New Document dialog box, then click **OK** to open a merged document containing all the form letters with the temporary filename **Letters** followed by a number

 close **Letters1.doc**
   CCLetter03.doc
   CCMailList01.doc

Figure 13-3: Match Fields dialog box

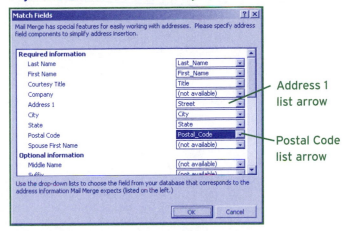

Address 1 list arrow

Postal Code list arrow

Figure 13-4: Reviewing the merged letters

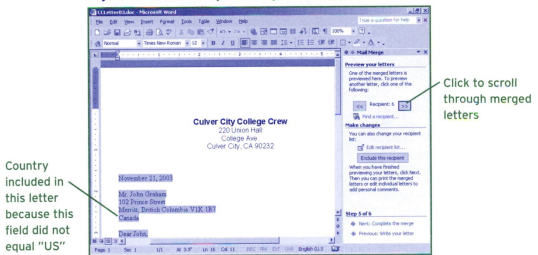

Click to scroll through merged letters

Country included in this letter because this field did not equal "US"

Skill Set 13

Using Mail Merge

Merge Labels with a Word, Excel, or Access Data Source

When you use the Mail Merge Wizard to merge letters and addresses, you still need a way to send those letters in the mail. You can use the Mail Merge Wizard to merge the names and addresses from the data source onto labels. Word has the dimensions and layouts of label sheets from over 14 companies, or you can create your own label format. The steps for merging the data source with a label's document are almost the same as those for merging a letter and a data source.

Note: This activity continues on page 298. Make sure you turn the page and complete all nine steps.

Activity Steps

1. Create a new blank document, click the **Show/Hide ¶ button** ¶ to display paragraph marks if necessary, click **Tools** on the menu bar, point to **Letters and Mailings**, click **Mail Merge Wizard**, click the **Labels option button** in the Mail Merge task pane, click the **Next: Starting document link**, make sure the **Change document layout option button** is selected, then click the **Label options link** to open the Label Options dialog box

Step 3
If you don't have any labels, use the default selections of Avery standard in the Label products list and 2162 Mini - Address in the Product number list.

2. Under Printer information, click the option button that corresponds to the printer attached to your computer, then, if you clicked the **Laser and ink jet option button**, click the **Tray list arrow** and click the tray used by your printer (**Default tray (Automatically Selected)** is a good choice)

3. Click the **Label products list arrow**, click the brand of labels you will be using, then click the type of label you are using in the **Product number list**
See Figure 13-5.

4. Click **OK**, click the **Next: Select recipients link** in the task pane, click the **Browse link** to open the Select Data Source dialog box, navigate to the drive and folder where your project files are stored, click **CCMailList02.doc**, click **Open** to open the Mail Merge Recipients dialog box, then click **OK**
See Figure 13-6.
The number after the filename Document may be a number other than 1.

Do not close the files. Continue with the step 5 on page 298.

Figure 13-5: Label Options dialog box

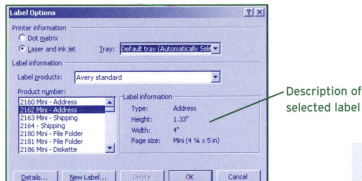

Description of selected label

Figure 13-6: Layout of labels

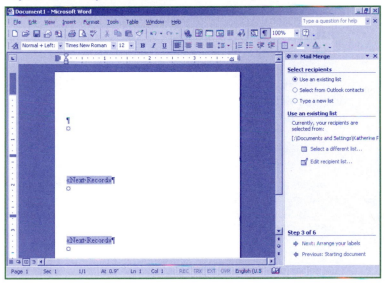

Skill Set 13

Using Mail Merge

Merge Labels with a Word, Excel, or Access Data Source (continued)

Now that you've chosen your label format and your data source, you need to insert the merge fields and complete the merge.

Activity Steps

5. Click the **Next: Arrange your labels link** in the task pane, click the **Address block link**, click the **Only include the country/ region if different than option button**, click in the text box below that option button, type **US**, click **Match Fields**, click the **Address 1 list arrow**, click **Street**, click the **Postal Code list arrow**, click **Postal_Code**, then click **OK** twice

6. Press **[Enter]**, click the **Postal bar code link** to open the Insert Postal Bar Code dialog box, then click **OK** to insert a bar code for US ZIP codes
   See Figure 13-7.

7. If the entire task pane is not visible on the screen, point to the **down arrow** in the thin bar at the bottom of the task pane to scroll down to the bottom of the task pane, click **Update all labels** to copy the format of the first label to the rest of the labels in the document, then click the **Next: Preview your labels link**

8. Click the **Next: Complete the merge link**, click the **Edit individual labels link**, make sure the **All option button** is selected in the Merge to New Document dialog box, then click **OK** to open a merged document containing all the form letters with the temporary filename **Labels** followed by a number

9. Scroll to the bottom of the document, click **Zip code not valid!** in the label addressed to England as shown in Figure 13-8, press **[Delete]**, click **Zip code not valid!** in the label addressed to Canada, press **[Delete]**, then click the **Show/Hide button** ¶

   file close Labels1.doc
   Document1.doc

Figure 13-7: Merge fields inserted in labels main document

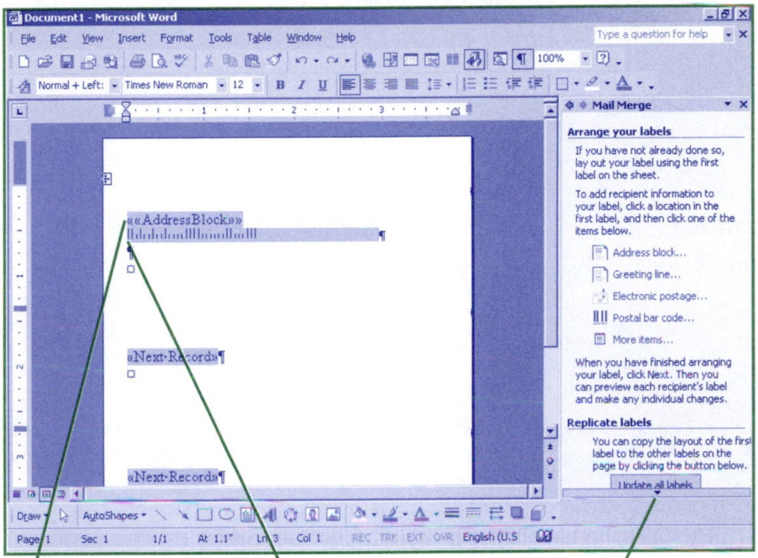

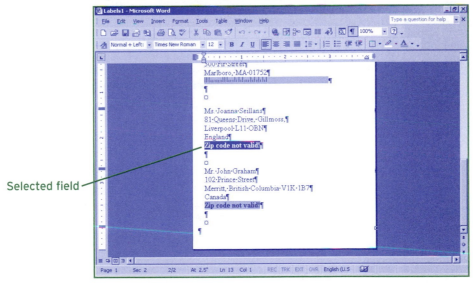

Address Block
merge field

Postal bar code
merge field

Point to this to scroll
to bottom of task pane

Figure 13-8: Invalid Zip code field selected

Selected field

Skill Set 13

Using Mail Merge

Use Outlook Data as a Mail Merge Data Source

Many people store names and addresses in the Contacts folder in Outlook. Using the Mail Merge Wizard, it is very simple to merge any names that you want with a main document. You can specify the Contacts folder or any folder within the Contacts folder as the data source. After you specify the data source and the Mail Merge Recipients dialog box opens, you can deselect any names in the list to exclude them from the merge.

Note: This activity continues on page 302. Make sure you turn the page and complete all nine steps.

Activity Steps

 open CCLetter04.doc

1. Click the **Start button** (start image) on the taskbar, point to **Programs, click Microsoft Outlook, click the New button list arrow**, click **Contact**, type **Mark Diaz**, click in the **Address box**, type **550 West Broad St.**, press **[Enter]**, then type **Oakhurst, CA 93644**
   See Figure 13-9.

2. Click the **Save and Close button**, click the **New button list arrow**, click **Contact**, type **Lena Yee**, click in the **Address box**, type **24 Washington St.**, press **[Enter]**, type **Phoenix, AZ 85001**, then click the **Save and Close button**

3. Click the **Word program button** on the taskbar, click **Tools** on the menu bar, point to **Letters and Mailings**, click **Mail Merge Wizard**, click the **Next: Starting document link** in the task pane, then click the **Next: Select recipients link**

4. Click the **Select from Outlook contacts option button**, click the **Choose Contacts Folder link** to open the Select Contact List folder dialog box, then make sure **Contacts** is selected in the list
   See Figure 13-10.

5. Click **OK** to open the Mail Merge Recipients dialog box, click **Clear All** to clear any check boxes that are selected, click the **check boxes** next to **Diaz, Mark** and **Yee, Lena** to select those two names to include them in the merge, then click **OK**

Do not close the files. Continue with step 6 on page 302.

tip

Step 5
Any names with a check in the check box next to them will be merged with the main document letter.

Figure 13-9: Contact dialog box in Outlook

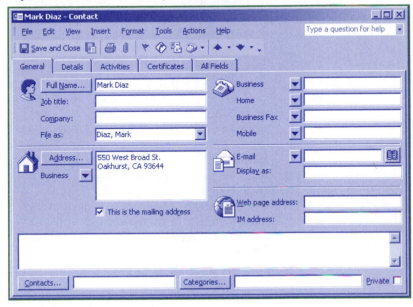

Figure 13-10: Select Contact List folder dialog box

Contacts folder selected

Skill Set 13

Using Mail Merge

Use Outlook Data as a Mail Merge Data Source (continued)

After you select the names from your Outlook contacts, you need to insert the merge fields as with an ordinary mail merge.

Activity Steps

6. Click the **Next: Write your letter link** in the task pane, position the insertion point in the main document below the date so that there is one blank line between it and the date, click the **Address block link**, click **Match Fields**, verify that each field in the Required information list contains a value except the Spouse First Name field, then click **OK** twice

7. Press **[Enter]** twice, click the **Greeting line link** to open the Greeting Line dialog box, click the list arrow next to **Mr. Randall**, scroll down and click **Joshua**, click **OK**, click the **Next: Preview your letters link**, then click >> in the task pane to see the second merged letter
   See Figure 13-11.

8. Click the **Next: Complete the merge link**, click the **Edit individual letters link**, make sure the **All option button** is selected in the Merge to New Document dialog box, then click **OK** to open a merged document containing all the form letters with the temporary filename Letters followed by a number
   See Figure 13-12.

9. Click the **Outlook program button** on the taskbar, click **Contacts** in the Outlook Shortcuts bar, click **Mark Diaz** in the Contacts list, click the **Delete button** ☒, click **Lena Yee** in the Contacts list, click the **Delete button** ☒, then click the **Close button** ☒ in the Outlook program window

      close Letters1.doc
                    CCLetter04.doc

Figure 13-11: Previewing the merged letters

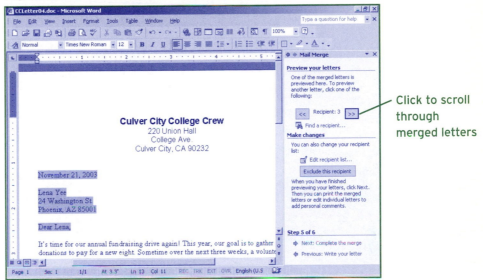

Click to scroll through merged letters

Figure 13-12: First merged letter after completing the merge process

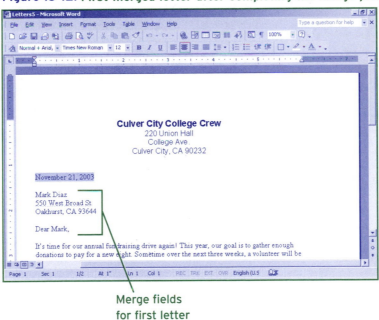

Merge fields for first letter

Skill Set 13
Using Mail Merge

Target Your Skills

 CCLetter05.doc

1 Merge the file CCLetter05 with the mailing list in CCMailList03. Make sure you open the Match Fields dialog box and set each merge field to the correct field in the data source. In the Greeting line merge field, match the merge field Courtesy Title to the data source field Title. Figure 13-13 shows the last letter in the final merged document.

Figure 13-13

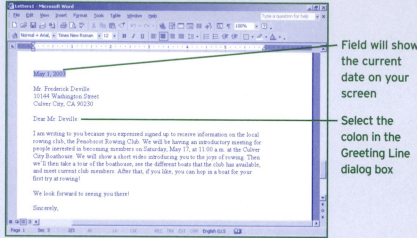

Field will show the current date on your screen

Select the colon in the Greeting Line dialog box

2 Create the merged labels document shown in Figure 13-14 by merging the data source CCMailList04 with a new, blank document. Use Avery standard 2160 Mini - Address labels. The figure shows the last three labels in the final merged document.

Figure 13-14

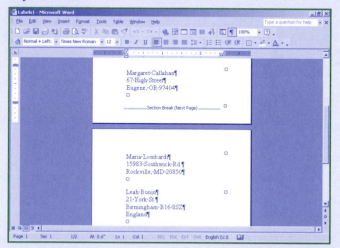

Projects List

Project 1 – Meeting Minutes for Mariposa Community Center

Project 2 – Advertising Bulletin for Skis 'n Boards

Project 3 – Newsletter for the Marine Educational Foundation

Project 4 – Memo for Lakeland Art Gallery

Project 5 – Information Sheet for Classic Car Races

Project 6 – Web Page for Allure Cosmetics

The Word Core skill sets cover a broad range of formatting and file management skills. Once you have mastered these skills, you can create many different document types. In the following projects, you will format a set of meeting minutes, an advertising bulletin, and a newsletter. You will also create a memo from one of Word's preset templates, add graphics to an information sheet, and save a Word document as a Web page that you can post to a Web site on the World Wide Web.

Project for Skill Set 1

Inserting and Modifying Text

Meeting Minutes for Mariposa Community Center

Each month a different staff member at the Mariposa Community Center in Carmel, California is responsible for recording the minutes of the monthly staff meeting. As the Office Manager at the Center, you receive and format each month's set of minutes before printing them for distribution to all staff. For this project, you will edit and format the minutes of the May 2004 meeting.

Activity Steps

 open WC_Project1.doc

1. Change **Mara Ramon** to **Darryl Cook** in the first bulleted item

2. Use the Find and Replace function to replace every instance of **Manjit Sidhu** with **Mitra Biazar**

3. Replace the second '**e**' in Hélene with **è** (in the bulleted item under "France Exchange Program")

4. Copy **report** in the first bullet under Fundraising Committee Report, use Paste Special to paste it after **Recreation Council** as unformatted text, capitalize **report**, then cut **Recreation Council Report** and its accompanying bulleted items and paste it below **Other Committee Reports**

5. Format the text **Mariposa Community Center** at the top of the page with **Bold**, then remove *Italics* from **Gym Fitness Program Builder** (in the first bulleted item below "Director's Report")

6. Use spell check to correct the spelling errors "**brekfast**" and "**oportunities**" and the grammatical error in the second bulleted item under Other Committee Reports
   Note that you should ignore the correction to "Mitra Biazar."

7. Enhance the text **May Meeting Minutes** with the Shadow font effect, then highlight the two names in the first bulleted item with **Turquoise**

8. Insert and center the current date below May Meeting Minutes; ensure the date is set to update automatically

9. Change the format of the date you just inserted to use the format that corresponds with **May 2, 2004**

10. Apply the Pacific character style to the text Pacific Marathon Boosters Association (under the Other Committee Reports heading)
    The completed minutes appear as shown in Figure WP 1-1.

 close WC_Project1.doc

Step 3
To insert the è symbol, click Insert on the menu bar, click Symbol, select the (normal text) font, click è, click Insert, then click Close.

Figure WP 1-1: Completed minutes for Mariposa Community Center

Mariposa Community Center
May Meeting Minutes
May 2, 2004

Approval of Minutes
- Minutes from the April 2004 meeting were approved by Darryl Cook and seconded by Mitra Biazar.

Fundraising Committee Report – Barry Deville
- Barry circulated a report on fundraising activities. The report provided information about the following topics:
  - Organizing a large fund-raising committee for the summer of 2004
  - Organizing a bingo night in partnership with Mitra Biazar, the Director of Athletics
  - Learning about the Charitable You Club, a local charity fundraising company

Other Committee Reports

P.M.B.A. (*Pacific Marathon Boosters Association*)
- The next run event will be held on June 2 and will include a marathon, a 10K fun run, and a 5K walk/run. The cost of the run will be $30.00, which includes a T-shirt, a hat, OR a water bottle.
- Tim Simmons, a world champion marathoner, will hold a Marathon Clinic on May 20. All registrants for the June 2 marathon are encouraged to attend.
- The next P.M.B.A. meeting is June 5, 2004.

Recreation Council Report
- The breakfast held for fitness instructors on Instructor Appreciation Day was a success
- The gym equipment committee will be cleaning and restoring equipment during the week of May 24 to May 31. Volunteers are requested.

France Exchange Program
- Marie-Hélène Rousseau will host a meeting for parents and students interested in participating in the 9th Annual France-California Exchange. This year, students will spend three weeks in the Loire Valley.

Director's Report
- The Professional Development day on May 1 was successful. Recreation instructors learned how to use the new Gym Fitness Program Builder to upload fitness information to the Mariposa Community Center Web site.
- A new large group room will be located in the lower hallway on the 200 floor. Multimedia presentations can be given in the room to audiences of up to 75 people.
- The post-secondary evening held on May 5 was fully attended. Parents and students from the area's high schools attended a lively presentation about career and educational opportunities.

Project for Skill Set 2
Creating and Modifying Paragraphs

Advertising Bulletin for Skis 'n Boards

Skis 'n Boards is a ski and snowboarding shop with three outlets in the Vancouver area. To celebrate the start of the ski season, each outlet will host a snowboarding demonstration given by two world-class snowboarders from International Snowboarding, the premier manufacturer of snowboarding equipment. The demonstrations will take place on three consecutive Saturdays in November at each of the three Skis 'n Boards outlets. You've been given a Word document containing a bulletin that advertises the event. Now you need to format the bulletin attractively so that each Skis 'n Boards outlet can distribute copies to customers, media people, and local businesses. The completed bulletin appears as shown in Figure WP 2-1.

Activity Steps

 open WC_Project2.doc

1. Apply the **Heading 1** style to the document heading **Snowboard Demo!**, increase the font size to **28 pt**, then center the heading

2. Apply the **Heading 3** style to the entire first paragraph

3. Indent the first paragraph **.5"** from both the left and the right margins of the page, apply the **Justified** alignment, then select **1.5 line spacing** for the first paragraph
   You can make all these changes in the Paragraph dialog box.

4. Apply **Gray-10% shading** to the entire first paragraph

5. Select the paragraph that begins "Two awesome world-class boarders...", then apply the same formatting you applied to the first paragraph

6. Select the line containing Day, Date, and Location, open the Tabs dialog box, clear all the current tabs, set **Center tabs** at **.9"**, **2.6"**, and **4.6"**, click to the left of Day, press **[Tab]** to position the three headings, then enhance the three headings with **Bold**

7. Select the information about the three locations, use the ruler bar to set **Left tabs** at **.5"**, **2"**, and **4"**, then indent the three lines to the first tab stop
   The .5 stop appears halfway between the left margin and the 1 on the ruler bar.

8. Apply bullets in the style shown in Figure WP 2-1 to the text that describes the events at each Snowboarding Demo

9. Use the Increase Indent button to indent the bulleted text to the 1" tab stop, then double-space the text

 close WC_Project2.doc

Step 6
To set tabs, click Format on the menu bar, click Tabs, click Clear All, type the required position, click the Center option button, then click Set. Type and set the remaining positions, then click OK.

Figure WP 2-1: Completed bulletin for Skis 'n Boards

Snowboard Demo!

Don't miss the Snowboard Demo at your local Skis 'n Boards outlet. You can also meet the Ski Bunny and win one of ten all-day lift tickets for Whistler-Blackcomb!

Day	Date	Location
Saturday	November 13, 2004	West Vancouver store
Saturday	November 20, 2004	Lonsdale Avenue store
Saturday	November 27, 2004	Kerrisdale store

Two awesome world-class boarders from International Snowboarding will be on hand to share tips and tricks while they perform an awesome series of stunts in our simulated half pipe. Each Snowboard Demo kicks off at noon. Here's an outline of events:

- Noon: The Ski Bunny mascot arrives to greet shoppers and pose for pictures
- 12:30: International Snowboarding experts Maury White and Adam Schreck arrive and sign autographs
- 1:00: First half pipe demo
- 1:30   Break; entertainment provided by the Powder Blues Band
- 2:00   Second half pipe demo
- 2:30   Maury and Adam sign autographs
- 3:00   Drawing for 10 discount lift tickets

Project for Skill Set 3

Formatting Documents

Newsletter for the Marine Educational Foundation

You work part-time in the administrative office of the Marine Educational Foundation, a non-profit educational organization that offers courses in marine ecology from its residential facility in Marathon, Florida. Your supervisor has just e-mailed you a copy of the Fall 2004 Newsletter and asked you to format it over two pages so it appears as shown in Figure WP 3-1 on pages 307 and 309.

Step 4
You will need to bold and center the text in Row 1, reduce the width of the columns, center the percentages in column 2, then center the table between the left and right margins of the newsletter column.

Activity Steps

 open WC_Project3a.doc

1. Change the orientation of the document to **Portrait**, then change the left and right margins to **1"**

2. Format the text from **2004 Educational Programs** to the end of the document in **two columns** of equal width

3. Remove the current header, then create a footer containing **your name** at the left margin and a **page number** at the right margin

4. Click below the first paragraph in the 2004 Educational Programs topic, create a table containing **seven rows** and **two columns**, then enter and format the text as shown in Figure WP 3-1

5. Apply the **Table Contemporary** AutoFormat to the table in the Leadership Programs section, remove the row containing information about **Angus Marsh**, insert a new column to the left of **State**, then enter the column head **Age** in bold and the ages of the students in the column cells, as shown in Figure WP 3-1

Figure WP 3-1: Completed newsletter for Marine Educational Foundation

Marine Educational Foundation

Fall 2004 Newsletter

2004 Educational Programs

In 2004, the Marine Educational Foundation hosted 300 student groups from all over the United States in its marine educational programs. Over 1000 students learned about the history and ecology of the mangrove, coral reef, and grass bed systems of the Florida Keys. Most student groups were from the state of Florida, followed closely by students from California and then New York and Georgia. The following table shows the states from which the highest percentage of our student groups traveled in 2004.

State	Percent of Students
Florida	43%
California	19%
New York	13%
Georgia	13%
South Carolina	7%
New Jersey	5%

New Facility

In 2005, we will begin construction of a new facility near San Diego in California to provide our west coast students with an ecological experience more related to their home environment.

Our members recognize the benefits of combining travel with study. The students who attend the Marine Educational Foundation enjoy a unique travel experience, while gaining knowledge that they can apply directly to their Marine Science classes.

Web Presence

Increasingly, our Web site is attracting interest from students and educators outside the United States. In 2005, we plan to expand our program to include students from Canada, England, Germany, Japan, and Brazil. Check out our site at: www.marinedfoundation.com.

Leadership Programs

The table shown below lists the students who participated in a special leadership group that was run at the Marine Educational Foundation in June 2004. The students were chosen on the basis of their teamwork skills, leadership potential, and academic achievement. The three-day program was a great success.

Last Name	First Name	Age	State
Amin	Zahra	16	CA
Flynn	Kate	17	NY
Leblanc	Michel	16	NY
McGraw	Andy	16	NJ
Penner	Marike	18	PA
Ramirez	Teresa	18	FL
Sanchez	Juan	17	FL
Yeung	Martha	17	CA

[Your Name]

1

Project for Skill Set 3

Formatting Documents

Newsletter for the Marine Educational Foundation (continued)

Step 7
To clear formatting, click the Styles list arrow on the Formatting toolbar, then click Clear Formatting.

6. In the table in the Upcoming Educational Program section, change the Green shading to **Light Green**, then change the font color of the text to **Black**

7. Increase the width of column 1 to **3.2"**, insert a page break before the Upcoming Educational Programs section, clear the formatting to remove the Heading 1 style at the bottom of page 1, then balance the columns on Page 1

8. Insert a column break at the beginning of the second paragraph of the Annual Meeting section on Page 2, view the newsletter in Print Preview, then print a copy of the document

9. Create and print a sheet of labels containing the address of the Marine Educational Foundation shown on Page 2 of the newsletter, then save the labels as **WC_Project3b.doc**

   close WC_Project3a.doc
WC_Project3b.doc

Figure WP 3-1 (continued): Completed newsletter for Marine Educational Foundation

Upcoming Educational Programs

We are anticipating the best season ever in the Spring of 2000 as over five-hundred groups are scheduled to go through the program! Here's the list of programs offered in 2005:

Study	Price
Mangroves, Coral Reefs, and Grass Beds	$300
Mangroves 3-days	$100
Coral Reefs 3-days	$100
Grass Beds 3-days	$100
Coral Reefs, Dolphins Plus	$200
Save the Manatee	$75
Grass Beds and Coral Reefs	$200

All programs, except for those listed as 3-day, last for five days and do not include the cost of transportation from the student's home town to Marathon, Florida. The program price includes all meals, books, transportation, and dormitory-style accommodation while students are participating in the programs.

Annual Meeting

On October 23 at 5 p.m., the Marine Educational Foundation will host its annual meeting and member get-together! As always, we will hold the meeting at the Marine Educational Foundation site in Marathon, Florida. We hope to see some new faces this year, so bring along your friends. For out-of-town members, we're offering a special weekend rate at one of our local hotels of $180 for two nights. You can also enjoy the gourmet delights of our student cafeteria. It's a deal you just can't pass up! Check out the beautiful Florida Keys! If you want to take advantage of this special offer, please call Mark at (305) 872-6641.

Our agenda for this year's meeting is as follows:

- Welcome to New Members
- Budget Report
- Detailed Program Schedule for 2005
- Slide Presentation by Scott Smith on his 2004 Teaching Experience
- New Business
- Adjournment
- Party Time!

We're counting on seeing all the Marine Educational Foundation members this year!

Marine Educational Foundation
P.O. Box 41
Marathon, Florida 33051

[Your Name]

2

Project for Skill Set 4

Managing Documents

Memo for Lakeland Art Gallery

You've just been hired as an Administrative Assistant at the Lakeland Art Gallery on the shores of Georgian Bay in Ontario. One of your first duties is to create a memo describing the upcoming winter exhibition of gallery artists. You decide to base the memo on a template and then create a new folder to contain the memos you create for the gallery. You'll also save the memo in Text (.txt) format so you can distribute it to artists who use other word processing programs that may not be compatible with Word 2002.

Activity Steps

1. Click **General Templates** in the New Document task pane, click the **Memos tab** in the Templates dialog box, then select the **Contemporary Memo** template

2. Modify the template so the completed memo appears as shown in Figure WP 4-1

3. Open the Save As dialog box, then create a new folder called **Art Gallery Memos**

4. Save the document as **WC_Project4.doc** in the Art Gallery Memos folder

5. Modify the document by changing the name of **Flora Wong** to **Flora Leung**

6. Save the changes to the document, then close the document

7. Open **WC_Project4.doc**, save the document in Plain Text (.txt) format with the default settings, then close the document

8. Open the **WC_Project4.txt** file
   Note that you'll need to click the Files of type list arrow and select All Files to see the .txt file.

     close WC_Project4.txt

Figure WP 4-1: Completed memo for Lakeland Art Gallery

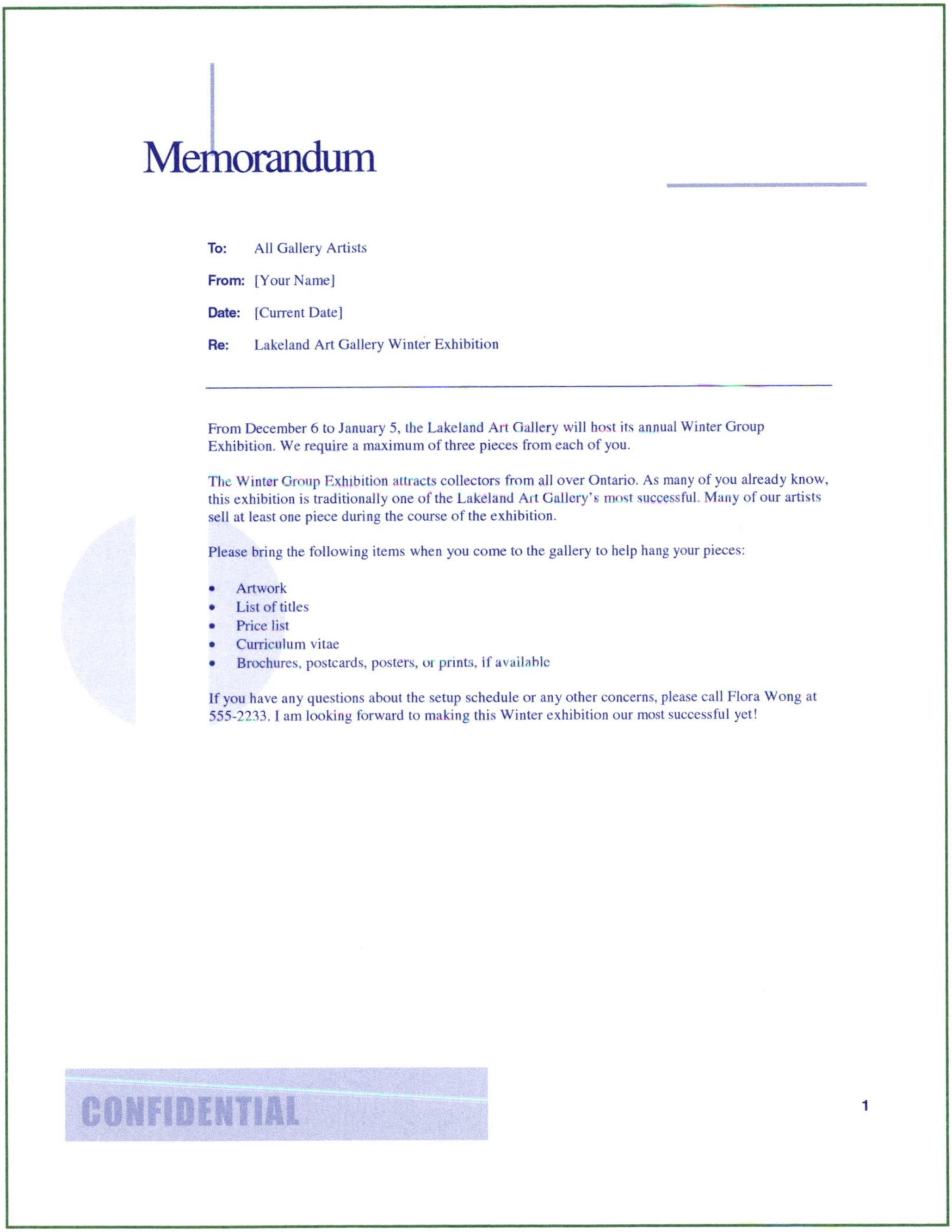

Memorandum

To: All Gallery Artists

From: [Your Name]

Date: [Current Date]

Re: Lakeland Art Gallery Winter Exhibition

From December 6 to January 5, the Lakeland Art Gallery will host its annual Winter Group Exhibition. We require a maximum of three pieces from each of you.

The Winter Group Exhibition attracts collectors from all over Ontario. As many of you already know, this exhibition is traditionally one of the Lakeland Art Gallery's most successful. Many of our artists sell at least one piece during the course of the exhibition.

Please bring the following items when you come to the gallery to help hang your pieces:

- Artwork
- List of titles
- Price list
- Curriculum vitae
- Brochures, postcards, posters, or prints, if available

If you have any questions about the setup schedule or any other concerns, please call Flora Wong at 555-2233. I am looking forward to making this Winter exhibition our most successful yet!

CONFIDENTIAL

1

Project for Skill Set 5

Working with Graphs

Information Sheet for Classic Car Races

The Adirondacks Raceway hosts a series of races for owners of classic sports racing cars of the 1950's and 1960's. As the Office Manager of the facility, you decide to create an information sheet for prospective racers. The sheet includes a pie chart, a clip art picture, a photograph of a classic car, and a diagram showing the steps required to register for a classic car race. The two pages of the completed information sheet appear in Figure WP 5-1 on pages 11 and 13.

Step 3
After you create the default column chart, click Chart on the menu bar, click Chart Type, click Pie, then click OK. You will then need to click Data on the Menu bar and then click Series in Columns.

Activity Steps

 open WC_Project5.doc

1. Insert the picture file called **Ferrari.jpg** at the beginning of paragraph 1, then change the layout to **Square**

2. Use your mouse to size and position the picture in paragraph 1 as shown in Figure WP 5-1

3. Create a **pie chart** that includes a legend from the data in the table, then delete the table

4. Increase the size of the pie chart and center it, as shown in Figure WP 5-1, double-click the **chart**, click just the **grey background** behind the pie, then press **[Delete]**

5. Insert, size, and position the **clip art image** shown in Figure WP 5-1
   Search for "racing car" in the Microsoft Clip Gallery. You will need to be online to access the full Microsoft Clip Gallery. If you are not able to go online, use another similar image of a car from the Microsoft Clip Gallery.

 close WC_Project5.doc

Figure WP 5-1: Completed information sheet for Classic Car Races

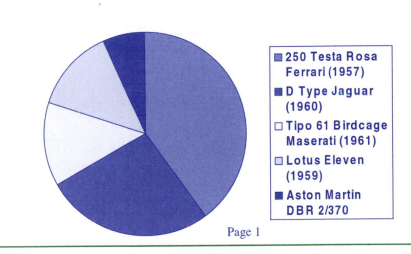

Adirondacks Raceway
Classic Sports Racing Car Competition

The Adirondacks Raceway located outside Saratoga Springs, New York hosts five classic sports racing car competitions each season. Drivers who own some of the most beautiful classic racing cars of the 1950's and 60's relive the glory days of racing, when the sleek design and ear-shattering power of front engine sports cars ruled the raceways. Famed drivers of the times make regular appearances to the delight of their many fans.

The pie chart shown below displays the breakdown of race winners over the past three years by car type.

- 250 Testa Rosa Ferrari (1957)
- D Type Jaguar (1960)
- Tipo 61 Birdcage Maserati (1961)
- Lotus Eleven (1959)
- Aston Martin DBR 2/370

Page 1

Project for Skill Set 6

Workgroup Collaboration

Web Page for Allure Cosmetics

Allure Cosmetics owns several shops in New Zealand. The company's rich, multi-scented soaps, gels, lotions, and cosmetics have become justly famous throughout the country. Now you and your colleagues are working on transforming existing marketing documents for use on the company's new Web site. In this project you will work on a description of the company's three top-selling cleansing products and insert a comment for your colleague, Joanne Plaice. You will then merge the document with another version edited by Joanne to produce a final copy that incorporates your comment and Joanne's comments and changes. Finally, you will save the document as a Web page and view it in your browser. Figure WP 6-1 shows the merged version of the document with two sets of comments.

Activity Steps

 open WC_Project6A.doc
WC_Project6B.doc

1. In the WC_Project6A document, select **Mango Cleansing Milk**, insert a comment with the text **What do you think of changing the name to Mango Wash?**, then save and close the document

2. In the WC_Project6B document, view the two comments inserted by Joanne

3. Merge to a new document the WC_Project6B document with the WC_Project6A document

4. Save the new document as **WC_Project6C.doc**, then print a copy
Figure WP 6-1 shows how the merged document appears when printed.

5. In response to the three comments, change the name of Mango Cleansing Milk to **Mango Wash** (two places), change tropical dawn to **tropical evening**, then change cool water to **warm water**

6. Use the appropriate buttons on the Reviewing toolbar to accept all the changes in the document, then delete all the comments in the document

7. Save the document as a Web page called **WC_Project6D.htm**, apply the Watermark theme, then view the document in your Web browser
Figure WCP 6-2 shows how the document appears in the browser.

 close WC_Project6B.doc
WC_Project6C.doc
WC_Project6D.htm

Figure WP 6-1: Merged document

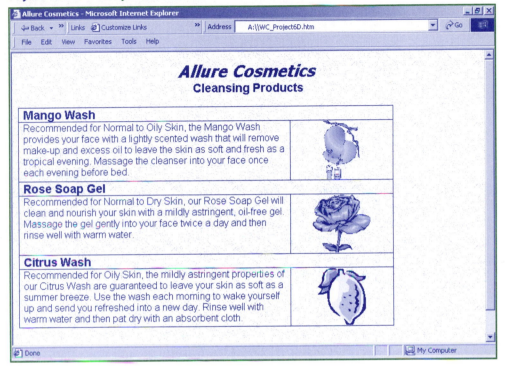

Word 2002 Expert Projects Appendix

Projects List

The Word Expert skill sets include features for customizing Word, applying advanced formatting options, creating and working with complex tables and graphics, working with multiple-page documents and different versions of documents, collaborating with one or more colleagues on a document, and using Mail Merge. In the following projects, you will practice these skills by creating and managing a variety of documents.

Project for Skill Set 7

Customizing Paragraphs

Architectural Heritage Campaign Information

The Architectural Heritage Campaign in Vancouver, British Columbia is working to preserve buildings of architectural and historical significance in the downtown core. As part of their campaign to raise public awareness about the many buildings that need saving, the organizers of the campaign have produced an information sheet. For this project, you will format the information sheet over two pages and then use the Sort feature to organize information about the buildings. The formatted document is shown in Figure WP 7-1.

Activity Steps

 open WE_Project7.doc

1. Remove the line breaks between each of the three subtitle lines at the top of page 1, then use the [Shift][Enter] keys to add manual line breaks so that the space between each item is closed up

2. Sort the items in the table on page 1 in alphabetical order by the information in column 1

3. Turn on widow and orphan control for the second paragraph that appears below the table on page 1
   The first line of the paragraph should now appear at the top of page 2.

4. Sort the five paragraphs describing the five heritage buildings on page 2 in alphabetical order

5. On page 1 insert a manual page break to the left of **Five buildings are slated ..."**
   The document is formatted over two pages as shown in Figure WP 7-1.

 close WE_Project7.doc

Figure WP 7-1: Document formatted over two pages

Architectural Heritage Campaign

Prepared by the Heritage Advisory Board
Vancouver, BC
September 20, 2004

The City Planning Department, in cooperation with the Heritage Advisory Board, is currently in the process of identifying heritage structures throughout the Vancouver area. In 2003, the Board plans to focus on saving as many good examples of the Modernist style (1933-1973) as possible. Several structures now slated for demolition should be placed in the Class A heritage list as good examples of the West Coast Modern style, which Vancouver as a city is internationally renowned.

The following buildings will be discussed at with the exception of the B.C. Binning house Vancouver city limits.

Building Name	Street
B.C. Binning House	Mathers Aven
Commonwealth Building	West Pender S
Customs House	Hastings Stree
Downtown Branch	Denman Stree
Marwell Construction Building	West Georgia
Mayor's Residence	Cambie Street
St. Andrew's United Church	Point Grey Rc
Waterfront Building	Burrard Street

Five buildings are slated for special campaigns in 2004. All of these buildings face imminent development bids.

B.C. Binning House: In an era which is finally waking up to the value of 20th Century architecture, this fine example of an early west coast Modernist house has long been on Vancouver's architectural heritage list. Artist and university instructor B.C. Binning lived in the house for forty years. The house remains under the ownership of his widow who is working with the heritage committees to save it.

Mayor's Residence: This turn of the century mansion is one of the few remaining examples of Victorian architecture in the city. Its classical columns and domed roof make it a prime candidate for inclusion in the city's heritage list. Plans are underway to preserve the structure for use as a public museum.

St. Andrew's United Church: This wooden church is another building from the Modernist 1950's era. The A-frame design includes a steep angled shingle roof and an open design that is complemented by vertical mahogany siding, reminiscent of the forest. The congregation and management of the church are currently seeking heritage protection for the structure.

Vancouver Public Library: Main Branch: This low-rise building in the center of Vancouver was awarded a Governor General's silver medal for design in 1957. The building's clean lines and classical proportions illustrate the most appealing side of Modernist architecture. Features of note include louvered front façade, unique roof elements, and original murals.

Waterfront Building: This excellent example of the late 1920's art deco style must be preserved as a prime example of its period. This building was once the tallest structure in the British Empire. Used as offices by the Port Authority for decades, the building is lavishly decorated with relief sculptures of marine life and other detailing which makes it a singular example of the use of ornamentation in 20th Century architecture.

Project for Skill Set 8

Formatting Documents

TV Documentary Proposal

Art Seen Productions, which produces TV documentaries about art and artists has created a proposal for a documentary about three art foundations. At present, the proposal consists of four documents that you need to format and organize into one document. You also will create a form that readers complete to provide feedback about the proposal.

Step 4
You'll need to add a space after you insert the cross-reference text "below."

Step 6
You'll need to add the text "Table of Contents" and "Index" as titles on the two pages and enhance them with the Documentary Title style, as shown in Figure 8-1. The index entries appear in the Gallery History section of the Episode 1 subdocument.

Activity Steps

  open WE_Project8A.doc

1. Use the Document Map to go to the **Production Schedule** section, verify that the line spacing in the numbered list is 1.5, then select the three numbered items and clear the formatting

2. Create a paragraph style called **Documentary Title** that centers text and formats it as **Times New Roman, 22 point, Bold** and **Dark Blue**, apply the style to the title **Art Seen Productions**, then modify the **Galleries** character style so that it formats text with the **Blue** font color

3. At the end of the first sentence, add a footnote that reads **The episodes are created for public television and so will span the full thirty minutes.**, delete the first sentence from footnote 3, then change the format of all the footnotes to the A, B, C style

4. Go to the **Schedule** bookmark, click after the text **Figure 1** in paragraph 1, then insert a cross-reference to **Figure 1**, using **Above/below** as the reference text

5. Switch to Outline view, move to the end of the document, then add three sub-documents: **WE_Project8B.doc**, **WE_Project8C.doc**, and **WE_Project8D.doc**

6. In Print Layout view, add a new page on a new section at the beginning of the document, insert a Table of Contents in the **Formal** format, find and mark **André Malraux** and **Samuel Beckett** for inclusion in an index, insert a new page at the end of the document, then insert an Index in the **Classic** format

7. Change the margins for section 1 to 2", update the table of contents as shown in Figure WP 8-1, then save, print, and close the document

8. Open **WE_Project8E.doc**, add a check box form field where indicated, then add a drop-down form field that includes the items shown in Figure WP 8-2

9. Protect the form, then save the file as a form template called **WE_Project8E.dot** and close it

  close WE_Project8E.dot

Project 8

TV Documentary Proposal

Figure WP 8-1: Completed table of contents

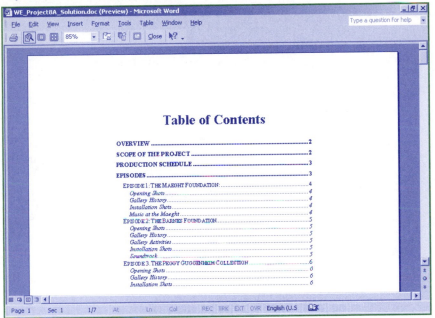

Figure WP 8-2: Items for the drop-down list

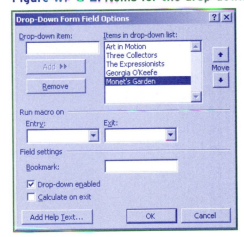

Project for Skill Set 9

Customizing Tables

Ohio Teen Choir Trip Information

The Ohio Teen Choir is California bound! During a 5-day tour of Los Angeles, the 60-person choir will perform at a variety of venues including Disneyland and Universal Studios. In this project, you need to add data to an information sheet that will be distributed to parents to inform them about the trip costs and performance schedule. As you work, refer to the completed information sheet shown in Figure WP 9-1.

Activity Steps

 open WE_Project9A.doc

1. Insert the Excel file **WE_Project9B.xls** as a linked worksheet object following paragraph 2

2. Enter a formula in cell **E9** of the worksheet object that adds the values in cells **E3** to **E8**, then center the worksheet object horizontally in the document
   The completed worksheet object appears as shown in Figure WP 9-1.

3. In the Concert Schedule Table that appears after the third paragraph in the document, merge the four cells in row 1 of the table

4. Split the last row of the table into two cells, then widen the first cell in that row so that it spans the first three columns

5. Enter the text **Total Performance Time** in the first cell of the last row, then format this text as shown in Figure WP 9-1

6. Enter a formula in the blank cell in the last row of the table that adds all the values in the rows above, then format the result as shown in Figure WP 9-1

 close WE_Project9A.doc
   WE_Project9B.xls

Figure WP 9-1: Completed information sheet

Ohio Teen Choir
California Bound!

In 2004, the Ohio Teen Choir will embark on a seven-day, five-concert tour of sunny California! The choir will perform four solo concerts and then participate in a massed choir at a grand finale concert hosted by Disneyland! Each choir member should bring both the casual and the concert uniform, along with two pairs of casual pants, three shirts, seven pairs of socks and underwear, a bathing suit, and personal toiletries. The tour will be fully chaperoned with three assistants in addition to the conductor.

The table shown below breaks down costs for the tour. Please make sure your teen has sufficient funds for the extra meals, attractions, and spending money. The suggested amount is $460.00. The prepaid amount is $850.00 for hotels, fifteen meals, and air fare, and is due on February 1, 2004.

Cost per Choir Member				
Expense	Unit	Unit Cost	Number	Total
Airfare from Cleveland	Ticket	$ 350.00	1	$ 350.00
Hotel	Night	50.00	7	350.00
Meals (prepaid)	Meal	10.00	15	150.00
Meals (extra)	Meal	15.00	7	105.00
Entrance Fees	Attraction	45.00	4	180.00
Spending Money	Day	25.00	7	175.00
			Total Cost	$ 1,310.00

The schedule shown below lists the locations of each concert and the total duration. Two concert programs will be performed—the *Jazz in the City* program and the *Classical Nights* program.

Concert Schedule			
Date	Location	Time	Duration (minutes)
March 2	Anaheim Convention Center	8:00 PM	40
March 4	Disneyland (Fantasyland)	4:30 PM	60
March 5	Marineland	3:00 PM	60
March 7	Universal Studios	5:00 PM	45
March 9	Disneyland (Massed choir)	7:00 PM	90
Total Performance Time			295

Project for Skill Set 10
Creating and Modifying Graphics

Flyer for Fascinatin' Rhythms Dance Studio

The Fascinatin' Rhythms dance studio teaches a variety of popular dance styles to couples and singles in the Milwaukee area. You've been asked to enhance a new flyer with some interesting graphics. In this project, you will draw and modify some AutoShapes in the drawing canvas and create a chart that includes data from an Excel worksheet. As you work, refer to the completed flyer shown in Figure WP 10-1.

Step 4
You'll find the arrow shape in the Block Arrows category on the AutoShapes menu.
Step 8
To change the color of a data series, right-click the data series, click Format Data Series, then select the color required.

Activity Steps

 open WE_Project10A.doc

1. Use the [ALT] key to position the picture of the dancers floating over the first paragraph so that it appears as shown in Figure WP 10-1

2. In the space below paragraph 1, draw and format an arrow as shown in Figure WP 10-1, then copy it twice

3. Use flip and rotate commands to position the three arrows as shown in Figure WP 10-1

4. Add a text box containing the text **Step-by-Step** in Arial 14-point Bold below the three arrows as shown in Figure WP 10-1, then remove the line from around the text box

5. Fit the drawing canvas to the contents, then center the drawing canvas between the left and right margins of the document

6. In the space below paragraph 2, insert a **Column chart** containing data from the Excel file **WE_Project10B.xls**

7. Move the chart legend below the chart by right-clicking it and clicking **Format Legend, Placement, Bottom**

8. Change the color of the **Ballroom data series** to **pink** and the color of the **Jazz and Pop data series** to **bright green**, then size and position the chart as shown in Figure WP 10-1

 close WE_Project10A.doc
WE_Project10B.xls

Figure WP 10-1: Completed flyer

Fascinatin' Rhythm Dance Studio
1600 Pine Drive, Milwaukee, WI 53223
www.fascinatinrhythm.com

Welcome to the *Fascinatin' Rhythm Dance Studio.* Here is the place where you can learn not only the new dances but also brush up on your mambo, waltz, and fox trot. We specialize in Latin and Jazz dance steps from samba to jive dancing. Learn from our accredited experts, who have had professional careers as performers and are also excellent instructors.

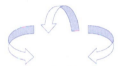

Step-by-Step

When you book your classes you can choose from three different series: Latin, Jazz and Pop, or Ballroom. Shown below is a chart of our classes.

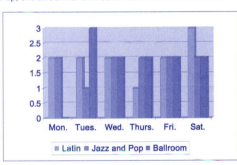

In the Latin classes, we teach Salsa, Mambo, Samba, Conga, and Cha-Cha. In the Jazz and Popular classes, we teach Jive dancing, Jitterbug, Swing Dancing, and Polka. In the Ballroom classes, we teach Waltz, Slow Dance, Tango, and Fox Trot.

Project for Skill Set 11

Phoenix Concert Society Posters

Each month, the Phoenix Concert Society presents an evening of classical music. However, several members of the society usually take turns creating posters for each month's concert with the result that formatting is not always the same. You decide to create a macro and a toolbar that can be used to apply consistent formatting to each month's poster. You'll then use the macro and toolbar to format concert posters for the new two months.

Step 2
You'll need to find the code line in the Visual Basic Editor that reads ".LineSpacingRule = wdLineSpace1pt5", then select 1pt5 and type Double.

Step 6
You will need to click the Grow Font 1 pt button twice to increase the font size to 18-point.

Activity Steps

   open WE_Project11.doc

1. Create a macro called **Poster** that is saved in the current document, runs with the **Alt + P** keystrokes, and performs the steps shown in Figure WP 11-1

2. Open the Visual Basic Editor and edit the macro by changing the line spacing from 1pt5 to **Double**

3. Run the revised Poster macro

4. Customize the Formatting toolbar by adding the button for **Grow Font 1 pt** (in the Format category) and save the customized toolbar with the current document

5. Create a new menu called **Concert** that is saved with the current document, appears to the right of the Help menu, and contains both the Small Caps menu item and the Double Underline menu item (both in the Format category)

6. Select the title of the document, use the Grow Font button on the Formatting toolbar to increase the font size of the title to 18-point, then use the Double Underline command in the Concert menu to format the title with double underlining

7. Select all the text in the table, then use the Small Caps selection in the Concert menu to enhance the text with Small Caps
The formatted document should appear as shown in Figure WP 11-2.

   close WE_Project11.doc

Figure WP 11-1: Macro steps

Macro Steps

1. Press [Ctrl][A] to select all the text in the document.
2. Open the Font dialog box, change the font to Arial, the font size to 16 point, and the font color to Blue, then click OK to close the Font dialog box.
3. Open the Paragraph dialog box, turn on 1.5 line spacing and centered alignment, then click OK to close the Paragraph dialog box.
4. Press the down arrow once to deselect the text.
5. Press [Ctrl][Home] to move to the top of the document.
6. Stop the macro recording.

Figure WP 11-2: Completed poster

An Evening of Beethoven

Be sure to catch the June performance by the Phoenix Concert Society at the Red Rock Theater on South Main Street. This month, you will be enveloped by the passion of Ludwig Von Beethoven. The all-Beethoven program includes two exquisite piano sonatas: the *Moonlight* and the **Pathetique** followed by the sublime 7th Symphony.

We are privileged this month to have the Four Corners Symphony as our special guest orchestra. Featured on the piano will be Gertrude Halliday, who has entertained Phoenix audiences for many years with her mesmerizing performances of the classics.

DATE	SATURDAY, NOVEMBER 27, 2004
TIME	8 P.M.
COST	$25.00

Project for Skill Set 12

Workgroup Collaboration

Short Story for Footloose Travel Magazine

As editor of a local travel magazine you collaborate with two other editors and an author to edit a short story. You use Word's collaboration features to edit a draft of the short story and then combine your changes with those made by two other editors (Melanie Reynolds and Florence Metz) and the author of the story (Lars Svensen). Finally, you open a document from Internet Explorer, edit it in Word, then upload it to a server.

Activity Steps

 open WE_Project12A.doc

1. Review the first formatting change made to the document, accept this change, review and accept the first change made by Melanie Reynolds, then reject her second change

2. With the Track Changes option turned on, enter a new line of text under the title that reads **By Lars Svensen**, press **[Enter]**, then save a version of the document with the comment **First version of the Print copy**

Step 3
Press [Enter] after typing the Web site address.
Step 8
If you do not have permission to save files to a Web server, navigate to the location where you are saving your project files, then click Save.

3. At the bottom of the document, add a centered hyperlink on a new line that goes to the top of the document and displays the text **Return to Top**, then save a new version with the comment **Print copy with hyperlink**

4. Use the **Compare and Merge Documents command** to merge the current document with **WE_Project12B.doc** and **WE_Project12C.doc**, so the first page of the merged version of WE_Project12C.doc appears as shown in Figure WP 12-1

5. View the changes made by the two other reviewers and your own changes, then accept all the changes

6. Add a digital signature to the document, if available, protect the document against tracked changes with the password **footloose**, save and close the document, then close the two other open documents without saving them

7. Open **WE_Project12D.htm** in Internet Explorer, edit the file in Word by editing the hyperlink at the bottom of the document so that it goes to the document top, then change the document title from Ocher to **Roussillon** as shown in Figure WP 12-2

8. Post the file to your Web server with the new name **RepostedStory.htm**

 close RepostedStory.htm

Project 12

Short Story for Footloose Travel Magazine

Figure WP 12-1: Merged document

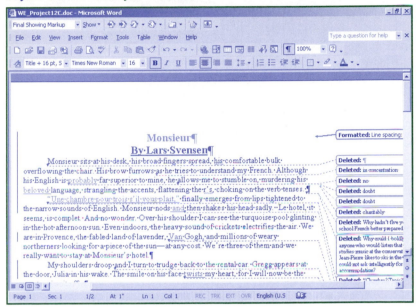

Figure WP 12-2: HTML document in Word

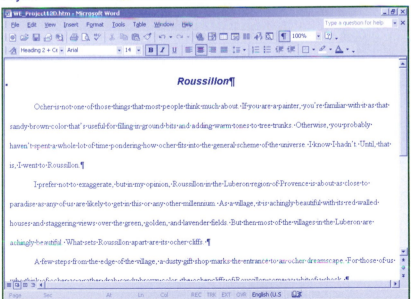

Project for Skill Set 13

Using Mail Merge

Film Location Form Letter

Pacific Drive is a Hollywood film production that plans to film on location in several residential neighborhoods throughout the Seattle area. As part of your job in the production office, you've been asked to create a form letter to send to homeowners in each of the neighborhoods where filming will occur. You will then merge the letter with an Access database containing the names and addresses of the homeowners and then you'll create a sheet of labels.

Activity Steps

 open WE_Project13A.doc

1. Set up the document as a form letter that uses the **Neighbors table** in the **WE_Project13B.mdb** file as the data source

2. Enter fields in the form letter as shown in Figure WP 13-1
   Make sure you enter the current date where indicated. Note that the fields are highlighted in Figure WP 13-1 so that you can easily see them. In your form letter, the fields will not appear highlighted.

3. Run the merge and print only letters to **Lara Drake** and **Ed Jefferson**

4. Save the form letter as **Neighbors Form Letter**, then close it

5. Create a sheet of labels using **3261R-Return Address** as the label type, the **Neighbors table** in the **WE_Project13b.mdb** file as the data source, and the Address Block field

6. Preview the sheet of labels, then compare it to WP 13-2

7. Save the labels as **Location Labels**, then print a copy

 close Location Labels.doc

Figure WP 13-1: Form letter with form fields

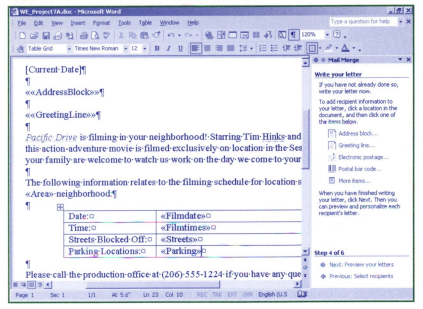

Figure WP 13-2: Form fields for label sheet

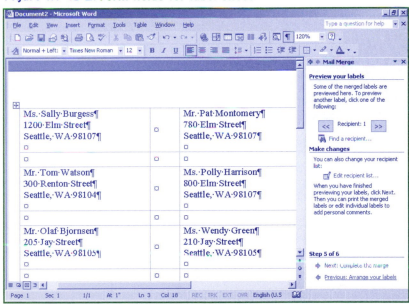

Glossary

.doc filename extension that identifies a file as one created in Microsoft Word

.dot filename extension that identifies a Microsoft Word template file

.htm filename extension that identifies a file as a file created using HyperText Markup Language

.rtf filename extension that identifies a file saved in Rich Text Format

active document the current document; the document in which you are currently entering or editing text

bookmark a named location in a document that you can jump to

cell the intersection of a row and column in a table or a datasheet

centered text or an object that is centered between the left and right margins

chart a visual representation of data in a datasheet

clip (clip art) a drawing, photograph, sound, or movie that you can insert into a document

clipboard an area in the computer in which cut and copied text is stored

comment notes that you add to a document that are not printed unless you specify that you want to print them

comments lines of code in Visual Basic that provide an explanation but do not execute

copy to place a duplicate of text or an object on the system or Office clipboard so that it may be pasted into another location

cross-reference a reference to a figure, table, or other element that appears somewhere else in the document

cut to remove text or an object and store it on the system or Office clipboard so that it may be pasted into another location

data label text that identifies any part of the chart

data marker the bar, column, or point that represents a single piece of data in a chart

data series the collection of all data markers in a row or column in a datasheet

data source the file that contains the list of data to be merged into the main document during the mail merge process

datasheet rows and columns in which you enter data to be graphed in Microsoft Graph

destination file the file into which data, an object, or a link is pasted

digital certificate electronic verification provided by a third-party company that verifies that the person or company whose name appears in the digital signature actually is the creator of the file

digital signature an encrypted key in a file or a macro that identifies the author of the document or macro and verifies that the file has not been changed since it was signed

docked toolbar a toolbar positioned along the edge of the screen

document a file that you create using a word-processing program

Document Map a pane that lists the headings in your document as links in outline form; you can click a heading link to jump to that location in the document

drawing canvas the area in a document in which a drawing or diagram is located or in which you draw a shape

embed to paste an object into a destination file document so that a copy of the object and the source file as well as a link to the source program actually become a part of the destination file

endnotes footnotes that are listed at the end of a document instead of at the bottom of the page on which the note is referenced

field a placeholder for something that might change in a document, such as the page number or the current date

filename extension three letters that follow a period after the filename; the extension identifies the file type, for example, the extension *.doc* identifies a file created using Word

floating object an object that is not anchored to text on a page; you can reposition it by dragging it anywhere on the page

floating toolbar a toolbar positioned in the middle of the screen

followed hyperlink a link formatted with a different color to indicate that it has been clicked

font the design of letters and numbers

font size the size of characters in a document

font style the way characters look, for example, bold, italic, or underlined

footer text that appears at the bottom of every page in a document

footnotes notes at the bottom of the page on which they are referenced

form a method of collecting data in a structured format

form control a field that displays or requests information in a form

format the way something looks; the size, color, and style of a word or paragraph in a document

frame a section of a Web page that acts as if it were a different window or pane on the screen

gutter margin the margin on the binding side of a document

hanging indent a paragraph in which all of the lines following the first line are indented a specified amount

header text that appears at the top of every page in a document

hyperlink (link) specially formatted text or object that, when clicked, moves you to another location in the document, in another document, or on the Web

inactive document an open document in which you are not currently entering or editing text

index entries words in a document that you mark by inserting an index field

index field a field inserted in a document when you mark a word to be part of the index; when you create the index, the words marked with index fields are compiled and sorted

inline object an object that is positioned at the insertion point and is moved with the text around it

insertion point the place on screen where the next character you type will appear

justified text text or an object aligned along both the left and right margins

keywords words that have a specific meaning in a program in Visual Basic

landscape orientation a page set up to print sideways so that the page is wider than it is tall

left-aligned text text or an object aligned along the left margin

link *See* hyperlink

macro a single command that you execute to perform a series of commands

Mail Merge Wizard a series of six steps that leads you through the process of merging a main document with a list of names and addresses from a data source

main document the file (for example, a form letter) that contains the information that will be in every final merged document after merging with a data source

master document a document that contains a set of subdocuments related to it; you can display the subdocuments as part of the master document or as links

merge fields placeholders for the data that you will use from the data source

mirror margins inside and outside margins set up for odd and even pages

object an item that can be manipulated as a whole, for example, an image or a chart in a document

Office Clipboard the clipboard that comes with Office and can store up to 24 of the most recently cut or copied items from any Office program

organizational chart a graphical representation of a hierarchical structure

orphan the first line of a paragraph that is printed by itself at the bottom of a page or column

paste to copy into a document the text or object stored on the system or Office clipboard

pica a measurement for text equal to approximately 12 points

placeholder a section in a template that you can click once to select then type to replace the existing text

point (pt) measurement for text equal to approximately $\frac{1}{72}$ of an inch

portrait orientation a page set up to print lengthwise so that the page is taller than it is wide

pt *See* point

read-only a document that is protected so that users can open it to read the contents but not make any changes or add any comments to it

right-aligned text text or an object aligned along the right margin

section a part of a document with separate page formatting

select to highlight a word or words in a document; also, to click a command

sizing handles small white circles that appear around an object when it is selected; you can drag a handle to resize the object

smart tag a button that appears on screen when Word recognizes a word or phrase as belonging to a certain category, for example, a name or address

source file the file from which data or an object is copied so that it can be pasted into or linked to a destination file

statements lines of programming code in Visual Basic that execute a task

style a defined set of formats that you can apply to words or paragraphs

subdocuments shorter, related documents that are usually referenced in a master document by links

subroutine a series of statements in a program in Visual Basic that, when executed, perform a specific task

symbol a character not included in the standard English alphabet or Arabic numerals

system clipboard the clipboard that contains only the most recently cut or copied item

tab leader a dotted, dashed, or solid line before a tab stop

tab stop the location on the ruler where text moves when you press [Tab]

table of authorities a list of citations in a legal document

table of figures a list of all the illustrations in a document

task pane a panel that appears along the left or right of the screen and contains a set of related hyperlinks to program commands

template a set of styles and formats that determines how a particular type of document will look

theme a background design and set of colors for headings and other text in a Web page or site

toggle turn something on or off; make something, such as a command or toolbar button, active or inactive

toolbar a row of buttons that provide one-click access to frequently used commands

undo to automatically reverse the previous action by clicking the Undo command or button

version a document saved at some point during its creation or while editing it; versions are saved as part of the document in which they are created; they are not saved as separate files

view a way of looking at a document; Word offers four views: Normal, Print Layout, Outline, and Web Layout

widow the last line of a paragraph printed by itself at the top of a page or column

wizard a series of dialog boxes in which you answer questions and choose options to customize a template

word-processing program a program that makes it easy to enter text and manipulate that text in documents

word-wrap the process where the insertion point automatically moves to the next line in a document when it reaches the end of a line

wrap points the vertexes of an object where two lines meet or the highest point in a curve

zoom magnification of the document on screen

Index